TALES OF TERROR
VOLUME I

TALES
Of
TERROR

THE SUPERNATURAL POEM
SINCE 1800

COLLECTED
BY
BRETT RUTHERFORD

IN TWO VOLUMES

A CONTINUATION OF THE WORK
OF MATTHEW GREGORY LEWIS
IN *TALES OF WONDER* (1801)

VOLUME I

YOGH &
THORN
BOOKS

PITTSBURGH, PENNSYLVANIA

Yogh & Thorn Edition 2015
Rev 1.3
Corrected second printing, 2016

The poems are in the Public Domain
Translations, Notes and Annotations
Copyright © 2015 by Brett Rutherford

Yogh & Thorn Books are published by
THE POET'S PRESS
2209 Murray Avenue #3/ Pittsburgh, PA 15217
www.poetspress.org

This is the 213th book from The Poet's Press

ISBN 0-922558-80-9 (paperback)

CONTENTS

INTRODUCTION

This new anthology is a continuation of a project started by Matthew Gregory Lewis in the late 1790s. His 1801 production, *Tales of Wonder*, was a landmark work in the history of Gothic literature, and a milestone in Romantic poetry. Percy Shelley owned the book as a young man, and drew ghosts and monsters in its margins; indeed, a cluster of Shelley's juvenile poems are imitations of the supernatural ballads collected here. Sir Walter Scott allowed himself to be tutored by its author and compiler, and both Scott and Robert Southey provided Gothic poems and ballads for the collection, originally to be titled *Tales of Terror*.

Tales of Wonder was published in 1801 in two volumes in London, printed by W. Bulmer and Co., and sold by J. Bell. A second edition was issued later that year, in one volume, with Robert Southey's poems removed.[1] The single-volume second edition was the bookseller's response to complaints about the price of the two-volume set, and the inclusion, in the second volume, of many poems readily available to readers. The first Dublin printing in 1801 was the one-volume version. The two-volume version did not lack for buyers, however: an 1805 printing in Dublin, "printed for P. Wogan," is based on the two-volume original, and includes Southey's poems once again.[2]

Another book, confusingly titled *Tales of Terror*, appeared later in 1801, and as the bookseller suggested it as a suitable companion for Lewis's *Tales of Wonder*, it was mistakenly assumed by many to be Lewis's own work. The authorship of the spurious *Tales of Terror* has never been determined, but I believe it to be the work of some of Lewis's friends, whose excesses of parody surprisingly did not provoke him to reply. The anthology contains a number of inflated spoofs of supernatural ballads, alongside some that seem to be in the Lewis vein. Aside from an interesting verse Apologia for the Gothic that reflects contemporaneous debates about horror and The Sublime, it is otherwise a sophomoric production.

In titling the present collection *Tales of Terror*, I shall take pride in contributing to another century of bibliographic confusion, since I am furthering Lewis's publishing plan with his original title, and pretty much thumbing my nose at the parody production.

In my edition of *Tales of Wonder*, I offered extensive annotations, and documented the origins of the poems Lewis translated or selected.

---

[1] "There is a sort of Imbroglio about Southey's ballads, which must be settled,"Lewis wrote to Walter Scott (Peck 119).

[2] Louis Peck notes an 1817 edition in London with 32 poems, an 1836 edition with only 23, and a 1925 "catchpenny" edition with only eight poems (133).

In some cases, I appended alternate translations or originals; in others I was content to point interested readers to the sources. The great mother lode of English and Scottish ballads can be found in Bishop Percy's *Reliques of Ancient English Poetry*, LeGrand's *Fabliaux*, and Evans' *A Collection of Old Ballads*. Child's *English and Scottish Popular Ballads*, although published later in the century (starting in 1868), was also cited frequently in my notes, since the Child ballad collection is comprehensive and the numbering of the ballads therein has become a standard cataloging reference.

It is worth keeping these early ballads in mind, even with the work of the later poets in the present collection, for it should not be forgotten that the literary ballad, where it is not a complete invention, is fossil evidence of a work intended to be sung, and accompanied by some kind of instrument. In the 18th century, some supernatural ballads were also transmitted in broadsheets and printed collections, often with musical notation. Ballad-singing was a tea-time entertainment, and sophisticated settings of such ballads by Haydn and Beethoven kept the text of the ballad in the public eye as song lyrics.

The leap from folk-lyric to literary ballad set a higher standard for the ballad-as-text, and Lewis and his peers made it their business to add metric regularity and poetic diction into the sometimes rougher-hewn originals. Sometimes the texts were Anglicised or modernized; other times a new-fangled poem was cast in archaic language, either for atmosphere or as an outright literary hoax.

One caveat for the reader weaned on modern poetry is that even the "Romantic" poets featured here employ forms, meters and language from an era earlier than their own, even sometimes to the extent of perpetrating a literary hoax à la Ossian. The Gothic esthetic by its nature is backward-looking. It takes some adjustment for today's reader to enjoy these poems for what they are, and read them in the context of their own time. Against the stifling moral and correct tone of most 18th century verse, this is pretty strong stuff, a bracing counter-esthetic.

A certain degree of macabre relish, what I call "the smile behind the skull," is always evident in this genre. The poems here are unlikely to frighten anyone other than the superstitious, or very small children; instead, they delight those of a Gothic predilection who enjoy the sublime frisson of danger and supernatural awe. Literal belief in the supernatural is actually rather rare among poets, who treat gods and monsters and fairies as their playthings.

THE PLAN OF "TALES OF TERROR"

In keeping with Lewis's original project, I have concerned myself principally with poems on overtly supernatural themes that are narrative in nature. Mood pieces, and poems that merely convey atmosphere without incident, are of less interest. On a few occasions, however, I have found poems that use the devices of the Gothic for other ends, and some of these are extraordinary enough to warrant inclusion. Indeed, as the 19th century progressed, poets began to employ the Gothic mode for purposes larger than the entertaining relation of a supernatural tale. Political, social or personal meanings layer over the Gothic.

One early example is the excerpt from Joel Barlow's epic *The Columbiad*, which I have titled "Cruelty." This passage employs classical allegory and personification akin to Milton's horrible representations of Sin and Death. It is a good reminder that the Monstrous Sublime has Classical origins, not just Gothic ones.

Samuel Taylor Coleridge, although many of his supernatural poems pre-date 1800, needs to be here, if only for the unforgettable "Rime of the Ancient Mariner," a poem cast in an intentionally arcane style, with both supernatural mood and allegorical intent. Lewis would not and could not have included Coleridge in his collection, as the two were hostile to one another. This collection, taking a slight step backward in time, remedies that.

Another reason that Coleridge merits a place of honor here is that he was the anonymous translator of one of the first English excerpts of Part 1 of Goethe's *Faust*. Coleridge, who recoiled from his own early enthusiasms, never acknowledged his role as translator.

Percy Shelley is represented by some juvenile ballads, as well as by his translation of The Witches' Sabbath from Goethe's *Faust*. At the time of his translation, no one else had rendered that scene into English. It is hard to comprehend today that parts of *Faust* were once considered obscene and blasphemous.

Although Sir Walter Scott's early supernatural ballads are in Lewis's 1801 collection, there are later supernatural poems, most placed within the *Waverly* novels. I chose the best of these that seem to stand on their own, and I also cobbled together a set I have titled "The White Lady," from verses scattered throughout Scott's novel, *The Monastery*. Scott was an ardent student of Norse mythology long before he met Monk Lewis, and we will see traces of that in his poems here.

The goodly chunk of Edgar Allan Poe to be found in these pages comprises all of his poems that I consider overtly supernatural: they are fewer than one might expect. Sarah Helen Whitman's poem, "The Raven," is her revision of a Valentine's Day poem she addressed to Poe, a work which initiated their mutually-tormented romance of 1848.

The American poet most in the same vein as Lewis and his Nordic-Germanic sources is, surprisingly, Longfellow, who was well-versed in Norse myth, Native American lore, and German literature. The encounter with hungry ghosts in *The Song of Hiawatha* also merits a place since, in addition to its content, it is cast in the meter of the Finnish epic *Kalevala*. Longfellow's poem on Torquemada gives us the Gothic trappings of the Spanish Inquisition, which, although not supernatural, combines superstition, intolerance and horror to the extent that the nobles and priests involved had might as well be demons. The poem "Enceladus" once again demonstrates the use of Cthonic myth with a political intent. Monsters always serve as a metaphor for current evils, but when such poems are well done, they can be enjoyed at multiple levels.

In the second edition of Rev. Griswold's massive anthology, *The Female Poets of America*, only two or three women poets demonstrate a knack for the Gothic or supernatural. Frances H. Green, born in Rhode Island and a descendent of that state's famed Whipple family, made her mark as journalist, editor and author on abolition, spiritualism, the Dorr Rebellion, and even, apparently, wrote a textbook on botany. Her poetic productions include an epic on the Narragansett Indians. Like Long-fellow, she was steeped in Norse mythology, and in the poem chosen here she joins in the line of Norse-inspired poems that Bishop Percy first collected, and which Lewis made a point of including in *Tales of Wonder*. The reference to Lapland with its legendary witches who can command the winds, shows that Green researched her myths well. Her poem also stands out from the far more conventional verses Griswold gathered from her contemporaries, in that it displays an unremitting paganism and a masculine, one might even say, blood-thirsty, pleasure in depicting the carnage inflicted by storm winds, in an era when sea travel was hazardous and frequently fatal.

The forthcoming second volume of this series will include American, British, Irish and Continental poets up to around 1930, followed by a clump of contemporaries writing poetry in the same vein. Some of the poets included in the second volume are Robert Graves, Madison Cawein, John Squire, William Butler Yeats, Oscar Wilde, H. P. Lovecraft. Clark Ashton Smith, Walter de la Mare, James Whitcomb Riley, Stephen Vincent Benét, Katherine Tynan, Barbara A. Holland, Shirley Powell, Jack Veasey, Claudia Dikinis, and Pieter Vanderbeck.

—Brett Rutherford
Pittsburgh, PA

FROM "TALES OF TERROR" (1801)[1]

The Defence of the Gothic

Anon. Introductory Dialogue.

Si erro, libenter erro, nec mihi hunc errorem, dum viro,
extorqueri volo — CICERO.[2]

FRIEND
What, scribble tales? Oh, cease to play the fool!
Christmas is past,[3] and children gone to school;
E'en active Harlequin abashed retires,[4]
Neglected witches quench the cauldron's fires,
Whilst fairy phantoms vanish swift away,
And sense and nature reassume their sway.
    What gain, what pleasure, can your labors crown?
A nursery's praise shall be your best renown;
Each feeble tale ingloriously expire,
A gossip's story at a winter's fire!

---

[1] *Tales of Terror,* issued in 1801 by the publisher of Matthew Gregory Lewis's *Tales of Wonder,* advertised the work as a suitable companion volume, causing many to believe that Lewis was the author or compiler. No one knows who edited the book, or who wrote the unattributed poems, many of which seem to be exaggerated parodies of Lewis's work.

[2] *Si erro...* "If I am in error, willingly do I err, and I would not wish this error to be torn from me, while I live." Perhaps ironic here, since the Latin words omitted from the quotation refer to Cicero's belief in the soul's immortality. Out of context, though, this quotation did become a badge of honor for stubborn belief of any kind.

[3] Ghost stories were customarily told at homes at Christmastime, so this accusation associates horror tales with childish custom.

[4] This may be a suggestion that Gothic plays may be out of favor in the theater.

<1>

AUTHOR
    Oh! cease this rage, this misapplied abuse,
Satire gives weapons[5] for a nobler use;
Why draw your sword against my harmless quill,
And strive, in vain, a ghostly muse to kill?
That task is ours: if I can augur well,
Each day grows weaker her unheeded spell,
Her eager votaries shall fix her doom,
And lay her spirit in Oblivion's tomb.

FRIEND
    Yes! thus I oft my drooping hopes revive,
Preprost'rous births are seldom known to thrive;
These scribblers soon shall mourn their useless pains,
And weep the short-lived product of their brains,
These active panders to perverted taste
Shall mar their purpose by too anxious haste.

    As earthquakes Nature's harmony restore,
And air grows purer in the tempest's roar,
So the strange workings of a monstrous mind
Will quickly fade, and leave no trace behind;
Like brilliant bubbles, glitter for a day,
Till, swoln[6] too big, they burst, and pass away.
We need not call ethereal spirits down
To rouse the torpid feelings of the town;
Or bid the dead their ghastly forms uprear,
To freeze some silly female breast with fear;
No — I have hopes you'll find this rage decreased,
And send a dish too much to Terror's feast;
The vicious taste, with such a rich supply
Quite surfeited, "will sicken, and so die."[7]

---

[5] Matthew Gregory Lewis, poet and compiler of *Tales of Wonder*, had literary
enemies in England. Coleridge scorned him, and the playwright and poet George
Colman, Jr., mocked the Gothic and even wrote verses satirizing Lewis's mode
(see Colman's poem in Volume II of *Tales of Wonder*.) The poet and caricaturist
Henry Bunbury, whose odd "Little Gray Man" is in Lewis's first volume,
illustrated the anonymous *Tales of Terror* and is another possible candidate for
authorship of this dialogue, or even of some of the poems in that volume.
[6] *swoln*: variant of swollen
[7] Shakespeare. *Twelfth Night*, i, 1

<2>

AUTHOR

My friend, believe me, with indifferent view
I mark opinion's ever-varying hue,
Let tasteless fashion guide the public heart,
And, without feeling, scan the poet's art.
Fashion! dread name in criticism's field,
Before whose sway both sense and judgment yield,
Whether she loves to hear, 'midst deserts bleak,
The untaught savage moral axioms speak;
O'er modern, six weeks, epic strains to doze,
To sigh in sonnets, or give wings to prose;
Or bids the bard, by leaden rules confined,
To freeze the bosom and confuse the mind,
While feeling stagnates in the drawler's veins,
And Fancy's fettered in didactic chains; —
Or rouses the dull German's gloomy soul,
And Pity leaves for Horror's wild control,
Pouring warm tears for visionary crimes,
And softening sins to mend these moral times;
It boots not me — my taste is still my own,
Nor heeds the gale by wavering fashion blown.
My mind unaltered views, with fixed delight,
The wreck of learning snatched from Gothic night;
Changed by no time, unsettled by no place,
It feels the Grecian fire, the Roman grace;
Exulting marks the flame of ancient days,
In Britain with triumphant brightness blaze!

Yet still the soul for various pleasure formed,
By Pity melted, and by Terror stormed,
Loves to roam largely through each distant clime,
And "leap the flaming bounds of space and time!"[8]
The mental eye, by constant lustre tires,
Forsakes, fatigued, the object it admires,
And, as it scans each various nation's doom,
From classic brightness turns to Gothic gloom.

---

[8] From Thomas Gray's "Progress of Poetry," a line alluding to Milton's Satan in transit to Eden.

<3>

Oh! it breathes awe and rapture o'er the soul
To mark the surge in wild confusion roll,
And when the forest groans, and tempest lours,
To wake Imagination's darkest powers!
How throbs the breast with terror and delight,
Filled with rude scenes of Europe's barbarous night!
When restless war with papal craft combined,
To shut each softening ray from lost mankind;
When nought but Error's fatal light was shown,
And taste and science were alike unknown;
To mark the soul, benumbed its active powers,
Chained at the foot of Superstition's towers;
To view the pale-eyed maid in penance pine,
To watch the votary at the sainted shrine;
And, while o'er blasted heaths the night-storm raves,
To hear the wizard wake the slumb'ring graves;
To view war's glitt'ring front, the trophied field,
The hallowed banner, and the red-cross shield;
The tourney's knights, the tyrant baron's crimes,
"Pomp, pride, and circumstance,"[9] of feudal times![10]

The enraptured mind with fancy loves to toil
O'er rugged Scandinavia's martial soil;
With eager joy the 'venturous spirit goes
O'er Morven's mountains, and through Lapland's snows;
Sees barbarous chiefs in fierce contention fall,
And views the blood-stained feasts of Odin's hall;
Hears Ossian's harp resound the deeds of war,
While each grey soldier glories in his scar;
Now marks the wand'ring ghost, at night's dull noon,
Howl out its woes beneath the silent moon;
Sees Danish pirates plough th' insulted main,
Whilst Rapine's outcry shakes the sacred fane!
Observes the Saxon baron's sullen state,
Where rival pride enkindles savage hate;
Each sound, each sight, the spell-bound sense appalls

[9] Shakespeare. *Othello*. III:3.
[10] This stanza's expression of Protestant disapproval of medieval, Roman Catholic superstition and power should be ample evidence that this poem is not by Lewis, who, despite his malevolent monks and ghostly knights, never engages in Catholic-bashing.

<4>

Amid some lonely abbey's ivied walls!
The night-shriek loud, wan ghost, and dungeon damp,
The midnight cloister, and the glim'ring lamp,
The pale procession fading on the sight,
The flaming tapers, and the chanted rite,
Rouse, in the trembling breast, delightful dreams,
And steep each feeling in romance's streams!
Streams, which afar in restless grandeur roll,
And burst tremendous on the wond'ring soul!
Now gliding smooth, now lashed by magic storms,
Lifting to light a thousand shapeless forms;
A vaporous glory floats each wave around,
The dashing waters breathe a mournful sound,
Pale Terror trembling guards the fountain's head,
And rouses Fancy on her wakeful bed;
"From realms of viewless spirits tears the veil,
And half reveals the unutterable tale!"[11]

—March 1, 1801

---

[11] The final quotation dates from 1800, from the text of a poem inserted in the middle of theater reviews in the February 1800 issue of *European Magazine and London Review*. William Sotheby's "Address to the Tragic Muse" was recited from a London stage and the entire poem was inserted in the middle of the review. The poem must have achieved some acclaim since the author of the poem above expects his readers to know the source of the quotation. The section of the poem in which the lines appear, almost verbatim as quoted here, is intriguing enough to excerpt here:

> Tamer of Man! Beneath thy boundless reign
> Wild Fancy shapes her visionary train,
> Embodies airy beings all her own,
> And rules, with wizard wand, the world unknown:
> Leagues the Weird Sisters where the night-storm raves,
> Drags howling spectres from reluctant graves;
> Bids fear, with icy dew-drops, freeze the frame,
> When horror broods o'er "deeds without a name";
> From realms of tortur'd spirits lifts the veil,
> And half reveals th' unutterable tale.

William Sotheby (1757-1833) translated Wieland's *Oberon*, and lived to complete his own translations of *The Iliad* and *The Odyssey*. He did not include the "Address to the Tragic Muse" in his collected poems.

<5>

JOEL BARLOW (1754-1812)

Cruelty

From Book VI of The Columbiad, *1809*

Cold-blooded Cruelty, first fiend of hell,
Ah think no more with savage hordes to dwell;
Quit the Caribian[1] tribes who eat their slain,
Fly that grim gang, the Inquisitors of Spain,
Boast not thy deeds in Moloch's shrines of old,
Leave Barbary's pirates to their blood-bought gold,
Let Holland steal her victims, force them o'er
To toils and death on Java's morbid shore;
Some cloak, some color all these crimes may plead;
'T is avarice, passion, blind religion's deed;
But Britons here, in this fraternal broil,
Grave, cool, deliberate in thy service toil.
Far from the nation's eye, whose nobler soul
Their wars would humanize, their pride control,
They lose the lessons that her laws impart,
And change the British for the brutal heart.
Fired by no passion, madden'd by no zeal,
No priest, no Plutus bids them not to feel;
Unpaid, gratuitous, on torture bent,
Their sport is death, their pastime to torment;
All other gods they scorn, but bow the knee,
And curb, well pleased, O Cruelty, to thee.[2]

Come then, curst goddess, where thy votaries reign,
Inhale their incense from the land and main;
Come to New York, their conquering arms to greet,

---

[1] *Caribian*, i.e., Caribbean.
[2] This section of Barlow's American history epic, *The Columbiad*, employs the classic device of personification. In depicting the savage treatment of American prisoners of war aboard British prison ships in New York harbor during the American Revolution, Barlow makes his Cruelty figure a cross between a mythological Fury and the Grim Reaper. It is a curious mixture of the classical and the Gothic, but all in keeping with neoclassical concepts of the Sublime.

<6>

Brood o'er their camp and breathe along their fleet;
The brother chiefs of Howe's illustrious name
Demand thy labors to complete their fame.
What shrieks of agony thy praises sound!
What grateless dungeons groan beneath the ground!
See the black Prison Ship's expanding womb
Impested thousands, quick and dead, entomb.
Barks after barks the captured seamen bear,
Transboard and lodge thy silent victims there;
A hundred scows, from all the neighboring shore,
Spread the dull sail and ply the constant oar,
Waft wrecks of armies from the well fought field,
And famisht garrisons who bravely yield;
They mount the hulk, and, cramm'd within the cave,
Hail their last house, their living, floating grave.

She comes, the Fiend! her grinning jaws expand,
Her brazen eyes cast lightning o'er the strand,
Her wings like thunder-clouds the welkin sweep,
Brush the tall spires and shade the shuddering deep;
She gains the deck, displays her wonted store,
Her cords and scourges wet with prisoners' gore;
Gripes, pincers, thumb-screws spread beneath her feet,
Slow poisonous drugs and loads of putrid meat;
Disease hangs drizzling from her slimy locks,
And hot contagion issues from her box.

O'er the closed hatches ere she takes her place,
She moves the massy planks a little space,
Opes a small passage to the cries below,
That feast her soul on messages of woe;
There sits with gaping ear and changeless eye,
Drinks every groan and treasures every sigh,
Sustains the faint, their miseries to prolong,
Revives the dying and unnerves the strong.

<7>

But as the infected mass resign their breath.
She keeps with joy the register of death.
As tost thro' portholes from the encumber'd cave,
Corpse after corpse fall dashing in the wave;
Corpse after corpse, for days and months and years,
The tide bears off, and still its current clears;
At last, o'erloaded with the putrid gore,
The slime-clad waters thicken round the shore.
Green Ocean's self, that oft his wave renews,
That drinks whole fleets with all their battling crews,
That laves, that purifies the earth and sky,
Yet ne'er before resign'd his natural dye,
Here purples, blushes for the race he bore
To rob and ravage this unconquer'd shore;
The scaly nations, as they travel by,
Catch the contagion, sicken, gasp and die.

<8>

SIR WALTER SCOTT (1771-1832)

The Dance of Death

I.

Night and morning were at meeting
    Over Waterloo;
Cocks had sung their earliest greeting;
    Faint and low they crew,
For no paly[1] beam yet shone
On the heights of Mount Saint John;
Tempest-clouds prolonged the sway
Of timeless darkness over day;
Whirlwind, thunder-clap, and shower
Marked it a predestined hour.
Broad and frequent through the night
Flashed the sheets of levin-light:[2]
Muskets, glancing lightnings back,
Showed the dreary bivouac
    Where the soldier lay,
Chill and stiff, and drenched with rain,
Wishing dawn of morn again,
  Though death should come with day.

II.

'Tis at such a tide and hour
Wizard, witch, and fiend have power,
And ghastly forms through mist and shower
    Gleam on the gifted ken;
And then the affrighted prophet's ear
Drinks whispers strange of fate and fear
Presaging death and ruin near
    Among the sons of men; —
Apart from Albyn's[3] war-array,
'Twas then grey Allan sleepless lay;

---

[1] *Paly.* Pale or somewhat pale.
[2] *Levin.* Lightning.
[3] *Albyn.* Scotland.

<9>

Grey Allan, who, for many a day,
    Had followed stout and stern,
Where, through battle's rout and reel,
Storm of shot and edge of steel,
Led the grandson of Lochiel,
    Valiant Fassiefern.
Through steel and shot he leads no more,
Low laid 'mid friends' and foemen's gore —
But long his native lake's wild shore,
And Sunart rough, and high Ardgower,
    And Morven long shall tell,
And proud Bennevis hear with awe
How, upon bloody Quatre-Bras,[4]
Brave Cameron[5] heard the wild hurra
  Of conquest as he fell.

III.
Lone on the outskirts of the host,
The weary sentinel held post,
And heard, through darkness far aloof,
The frequent clang of courser's hoof,
Where held the cloaked patrol their course,
And spurred 'gainst storm the swerving horse;
But there are sounds in Allan's ear,
Patrol nor sentinel may hear,
And sights before his eye aghast
Invisible to them have passed,
    When down the destined plain,
'Twixt Britain and the bands of France,
Wild as marsh-borne meteor's glance,
Strange phantoms wheeled a revel dance,
    And doomed the future slain. —
Such forms were seen, such sounds were heard,
When Scotland's James his march prepared
    For Flodden's fatal plain;
Such, when he drew his ruthless sword,
As Choosers of the Slain, adored

---

[4] *Quatre Bras.* The Battle of Quatre Bras, June 16th, 1815, at a crossroad on the Charleroi-Brussels road.
[5] *Cameron.* Donald Cameron, 23rd chirf of Clan Cameron, fought at Waterloo.

<10>

The yet unchristened Dane.
An indistinct and phantom band,
They wheeled their ring-dance hand in hand,
    With gestures wild and dread;
The Seer, who watched them ride the storm,
Saw through their faint and shadowy form
        The lightning's flash more red;
And still their ghastly roundelay
Was of the coming battle-fray,
        And of the destined dead.

IV. SONG.

Wheel the wild dance
While lightnings glance,
        And thunders rattle loud,
And call the brave
To bloody grave,
        To sleep without a shroud.
Our airy feet,
So light and fleet,
        They do not bend the rye
That sinks its head when whirlwinds rave,
And swells again in eddying wave,
        As each wild gust blows by;
But still the corn,
At dawn of morn,
        Our fatal steps that bore,
At eve lies waste,
A trampled paste
        Of blackening mud and gore.
Wheel the wild dance
While lightnings glance,
        And thunders rattle loud,
And call the brave
To bloody grave,
        To sleep without a shroud.

<11>

V.

Wheel the wild dance!
Brave sons of France,
 For you our ring makes room;
Make space full wide
For martial pride,
 For banner, spear, and plume.
Approach, draw near,
Proud cuirassier!
 Room for the men of steel!
Through crest and plate
The broadsword's weight
 Both head and heart shall feel.

VI.

Wheel the wild dance
While lightnings glance,
 And thunders rattle loud,
And call the brave
To bloody grave,
 To sleep without a shroud.
Sons of the spear!
You feel us near
 In many a ghastly dream;
With fancy's eye
Our forms you spy,
 And hear our fatal scream.
With clearer sight
Ere falls the night,
 Just when to weal or woe
Your disembodied souls take flight
On trembling wing — each startled sprite
 Our choir of death shall know.

<12>

VII.

Wheel the wild dance
While lightnings glance,
 And thunders rattle loud,
And call the brave
To bloody grave,
 To sleep without a shroud.
Burst, ye clouds, in tempest showers,
Redder rain shall soon be ours —
 See the east grows wan —
Yield we place to sterner game,
Ere deadlier bolts and direr flame
Shall the welkin's[6] thunders shame,
Elemental rage is tame
 To the wrath of man.

VIII.

At morn, grey Allan's mates with awe
Heard of the visioned sights he saw,
 The legend heard him say;
But the Seer's gifted eye was dim,
Deafened his ear, and stark his limb,
 Ere closed that bloody day.
He sleeps far from his Highland heath,
But often of the Dance of Death
 His comrades tell the tale
On picquet-post, when ebbs the night,
And waning watch-fires glow less bright,
 And dawn is glimmering pale.

        — 1815

---

6 *Welkin.* Sky.

<13>

St. Swithin's Chair

On Hallow-Mass Eve, ere you boune[7] ye to rest,
Ever beware that your couch be bless'd;
Sign it with cross, and sain it with bead,
Sing the *Ave*, and say the Creed.

For on Hallow-Mass Eve the Night-Hag will ride,
And all her nine-fold sweeping on by her side,
Whether the wind sing lowly or loud,
Sailing through moonshine or swath'd in the cloud.

The Lady she sate in Saint Swithin's Chair,[8]
The dew of the night has damp'd her hair:
Her cheek was pale — but resolved and high
Was the word of her lip and the glance of her eye.

She mutter'd the spell of Swithin bold,
When his naked foot traced the midnight wold,
When he stopp'd the Hag as she rode the night,
And bade her descend, and her promise plight.

He that dare sit on Saint Swithin's Chair,
When the Night-Hag wings the troubled air.
Questions three, when he speaks the spell,
He may ask, and she must tell.

The Baron has been with King Robert his liege.
These three long years, in battle and siege;
News are there none of his weal or his woe,
And fain the Lady his fate would know.

---

[7] *Boune.* Prepare.
[8] *Saint Swithin.* Saint Swithin (d. 861 CE) was patron saint of Winchester
Cathedral. Various parts of his body are located in different shrines in England.
The locale of this poem might be the empty tomb of Swithin in the ruins of the
Old Minster, but considering how many fragments might have had separate
burial, removal and reburial, the locale is uncertain.

<14>

She shudders and stops as the charm she speaks; —
Is it the moody owl that shrieks?
Or is that sound, betwixt laughter and scream,
The voice of the Demon who haunts the stream?

The moan of the wind sunk silent and low.
And the roaring torrent had ceased to flow;
The calm was more dreadful than raging storm,
When the cold grey mist brought the ghastly form!

—*Waverly*, Chapter XIII

<15>

The Dead Man's Lea

[They came upon us in the night.
And brake my bower and slew my knight;
My servants a' for life did flee
And left us in extremitie.
They slew my knight to me sae dear;
They slew my knight, and drave his gear;]
The moon may set, the sun may rise.
But a deadly sleep has closed his eyes.

★ ★ ★

But follow, follow me,
While glowworms light the lea,[9]
I'll show ye where the dead should be —
    Each in his shroud.
    While winds pipe loud,
    And the red moon peeps dim through the cloud.

Follow, follow me;
Brave should he be
That treads by night the dead man's lea.

—Waverly, Chap. lxiii.

---

[9] *Lea.* An open, grassy area.

<16>

Proud Maisie

Proud Maisie is in the wood,
   Walking so early;
Sweet Robin sits on the bush,
   Singing so rarely.

"Tell me, thou bonny bird,
   When shall I marry me?" —
"When six braw[10] gentlemen
   Kirkward shall carry ye."

"Who makes the bridal bed,
   Birdie, say truly?" —
"The grey-headed sexton
   That delves the grave duly.

"The glow-worm o'er grave and stone
   Shall light thee steady.
The owl from the steeple sing,
   'Welcome, proud lady.'"

—From *The Heart of Midlothian*, xiv – xxxix

---

[10] *Braw.* Finely-dressed.

<17>

The Maidens of Valhalla

Whet the bright steel.
Sons of the White Dragon![11]
Kindle the torch.
Daughter of Hengist![12]

The steel glimmers not for the carving of the banquet.
It is hard, broad, and sharply pointed;
The torch goeth not to the bridal chamber,
It steams and glitters blue with sulphur.
Whet the steel, the raven croaks!
Light the torch, Zernebock[13] is yelling!
Whet the steel, sons of the Dragon!
Kindle the torch, daughter of Hengist!

The black clouds are low over the thane's castle:
The eagle screams — he rides on their bosom.
Scream not, grey rider of the sable cloud.
Thy banquet is prepared!
The maidens of Valhalla look forth.
The race of Hengist will send them guests.
Shake your black tresses, maidens of Valhalla!
And strike your loud timbrels for joy!
Many a haughty step bends to your halls.
Many a helmed head.

Dark sits the evening upon the thane's castle.
The black clouds gather round;
Soon shall they be red as the blood of the valiant!
The destroyer of forests shall shake his red crest against them;
He, the bright consumer of palaces.
Broad waves he his blazing banner,

---

[11] *White Dragon.* The white dragon is a symbol of the Anglo-Saxons. This poem has also appeared with the alternate title, "The Saxon War Song."
[12] Hengist and Horsa were the legendary Saxon invaders of England.
[13] *Zernebock.* Scott believes that Zernebock is a Saxon pagan god, but it is actually a Slavic word for the Devil.

<18>

Red, wide, and dusky,
Over the strife of the valiant;
His joy is in the clashing swords and broken bucklers;
He loves to lick the hissing blood as it bursts warm
      from the wound!

All must perish!
The sword cleaveth the helmet;
The strong armour is pierced by the lance:
Fire devoureth the dwelling of princes.
Engines break down the fences of the battle.
All must perish!
The race of Hengist is gone —
The name of Horsa is no more!
Shrink not then from your doom, sons of the sword!

Let your blades drink blood like wine;
Feast ye in the banquet of slaughter,
By the light of the blazing halls!
Strong be your swords while your blood is warm,
And spare neither for pity nor fear,
For vengeance hath but an hour;
Strong hate itself shall expire!
I also must perish.

                  —From *Ivanhoe*, Chap. xxxii

<19>

Merrily Swim We: – The Kelpy

Merrily swim we, the moon shines bright,
Both current and ripple are dancing in light:
We have roused the night raven; I heard him croak
As we plashed along beneath the oak
That flings its broad branches so far and so wide,
Their shadows are dancing in midst of the tide.
"Who wakens my nestlings?" the raven he said,
"My beak shall 'ere morn in his blood be red!
For a blue swollen corpse is a dainty meal,
And I'll have my share with the pike and the eel."

Merrily swim we, the moon shines bright,
There's a golden gleam on the distant height:
There's a silver shower on the alders dank,
And the drooping willows that wave on the bank.
I see the Abbey, both turret and tower,
It is all astir for the vesper hour;
The monks for the chapel are leaving each cell,
But where's Father Philip should toll the bell?

Merrily swim we, the moon shines bright.
Downward we drift through shadow and light;
Under yon rock the eddies sleep.
Calm and silent, dark and deep.
The Kelpy has risen from the fathomless pool,
He has lighted his candle of death and of dool:[14]
Look, Father, look, and you'll laugh to see
How he gapes and glares with his eyes on thee!

---

[14] *Dool.* Variant of dole, for grief or mourning.

<20>

Good luck to your fishing, whom watch ye to-night?
A man of mean or a man of might?
Is it layman or priest that must float in your cove,
Or lover who crosses to visit his love?
Hark! heard ye the Kelpy reply as we pass'd, —
"God's blessing on the warder — he lock'd the bridge fast!
All that come to my cove are sunk,
Priest or layman, lover or monk."

Landed — landed! the black book hath won.
Else had you seen Berwick[15] with morning sun
Sain ye, and save ye, and blithe mot ye be,
For seldom they land that go swimming with me.

—From From the Monastery, Chap. V

---

[15] *Berwick*. Berwick-upon-Tweed, Northumberland. Most malevolent kelpies
were associated with ponds or lochs, but Scott and others permit kelpies to haunt
rivers. The reference to tide places this poem near the coast. Berwick Bridge,
rebuilt at least five times since the 12th century, is a likely locale.

<21>

To the White Lady

I. INVOCATION
Thrice to the holly brake,
Thrice to the well —
I bid thee awake,
White Maid of Avenel!

Noon gleams on the lake,
Noon glows on the fell, —
Wake thee, O wake,
White Maid of Avenel.

II. THE WHITE LADY SPEAKS
Youth of the dark eye, wherefore didst thou call me?
Wherefore art thou here, if terrors can appal thee?
He that seeks to deal with us must know no fear nor failing;
To coward and churl our speech is dark, our gifts are unavailing.
The breeze that brought me hither now must sweep
    Egyptian ground,
The fleecy cloud on which I ride for Araby is bound;
The fleecy cloud is drifting by, the breeze sighs for my stay,
For I must sail a thousand miles before the close of day.

What I am I must not show —
What I am thou couldst not know —
Something betwixt heaven and hell —
Something that neither stood nor fell —
Something that through thy wit or will
May work thee good — may work thee ill.
Neither substance quite, nor shadow,
Haunting lonely moor and meadow.
Dancing by the haunted spring.
Riding on the whirlwind's wing;
Aping in fantastic fashion
Every change of human passion,
While o'er our frozen minds they pass
Like shadows from the mirror'd glass.

<22>

Wayward, fickle, is our mood,
Hovering betwixt bad and good,
Happier than brief-dated man,
Living twenty times his span;
Far less happy, for we have
Help nor hope beyond the grave!
Man awakes to joy or sorrow;
Ours the sleep that knows no morrow.
This is all that I can show —
This is all that thou may'st know.

Ay! and I taught thee the word and the spell,
To waken me here by the Fairies' Well:
But thou hast loved the heron and hawk,
More than to seek my haunted walk;
And thou hast loved the lance and the sword,
More than good text and holy word;
And thou hast loved the deer to track,
More than the lines and the letters black;
And thou art a ranger of moss and of wood.
And scornest the nurture of gentle blood.

Thy craven fear my truth accused;
Thine idlehood my trust abused;
He that draws to harbour late,
Must sleep without, or burst the gate.
There is a star for thee which burn'd,
Its influence wanes, its course is turn'd;
Valour and constancy alone
Can bring thee back the chance that 's flown.

Within that awful volume lies
The mystery of mysteries!
Happiest they of human race.
To whom God has granted grace
To read, to fear, to hope, to pray,
To lift the latch, and force the way;
And better had they ne'er been born,
Who read to doubt, or read to scorn.

<23>

Many a fathom dark and deep
I have laid the book to sleep;
Ethereal fires around it glowing —
Ethereal music ever flowing —
The sacred pledge of Heav'n
    All things revere.
    Each in his sphere,
Save man for whom 'twas giv'n:
Lend thy hand, and thou shalt spy
Things ne'er seen by mortal eye.

Fear'st thou to go with me?
Still it is free to thee
    A peasant to dwell;
Thou may'st drive the dull steer,
And chase the king's deer,
But never more come near
    This haunted well.

Here lies the volume thou boldly hast sought;
Touch it, and take it, — 'twill dearly be bought.

      Rash thy deed,
      Mortal weed
    To immortal flames applying;
      Rasher trust
      Has thing of dust.
    On his own weak worth relying:
Strip thee of such fences vain,
Strip, and prove thy luck again.

Mortal warp and mortal woof
Cannot brook this charmed roof;
All that mortal art hath wrought
In our cell returns to nought.
The molten gold returns to clay.
The polish'd diamond melts away;
All is altered, all is flown.
Nought stands fast but truth alone.

<24>

Not for that thy quest give o'er:
Courage ! prove thy chance once more.

Alas! alas!
Not ours the grace
These holy characters to trace:
    Idle forms of painted air.
    Not to us is given to share
The boon bestow'd on Adam's race.

With patience bide,
Heaven will provide
The fitting time, the fitting guide.

III. THE FAIRIES ON GOOD FRIDAY
This is the day when the fairy kind
Sit weeping alone for their hopeless lot,
And the wood-maiden sighs to the sighing wind,
And the mermaiden weeps in her crystal grot;

For this is a day that the deed was wrought,
In which we have neither part nor share.
For the children of clay was salvation bought,
But not for the forms of sea or air!
And ever the mortal is most forlorn.
Who meeteth our race on the Friday morn.

IV. THE SECRET OF AVENEL
By ties mysterious link'd, our fated race
Holds strange connexion with the sons of men.
The star that rose upon the House of Avenel,
When Norman Ulric first assumed the name,
That star, when culminating in its orbit.
Shot from its sphere a drop of diamond dew.

And this bright font received it — and a Spirit
Rose from the fountain, and her date of life
Hath co-existence with the House of Avenel,
And with the star that rules it.

<25>

Look on my girdle — on this thread of gold —
'Tis fine as web of lightest gossamer.
And, but there is a spell on 't, would not bind,
Light as they are, the folds of my thin robe.
But when 'twas donn'd, it was a massive chain,
Such as might bind the champion of the Jews,[16]
Even when his locks were longest: it hath dwindled,
Hath 'minish'd in its substance and its strength,
As sunk the greatness of the House of Avenel.
When this frail thread gives way, I to the elements
Resign the principles of life they lent me.
Ask me no more of this! — the stars forbid it.

Dim burns the once bright star of Avenel,
Dim as the beacon when the morn is nigh.
And the o'er-wearied warder leaves the light-house;
There is an influence sorrowful and fearful,
That dogs its downward course. Disastrous passion.
Fierce hate and rivalry, are in the aspect
That lowers upon its fortunes.
Complain not on me, child of clay,
If to thy harm I yield the way.
We, who soar thy sphere above,
Know not aught of hate or love;
As will or wisdom rules thy mood,
My gift to evil turn or good.

[16] *Champion of the Jews.* Samson, who was chained to the temple of the Philistines.

<26>

V. SHE COMES AT WILL

You have summone'd me once, you have summon'd me twice.
And without e'er a summons I come to you thrice;
Unask'd for, unsued for, you come to my glen;
Unsued and unask'd, I am with you agen.

VI. THE WHITE LADY'S FAREWELL

Fare thee well, thou Holly green!
Thou shalt seldom now be seen,
With all thy glittering garlands bending,
As to greet my slow descending,
Startling the bewilder'd hind
Who sees thee wave without a wind.

Farewell, Fountain! now not long
Shalt thou murmur to my song,
While thy crystal bubbles glancing.
Keep the time in mystic dancing.
Rise and swell, are burst and lost.
Like mortal schemes by fortune cross'd.

The knot of fate at length is tied.
The Churl is Lord, the Maid is Bride!
Vainly did my magic sleight
Send the lover from her sight;
Wither bush, and perish well,
Fall'n is lofty Avenel.

—From *From the Monastery*, Chaps xi-xxx.

<27>

The Song of the Reim-Kennar

Stern eagle of the far north-west,
Thou that bearest in thy grasp the thunderbolt,
Thou whose rushing pinions stir ocean to madness,
Thou the destroyer of herds, thou the scatterer of navies.
Amidst the scream of thy rage.
Amidst the rushing of thy onward wings.
Though thy scream be loud as the cry of a perishing nation,
Though the rushing of thy wings be like the roar
      of ten thousand waves.
Yet hear, in thine ire and thy haste.
Hear thou the voice of the Reim-kennar
Thou hast met the pine-trees of Drontheim,[17]
Their dark-green heads lie prostrate beside their up-rooted stems;
Thou hast met the rider of the ocean,
The tall, the strong bark of the fearless rover,
And she has struck to thee the topsail
That she had not veil'd to a royal armada.
Thou hast met the tower that bears its crest among the clouds,
The battled massive tower of the Jarl of former days,
And the cope-stone of the turret
Is lying upon its hospitable hearth;
But thou too shalt stoop, proud compeller of clouds.
When thou hearest the voice of the Reim-kennar.

There are verses that can stop the stag in the forest.
Ay, and when the dark-colour'd dog is opening on his track;
There are verses can make the wild hawk pause on the wing,
Like the falcon that wears the hood and the jesses,
And who knows the shrill whistle of the fowler.
Thou who canst mock at the scream of the drowning mariner,
And the crash of the ravaged forest,
And the groan of the overwhelmed crowds,
When the church hath fallen in the moment of prayer;
There are sounds which thou also must list,
When they are chanted by the voice of the Reim-kennar.

---

[17] *Drontheim.* Capital of Norway during the Viking era.

<28>

Enough of woe hast thou wrought on the ocean.
The widows wring their hands on the beach;
Enough of woe hast thou wrought on the land,
The husbandman folds his arms in despair;
Cease thou the waving of thy pinions,
Let the ocean repose in her dark strength;
Cease thou the flashing of thine eye,
Let the thunderbolt sleep in the armoury of Odin;
Be thou still at my bidding, viewless racer
     of the north-western heaven, —
Sleep thou at the voice of Norna the Reim-kennar.

Eagle of the far north-western waters,
Thou hast heard the voice of the Reim-kennar,
Thou hast closed thy wide sails at her bidding,
And folded them in peace by thy side.
My blessing be on thy retiring path;
When thou stoopest from thy place on high.
Soft be thy slumbers in the caverns of the unknown ocean,
Rest till destiny shall again awaken thee;
Eagle of the north-west, thou hast heard the voice
    of the Reim-kennar

—From *The Pirate*, Chap vi

<29>

SAMUEL TAYLOR COLERIDGE (1772-1834)

The Rime of the Ancient Mariner

IN SEVEN PARTS

*Facile credo, plures esse Naturas invisibiles quam visibiles in rerum universitate.
Sed horum omnium familiam quis nobis enarrabit? et gradus et cognationes et
discrimina et singulorum munera? Quid agunt? quæ loca habitant? Harum
rerum notitiam semper ambivit ingenium humanum, nunquam attigit. Juvat,
interea, non diffiteor, quandoque in animo, tanquam in tabulâ, majoris et
melioris mundi imaginem contemplari: ne mens assuefacta hodiernæ vitæ
minutiis se contrahat nimis, et tota subsidat in pusillas cogitationes. Sed veritati
interea invigilandum est, modusque servandus, ut certa ab incertis, diem a nocte,
distinguamus.*

— *T. BURNET, Archæol Phil. p. 68.*[1]

ARGUMENT

*How a Ship having passed the Line was driven by storms to the cold
Country towards the South Pole; and how from thence she made her
course to the tropical Latitude of the Great Pacific Ocean; and of the
strange things that befell; and in what manner the Ancyent Marinere
came back to his own Country.*

---

[1] *Facile credo* ... "I easily believe, that there are more invisible Entities in the
universe than visible ones. But who can describe how they are grouped together?
and their ranks and relationships and distinguishing features and qualities?
What they do? In which places do they live? The mind of man has always circled
about knowledge of these things, without ever attaining it. Nevertheless, I do not
doubt that on occasion it is good for us to imagine, as if it were pictured upon a
tablet, the image of a greater and better world; lest the intellect, habituated to
the banalities of everyday life, contract itself too and be overwhelmed with trivia.
But at the same time we must be vigilant for truth, and maintain a proper
proportion, so that we may distinguish certainty from uncertainty, day from
night." —Thomas Burnet (1635-1715). The text was published in Latin in 1684
and in English in 1689. As if often the case with poetic epigraphs, Coleridge
selected only those sentences and phrases he wanted and removed the Burnet
lines from their original context, a lengthy discussion of the Hebrew Cabala.

<30>

PART I

It is an ancient Mariner,
And he stoppeth one of three.
"By thy long grey beard and glittering eye,
Now wherefore stopp'st thou me?

"The Bridegroom's doors are opened wide,
And I am next of kin;
The guests are met, the feast is set:
May'st hear the merry din."

He holds him with his skinny hand,
"There was a ship," quoth he.
"Hold off! unhand me, grey-beard loon!"
Eftsoons his hand dropt he.

He holds him with his glittering eye
The Wedding-Guest stood still,
And listens like a three years' child:
The Mariner hath his will.

The Wedding-Guest sat on a stone:
He cannot choose but hear;
And thus spake on that ancient man,
The bright-eyed Mariner.

"The ship was cheered, the harbour cleared,
Merrily did we drop
Below the kirk, below the hill,
Below the lighthouse top.

The sun came up upon the left,
Out of the sea came he!
And he shone bright, and on the right
Went down into the sea.

Higher and higher every day,
Till over the mast at noon —"
The Wedding-Guest here beat his breast,
For he heard the loud bassoon.

<31>

The bride hath paced into the hall,
Red as a rose is she;
Nodding their heads before her goes
The merry minstrelsy.

The Wedding-Guest he beat his breast,
Yet he cannot choose but hear;
And thus spake on that ancient man,
The bright-eyed Mariner: —

And now the Storm-blast came, and he
Was tyrannous and strong:
He struck with his o'ertaking wings
And chased us south along.

With sloping masts and dipping prow,
As who pursued with yell and blow
Still treads the shadow of his foe,
And forward bends his head,
The ship drove fast, loud roared the blast,
And southward aye we fled.

And now there came both mist and snow,
And it grew wondrous cold:
And ice, mast-high, came floating by,
As green as emerald.

And through the drifts the snowy clifts
Did send a dismal sheen:
Nor shapes of men nor beasts we ken —
The ice was all between.

The ice was here, the ice was there,
The ice was all around:
It cracked and growled, and roared and howled,
Like noises in a swound!

At length did cross an Albatross,
Thorough the fog it came;
As if it had been a Christian soul,
We hailed it in God's name.

<32>

It ate the food it ne'er had eat,
And round and round it flew.
The ice did split with a thunder-fit;
The helmsman steered us through!

And a good south wind sprung up behind;
The Albatross did follow,
And every day, for food or play,
Came to the mariners' hollo!

In mist or cloud, on mast or shroud,
It perched for vespers nine;
Whiles all the night, through fog-smoke white,
Glimmered the white moon-shine."
 "God save thee, ancient Mariner!
From the fiends, that plague thee thus! —
Why look'st thou so?" — With my cross-bow
I shot the Albatross.

     ★   ★   ★   ★   ★

PART II
The Sun now rose upon the right:
Out of the sea came he,
Still hid in mist, and on the left
Went down into the sea.

And the good south wind still blew behind,
But no sweet bird did follow,
Nor any day for food or play
Came to the mariners' hollo!

And I had done a hellish thing,
And it would work 'em woe:
For all averred, I had killed the bird
That made the breeze to blow.
Ah wretch! said they, the bird to slay,
That made the breeze to blow!

<33>

Nor, dim nor red, like God's own head,
The glorious Sun uprist:
Then all averred, I had killed the bird
That brought the fog and mist.
'Twas right, said they, such birds to slay,
That bring the fog and mist.

The fair breeze blew, the white foam flew,
The furrow followed free;
We were the first that ever burst
Into that silent sea.

Down dropt the breeze, the sails dropt down,
'Twas sad as sad could be;
And we did speak only to break
The silence of the sea!

All in a hot and copper sky,
The bloody Sun, at noon,
Right up above the mast did stand,
No bigger than the Moon.

Day after day, day after day,
We stuck, nor breath nor motion;
As idle as a painted ship
Upon a painted ocean.

Water, water, every where,
And all the boards did shrink;
Water, water, every where
Nor any drop to drink.

The very deep did rot: O Christ!
That ever this should be!
Yea, slimy things did crawl with legs
Upon the slimy sea.

About, about, in reel and rout
The death-fires danced at night;
The water, like a witch's oils,
Burnt green, and blue and white.

<34>

And some in dreams assured were,
Of the Spirit that plagued us so;
Nine fathom deep he had followed us
From the land of mist and snow.

And every tongue, through utter drought,
Was withered at the root;
We could not speak, no more than if
We had been choked with soot.

Ah! well a-day! what evil looks
Had I from old and young!
Instead of the cross, the Albatross
About my neck was hung.

PART III
There passed a weary time. Each throat
Was parched, and glazed each eye.
A weary time! a weary time!
How glazed each weary eye,
When looking westward, I beheld
A something in the sky.

At first it seemed a little speck,
And then it seemed a mist;
It moved and moved, and took at last
A certain shape, I wist.

A speck, a mist, a shape, I wist!
And still it neared and neared:
As if it dodged a water-sprite,
It plunged and tacked and veered.

With throats unslaked, with black lips baked,
We could nor laugh nor wail;
Through utter drought all dumb we stood!
I bit my arm, I sucked the blood,
And cried, A sail! a sail!

<35>

With throats unslaked, with black lips baked,
Agape they heard me call:
Gramercy! they for joy did grin,
And all at once their breath drew in,
As they were drinking all.

See! see! (I cried) she tacks no more!
Hither to work us weal;
Without a breeze, without a tide,
She steadies with upright keel!

The western wave was all a-flame,
The day was well nigh done!
Almost upon the western wave
Rested the broad bright Sun;

When that strange shape drove suddenly
Betwixt us and the Sun.
And straight the Sun was flecked with bars,
(Heaven's Mother send us grace!)
As if through a dungeon-grate he peered
With broad and burning face.

Alas! (thought I, and my heart beat loud)
How fast she nears and nears!
Are those her sails that glance in the Sun,
Like restless gossameres?

Are those her ribs through which the Sun
Did peer, as through a grate?
And is that Woman all her crew?
Is that a Death? and are there two?
Is Death that Woman's mate?

Her lips were red, her looks were free,
Her locks were yellow as gold:
Her skin was as white as leprosy,
The Night-mare Life-in-Death was she,
Who thicks man's blood with cold.

<36>

The naked hulk alongside came,
And the twain were casting dice;
"The game is done! I've won! I've won!"
Quoth she, and whistles thrice.

The Sun's rim dips; the stars rush out:
At one stride comes the dark;
With far-heard whisper, o'er the sea,
Off shot the spectre-bark.

We listened and looked sideways up!
Fear at my heart, as at a cup,
My life-blood seemed to sip!
The stars were dim, and thick the night,
The steersman's face by his lamp gleamed white;

From the sails the dew did drip —
Till clomb above the eastern bar
The horned Moon, with one bright star
Within the nether tip.

One after one, by the star-dogged Moon,
Too quick for groan or sigh,
Each turned his face with a ghastly pang,
And cursed me with his eye.

Four times fifty living men,
(And I heard nor sigh nor groan)
With heavy thump, a lifeless lump,
They dropped down one by one.

The souls did from their bodies fly, —
They fled to bliss or woe!
And every soul, it passed me by,
Like the whizz of my cross-bow! —

<37>

PART IV
"I fear thee, ancient Mariner!
I fear thy skinny hand!
And thou art long, and lank, and brown,
As is the ribbed sea-sand.[2]

I fear thee and thy glittering eye,
And thy skinny hand, so brown." —
Fear not, fear not, thou Wedding-Guest!
This body dropt not down.

Alone, alone, all, all alone,
Alone on a wide wide sea!
And never a saint took pity on
My soul in agony.

The many men, so beautiful!
And they all dead did lie:
And a thousand thousand slimy things
Lived on; and so did I.

I looked upon the rotting sea,
And drew my eyes away;
I looked upon the rotting deck,
And there the dead men lay.

I looked to heaven, and tried to pray;
But or ever a prayer had gusht,
A wicked whisper came, and made
My heart as dry as dust.

I closed my lids, and kept them close,
And the balls like pulses beat;
For the sky and the sea, and the sea and the sky,
Lay like a load on my weary eye,
And the dead were at my feet.

---

[2] For the last two lines of this stanza, I am indebted to Mr. Wordsworth. It was on a delightful walk from Nether Stowey to Dulverton, with him and his sister, in the autumn of 1797, that this poem was planned, and in part composed — STC.

<38>

The cold sweat melted from their limbs,
Nor rot nor reek did they:
The look with which they looked on me
Had never passed away.

An orphan's curse would drag to hell
A spirit from on high;
But oh! more horrible than that
Is a curse in a dead man's eye!
Seven days, seven nights, I saw that curse,
And yet I could not die.

The moving Moon went up the sky,
And no where did abide:
Softly she was going up,
And a star or two beside —

Her beams bemocked the sultry main,
Like April hoar-frost spread;
But where the ship's huge shadow lay,
The charmed water burnt always
A still and awful red.

Beyond the shadow of the ship,
I watched the water-snakes:
They moved in tracks of shining white,
And when they reared, the elfish light
Fell off in hoary flakes.

Within the shadow of the ship
I watched their rich attire:
Blue, glossy green, and velvet black,
They coiled and swam; and every track
Was a flash of golden fire.

<39>

O happy living things! no tongue
Their beauty might declare:
A spring of love gushed from my heart,
And I blessed them unaware:
Sure my kind saint took pity on me,
And I blessed them unaware.

The selfsame moment I could pray;
And from my neck so free
The Albatross fell off, and sank
Like lead into the sea.

PART V
Oh sleep! it is a gentle thing,
Beloved from pole to pole!
To Mary Queen the praise be given!
She sent the gentle sleep from Heaven,
That slid into my soul.

The silly buckets on the deck,
That had so long remained,
I dreamt that they were filled with dew;
And when I awoke, it rained.

My lips were wet, my throat was cold,
My garments all were dank;
Sure I had drunken in my dreams,
And still my body drank.

I moved, and could not feel my limbs:
I was so light — almost
I thought that I had died in sleep;
And was a blessed ghost.

And soon I heard a roaring wind:
It did not come anear;
But with its sound it shook the sails,
That were so thin and sere.

<40>

The upper air burst into life!
And a hundred fire-flags sheen,
To and fro they were hurried about!
And to and fro, and in and out,
The wan stars danced between.

And the coming wind did roar more loud,
And the sails did sigh like sedge;
And the rain poured down from one black cloud;
The Moon was at its edge.

The thick black cloud was cleft, and still
The Moon was at its side:
Like waters shot from some high crag,
The lightning fell with never a jag,
A river steep and wide.

The loud wind never reached the ship,
Yet now the ship moved on!
Beneath the lightning and the Moon
The dead men gave a groan.

They groaned, they stirred, they all uprose,
Nor spake, nor moved their eyes;
It had been strange, even in a dream,!
To have seen those dead men rise.

The helmsman steered, the ship moved on;
Yet never a breeze up blew;
The mariners all 'gan work the ropes,
Where they were wont to do;
They raised their limbs like lifeless tools —
We were a ghastly crew.

The body of my brother's son
Stood by me, knee to knee:
The body and I pulled at one rope
But he said nought to me. —

<41>

"I fear thee, ancient Mariner!" —
Be calm, thou Wedding-Guest!
'Twas not those souls that fled in pain,
Which to their corses came again,
But a troop of spirits blest:

For when it dawned — they dropped their arms,
And clustered round the mast;
Sweet sounds rose slowly through their mouths,
And from their bodies passed.

Around, around, flew each sweet sound,
Then darted to the Sun;
Slowly the sounds came back again,
Now mixed, now one by one.

Sometimes a-dropping from the sky
I heard the sky-lark sing;
Sometimes all little birds that are,
How they seemed to fill the sea and air
With their sweet jargoning!

And now 'twas like all instruments,
Now like a lonely flute;
And now it is an angel's song,
That makes the heavens be mute.

It ceased; yet still the sails made on
A pleasant noise till noon,
A noise like of a hidden brook
In the leafy month of June,
That to the sleeping woods all night
Singeth a quiet tune.

Till noon we quietly sailed on,
Yet never a breeze did breathe:
Slowly and smoothly went the ship,
Moved onward from beneath.

<42>

Under the keel nine fathom deep,
From the land of mist and snow,
The spirit slid: and it was he
That made the ship to go.
The sails at noon left off their tune,
And the ship stood still also.

The Sun, right up above the mast,
Had fixed her to the ocean:
But in a minute she 'gan stir,
With a short uneasy motion —
Backwards and forwards half her length
With a short uneasy motion.

Then like a pawing horse let go,
She made a sudden bound:
It flung the blood into my head,
And I fell down in a swound.

How long in that same fit I lay,
I have not to declare;
But ere my living life returned,
I heard and in my soul discerned
Two voices in the air.

"Is it he?" quoth one, "Is this the man?
By him who died on cross,
With his cruel bow he laid full low
The harmless Albatross.

The spirit who bideth by himself
In the land of mist and snow,
He loved the bird that loved the man
Who shot him with his bow."

The other was a softer voice,
As soft as honey-dew:
Quoth he, "The man hath penance done,
And penance more will do."

<43>

PART VI
FIRST VOICE
"But tell me, tell me! speak again,
Thy soft response renewing —
What makes that ship drive on so fast?
What is the ocean doing?"

SECOND VOICE
"Still as a slave before his lord,
The ocean hath no blast;
His great bright eye most silently
Up to the Moon is cast —

If he may know which way to go;
For she guides him smooth or grim.
See, brother, see! how graciously
She looketh down on him."

FIRST VOICE
"But why drives on that ship so fast,
Without or wave or wind?"

SECOND VOICE
"The air is cut away before,
And closes from behind.

Fly, brother, fly! more high, more high!
Or we shall be belated:
For slow and slow that ship will go,
When the Mariner's trance is abated."

I woke, and we were sailing on
As in a gentle weather:
'Twas night, calm night, the moon was high,
The dead men stood together.

All stood together on the deck,
For a charnel-dungeon fitter:
All fixed on me their stony eyes,
That in the Moon did glitter.

<44>

The pang, the curse, with which they died,
Had never passed away:
I could not draw my eyes from theirs,
Nor turn them up to pray.

And now this spell was snapt: once more
I viewed the ocean green,
And looked far forth, yet little saw
Of what had else been seen —

Like one, that on a lonesome road
Doth walk in fear and dread,
And having once turned round walks on,
And turns no more his head;
Because he knows, a frightful fiend
Doth close behind him tread.

But soon there breathed a wind on me,
Nor sound nor motion made:
Its path was not upon the sea,
In ripple or in shade.

It raised my hair, it fanned my cheek
Like a meadow-gale of spring —
It mingled strangely with my fears,
Yet it felt like a welcoming.

Swiftly, swiftly flew the ship,
Yet she sailed softly too:
Sweetly, sweetly blew the breeze —
On me alone it blew.

Oh! dream of joy! is this indeed
The light-house top I see?
Is this the hill? is this the kirk?
Is this mine own countree?

We drifted o'er the harbour-bar,
And I with sobs did pray —
O let me be awake, my God!
Or let me sleep alway.

<45>

The harbour-bay was clear as glass,
So smoothly it was strewn!
And on the bay the moonlight lay,
And the shadow of the Moon.

The rock shone bright, the kirk no less,
That stands above the rock:
The moonlight steeped in silentness
The steady weathercock.

And the bay was white with silent light
Till rising from the same,
Full many shapes, that shadows were,
In crimson colours came.

A little distance from the prow
Those crimson shadows were:
I turned my eyes upon the deck —
Oh, Christ! what saw I there!

Each corse lay flat, lifeless and flat,
And, by the holy rood!
A man all light, a seraph-man,
On every corse there stood.

This seraph-band, each waved his hand:
It was a heavenly sight!
They stood as signals to the land,
Each one a lovely light;

This seraph-band, each waved his hand,
No voice did they impart —
No voice; but oh! the silence sank
Like music on my heart.

But soon I heard the dash of oars,
I heard the Pilot's cheer;
My head was turned perforce away,
And I saw a boat appear.

<46>

The Pilot and the Pilot's boy,
I heard them coming fast:
Dear Lord in Heaven! it was a joy
The dead men could not blast.

I saw a third — I heard his voice:
It is the Hermit good!
He singeth loud his godly hymns
That he makes in the wood.
He'll shrieve my soul, he'll wash away
The Albatross's blood.

PART VII

This Hermit good lives in that wood
Which slopes down to the sea.
How loudly his sweet voice he rears!
He loves to talk with marineres
That come from a far countree.

He kneels at morn, and noon, and eve —
He hath a cushion plump.
It is the moss that wholly hides
The rotted old oak-stump.

The skiff-boat neared: I heard them talk,
"Why, this is strange, I trow!
Where are those lights so many and fair,
That signal made but now?"

"Strange, by my faith!" the Hermit said —
"And they answered not our cheer!
The planks looked warped! and see those sails,
How thin they are and sere!
I never saw aught like to them,
Unless perchance it were

"Brown skeletons of leaves that lag
My forest-brook along;
When the ivy-tod is heavy with snow,
And the owlet whoops to the wolf below,
That eats the she-wolf's young."

<47>

"Dear Lord! it hath a fiendish look —
(The Pilot made reply)
I am a-feared" — "Push on, push on!"
Said the Hermit cheerily.

The boat came closer to the ship,
But I nor spake nor stirred;
The boat came close beneath the ship,
And straight a sound was heard.

Under the water it rumbled on,
Still louder and more dread:
It reached the ship, it split the bay;
The ship went down like lead.

Stunned by that loud and dreadful sound,
Which sky and ocean smote,
Like one that hath been seven days drowned
My body lay afloat;
But swift as dreams, myself I found
Within the Pilot's boat.

Upon the whirl, where sank the ship,
The boat spun round and round;
And all was still, save that the hill
Was telling of the sound.

I moved my lips — the Pilot shrieked
And fell down in a fit;
The holy Hermit raised his eyes,
And prayed where he did sit.

I took the oars: the Pilot's boy,
Who now doth crazy go,
Laughed loud and long, and all the while
His eyes went to and fro.
"Ha! ha!" quoth he, "full plain I see,
The Devil knows how to row."

<48>

And now, all in my own countree,
I stood on the firm land!
The Hermit stepped forth from the boat,
And scarcely he could stand.

"O shrieve me, shrieve me, holy man!"
The Hermit crossed his brow.
"Say quick," quoth he, "I bid thee say
What manner of man art thou?"

Forthwith this frame of mine was wrenched
With a woful agony,
Which forced me to begin my tale;
And then it left me free.

Since then, at an uncertain hour,
That agony returns:
And till my ghastly tale is told,
This heart within me burns.

I pass, like night, from land to land;
I have strange power of speech;
That moment that his face I see,
I know the man that must hear me:
To him my tale I teach.

What loud uproar bursts from that door!
The wedding-guests are there:
But in the garden-bower the bride
And bride-maids singing are:
And hark the little vesper bell,
Which biddeth me to prayer!

O Wedding-Guest! this soul hath been
Alone on a wide wide sea:
So lonely 'twas, that God himself
Scarce seemed there to be.

<49>

O sweeter than the marriage-feast,
'Tis sweeter far to me,
To walk together to the kirk
With a goodly company! —

To walk together to the kirk,
And all together pray,
While each to his great Father bends,
Old men, and babes, and loving friends,
And youths and maidens gay!

Farewell, farewell! but this I tell
To thee, thou Wedding-Guest!
He prayeth well, who loveth well
Both man and bird and beast.

He prayeth best, who loveth best
All things both great and small;
For the dear God who loveth us,
He made and loveth all.

The Mariner, whose eye is bright,
Whose beard with age is hoar,
Is gone: and now the Wedding-Guest
Turned from the bridegroom's door.

He went like one that hath been stunned,
And is of sense forlorn:
A sadder and a wiser man,
He rose the morrow morn.

1797-1798

<50>

Christabel

PART THE FIRST

'Tis the middle of night by the castle clock,
And the owls have awakened the crowing cock,"
Tu — whit! — Tu — whoo!
And hark, again! the crowing cock,
How drowsily it crew.

Sir Leoline; the Baron rich,
Hath a toothless mastiff, which
From her kennel beneath the rock
Maketh answer to the clock,
Four for the quarters, and twelve for the hour;
Ever and aye, by shine and shower,
Sixteen short howls, not over loud;
Some say, she sees my lady's shroud.

Is the night chilly and dark?
The night is chilly, but not dark.
The thin gray cloud is spread on high,
It covers but not hides the sky.
The moon is behind, and at the full;
And yet she looks both small and dull.
The night is chill, the cloud is gray:
'Tis a month before the month of May,
And the Spring comes slowly up this way.

The lovely lady, Christabel,
Whom her father loves so well,
What makes her in the wood so late,
A furlong from the castle gate?
She had dreams all yesternight
Of her own betrothed knight;
And she in the midnight wood will pray
For the weal of her lover that's far away.

<51>

She stole along, she nothing spoke,
The sighs she heaved were soft and low,
And naught was green upon the oak
But moss and rarest misletoe:
She kneels beneath the huge oak tree,
And in silence prayeth she.

The lady sprang up suddenly,
The lovely lady, Christabel!
It moaned as near, as near can be,
But what it is she cannot tell. —
On the other side it seems to be,
Of the huge, broad-breasted, old oak tree.

The night is chill; the forest bare;
Is it the wind that moaneth bleak?
There is not wind enough in the air
To move away the ringlet curl
From the lovely lady's cheek —
There is not wind enough to twirl
The one red leaf, the last of its clan,
That dances as often as dance it can,
Hanging so light, and hanging so high,
On the topmost twig that looks up at the sky.

Hush, beating heart of Christabel!
Jesu, Maria, shield her well!
She folded her arms beneath her cloak,
And stole to the other side of the oak.
What sees she there?

There she sees a damsel bright,
Drest in a silken robe of white,
That shadowy in the moonlight shone:
The neck that made that white robe wan,
Her stately neck, and arms were bare;
Her blue-veined feet unsandal'd were,
And wildly glittered here and there
The gems entangled in her hair.
I guess, 'twas frightful there to see

<52>

A lady so richly clad as she —
Beautiful exceedingly!

Mary mother, save me now!
(Said Christabel,) And who art thou?

The lady strange made answer meet,
And her voice was faint and sweet: —
Have pity on my sore distress,
I scarce can speak for weariness:
Stretch forth thy hand, and have no fear!
Said Christabel, How camest thou here?
And the lady, whose voice was faint and sweet,
Did thus pursue her answer meet: —

My sire is of a noble line,
And my name is Geraldine:
Five warriors seized me yestermorn,
Me, even me, a maid forlorn:
They choked my cries with force and fright,
And tied me on a palfrey white.

The palfrey was as fleet as wind,
And they rode furiously behind.
They spurred amain, their steeds were white:
And once we crossed the shade of night.
As sure as Heaven shall rescue me,
I have no thought what men they be;
Nor do I know how long it is
(For I have lain entranced I wis)
Since one, the tallest of the five,
Took me from the palfrey's back,
A weary woman, scarce alive.
Some muttered words his comrades spoke:
He placed me underneath this oak;
He swore they would return with haste;
Whither they went I cannot tell
I thought I heard, some minutes past,
Sounds as of a castle bell.

<53>

Stretch forth thy hand (thus ended she),
And help a wretched maid to flee.

Then Christabel stretched forth her hand,
And comforted fair Geraldine:
O well, bright dame! may you command
The service of Sir Leoline;
And gladly our stout chivalry
Will he send forth and friends withal
To guide and guard you safe and free
Home to your noble father's hall.

She rose: and forth with steps they passed
That strove to be, and were not, fast.
Her gracious stars the lady blest,
And thus spake on sweet Christabel:
All our household are at rest,
The hall as silent as the cell;
Sir Leoline is weak in health,
And may not well awakened be,
But we will move as if in stealth,
And I beseech your courtesy,
This night, to share your couch with me.

They crossed the moat, and Christabel
Took the key that fitted well;
A little door she opened straight,
All in the middle of the gate;
The gate that was ironed within and without
Where an army in battle array had marched out.
The lady sank, belike through pain,
And Christabel with might and main
Lifted her up, a weary weight,
Over the threshold of the gate:
Then the lady rose again,
And moved, as she were not in pain.

So free from danger, free from fear,
They crossed the court: right glad they were.
And Christabel devoutly cried

<54>

To the lady by her side,
Praise we the Virgin all divine
Who hath rescued thee from thy distress!
Alas! alas! said Geraldine,
I cannot speak for weariness.
So free from danger, free from fear,
They crossed the court: right glad they were.

Outside her kennel, the mastiff old
Lay fast asleep, in moonshine cold.
The mastiff old did not awake,
Yet she an angry moan did make!
And what can ail the mastiff bitch?
Never till now she uttered yell
Beneath the eye of Christabel.
Perhaps it is the owlet's scritch:
For what can ail the mastiff bitch?

They passed the hall, that echoes still,
Pass as lightly as you will!
The brands were flat, the brands were dying,
Amid their own white ashes lying;
But when the lady passed, there came
A tongue of light, a fit of flame
And Christabel saw the lady's eye,
And nothing else saw she thereby,
Save the boss of the shield of Sir Leoline tall,
Which hung in a murky old niche in the wall.
O softly tread, said Christabel,
My father seldom sleepeth well.

Sweet Christabel her feet doth bare,
And jealous of the listening air
They steal their way from stair to stair,
Now in glimmer, and now in gloom,
And now they pass the Baron's room,
As still as death with stifled breath!
And now have reached her chamber door;
And now doth Geraldine press down
The rushes of the chamber floor.

<55>

The moon shines dim in the open air,
And not a moonbeam enters here.
But they without its light can see
The chamber carved so curiously,
Carved with figures strange and sweet,
All made out of the carver's brain,
For a lady's chamber meet:
The lamp with twofold silver chain
Is fastened to an angel's feet.

The silver lamp burns dead and dim;
But Christabel the lamp will trim.
She trimmed the lamp, and made it bright,
And left it swinging to and fro,
While Geraldine, in wretched plight,
Sank down upon the floor below.

O weary lady, Geraldine,
I pray you, drink this cordial wine!
It is a wine of virtuous powers;
My mother made it of wild flowers.
And will your mother pity me,
Who am a maiden most forlorn?
Christabel answered — Woe is me!
She died the hour that I was born.
I have heard the grey-haired friar tell
How on her death-bed she did say,
That she should hear the castle-bell
Strike twelve upon my wedding-day.
O mother dear! that thou wert here!
I would, said Geraldine, she were!

But soon with altered voice, said she —
"Off, wandering mother! Peak and pine!
I have power to bid thee flee."
Alas! what ails poor Geraldine?
Why stares she with unsettled eye?
Can she the bodiless dead espy?

<56>

And why with hollow voice cries she,
"Off, woman, off! this hour is mine —
Though thou her guardian spirit be,
Off, woman, off! 'tis given to me."

Then Christabel knelt by the lady's side,
And raised to heaven her eyes so blue — ,
Alas! said she, this ghastly ride —
Dear lady! it hath wildered you!
The lady wiped her moist cold brow,
And faintly said, " 'Tis over now!"
Again the wild-flower wine she drank:
Her fair large eyes 'gan glitter bright,
And from the floor whereon she sank,
The lofty lady stood upright:
She was most beautiful to see,
Like a lady of a far countrée.
And thus the lofty lady spake —
"All they who live in the upper sky,
Do love you, holy Christabel!
And you love them, and for their sake
And for the good which me befel,
Even I in my degree will try,
Fair maiden, to requite you well.
But now unrobe yourself; for I
Must pray, ere yet in bed I lie."

Quoth Christabel, So let it be!
And as the lady bade, did she.
Her gentle limbs did she undress,
And lay down in her loveliness.

But through her brain of weal and woe
So many thoughts moved to and fro,
That vain it were her lids to close;
So half-way from the bed she rose,
And on her elbow did recline
To look at the lady Geraldine.

<57>

Beneath the lamp the lady bowed,
And slowly rolled her eyes around
Then drawing in her breath aloud,
Like one that shuddered, she unbound
The cincture from beneath her breast:
Her silken robe, and inner vest,
Dropt to her feet, and full in view,
Behold! her bosom and half her side —
A sight to dream of, not to tell!
O shield her! shield sweet Christabel!

Yet Geraldine nor speaks nor stirs;
Ah! what a stricken look was hers!
Deep from within she seems half-way
To lift some weight with sick assay,
And eyes the maid and seeks delay;
Then suddenly, as one defied,
Collects herself in scorn and pride,
And lay down by the Maiden's side! —
And in her arms the maid she took,
Ah wel-a-day!
And with low voice and doleful look
These words did say:
"In the touch of this bosom there worketh a spell,
Which is lord of thy utterance, Christabel!
Thou knowest to-night, and wilt know to-morrow,
This mark of my shame, this seal of my sorrow;
But vainly thou warrest,
For his is alone in
Thy power to declare,
That in the dim forest
Thou heard'st a low moaning,
And found'st a bright lady, surpassingly fair;
And didst bring her home with thee in love
        and in charity,
To shield her and shelter her from the damp air."

<58>

THE CONCLUSION TO PART THE FIRST

It was a lovely sight to see
The lady Christabel, when she
Was praying at the old oak tree.
Amid the jagged shadows
Of mossy leafless boughs,
Kneeling in the moonlight,
To make her gentle vows;
Her slender palms together prest,
Heaving sometimes on her breast;
Her face resigned to bliss or bale —
Her face, oh call it fair not pale,
And both blue eyes more, bright than clear,
Each about to have a tear.

With open eyes (ah woe is me!)
Asleep, and dreaming fearfully,
Fearfully dreaming, yet, I wis,
Dreaming that alone, which is —
O sorrow and shame! Can this be she,
The lady, who knelt at the old oak tree?
And lo! the worker of these harms,
That holds the maiden in her arms,
Seems to slumber still and mild,
As a mother with her child.

A star hath set, a star hath risen,
O Geraldine! since arms of thine
Have been the lovely lady's prison.
O Geraldine! one hour was thine
Thou'st had thy will! By tairn and rill,
The night-birds all that hour were still.
But now they are jubilant anew,
From cliff and tower, *tu-whoo! tu-whoo!*
Tu-whoo! tu-whoo! from wood and fell!

And see! the lady Christabel
Gathers herself from out her trance;
Her limbs relax, her countenance

<59>

Grows sad and soft; the smooth thin lids
Close o'er her eyes; and tears she sheds
Large tears that leave the lashes bright!
And oft the while she seems to smile
As infants at a sudden light!

Yea, she doth smile, and she doth weep,
Like a youthful hermitess,
Beauteous in a wilderness,
Who, praying always, prays in sleep.
And, if she move unquietly,
Perchance, 'tis but the blood so free
Comes back and tingles in her feet.
No doubt, she hath a vision sweet.
What if her guardian spirit 'twere,
What if she knew her mother near?
But this she knows, in joys and woes,
That saints will aid if men will call:
For the blue sky bends over all!

—1797

PART THE SECOND

Each matin bell, the Baron saith,
Knells us back to a world of death.
These words Sir Leoline first said,
When he rose and found his lady dead:
These words Sir Leoline will say
Many a morn to his dying day!

And hence the custom and law began
That still at dawn the sacristan,
Who duly pulls the heavy bell,
Five and forty beads must tell
Between each stroke — a warning knell,
Which not a soul can choose but hear
From Bratha Head to Wyndermere.
Saith Bracy the bard, So let it knell!

<60>

And let the drowsy sacristan
Still count as slowly as he can!
There is no lack of such, I ween,
As well fill up the space between.
In Langdale Pike and Witch's Lair,
And Dungeon-ghyll so foully rent,
With ropes of rock and bells of air
Three sinful sextons' ghosts are pent,
Who all give back, one after t'other,
The death-note to their living brother;
And oft too, by the knell offended,
Just as their one! two! three! is ended,
The devil mocks the doleful tale
With a merry peal from Borrowdale.

The air is still! through mist and cloud
That merry peal comes ringing loud;
And Geraldine shakes off her dread,
And rises lightly from the bed;
Puts on her silken vestments white,
And tricks her hair in lovely plight,
And nothing doubting of her spell
Awakens the lady Christabel
"Sleep you, sweet lady Christabel?
I trust that you have rested well."

And Christabel awoke and spied
The same who lay down by her side —
O rather say, the same whom she
Raised up beneath the old oak tree!
Nay, fairer yet! and yet more fair!
For she belike hath drunken deep
Of all the blessedness of sleep!
And while she spake, her looks, her air,
Such gentle thankfulness declare,
That (so it seemed) her girded vests
Grew tight beneath her heaving breasts.
"Sure I have sinn'd!" said Christabel,
"Now heaven be praised if all be well!"
And in low faltering tones, yet sweet,

<61>

Did she the lofty lady greet
With such perplexity of mind
As dreams too lively leave behind.

So quickly she rose, and quickly arrayed
Her maiden limbs, and having prayed
That He, who on the cross did groan,
Might wash away her sins unknown,
She forthwith led fair Geraldine
To meet her sire, Sir Leoline.

The lovely maid and the lady tall
Are pacing both into the hall,
And pacing on through page and groom,
Enter the Baron's presence-room.

The Baron rose, and while he prest
His gentle daughter to his breast,
With cheerful wonder in his eyes
The lady Geraldine espies,
And gave such welcome to the same,
As might beseem so bright a dame!

But when he heard the lady's tale,
And when she told her father's name,
Why waxed Sir Leoline so pale,
Murmuring o'er the name again,
Lord Roland de Vaux of Tryermaine?

Alas! they had been friends in youth;
But whispering tongues can poison truth;
And constancy lives in realms above;
And life is thorny; and youth is vain;
And to be wroth with one we love
Doth work like madness in the brain.
And thus it chanced, as I divine,
With Roland and Sir Leoline.
Each spake words of high disdain
And insult to his heart's best brother:
They parted — ne'er to meet again!

<62>

But never either found another
To free the hollow heart from paining —
They stood aloof, the scars remaining,
Like cliffs which had been rent asunder;
A dreary sea now flows between.
But neither heat, nor frost, nor thunder,
Shall wholly do away, I ween,
The marks of that which once hath been.
Sir Leoline, a moment's space,
Stood gazing on the damsel's face:
And the youthful Lord of Tryermaine
Came back upon his heart again.

O then the Baron forgot his age,
His noble heart swelled high with rage;
He swore by the wounds in Jesu's side
He would proclaim it far and wide,
With trump and solemn heraldry,
That they, who thus had wronged the dame
Were base as spotted infamy!
"And if they dare deny the same,
My herald shall appoint a week,
And let the recreant traitors seek
My tourney court — that there and then
I may dislodge their reptile souls
From the bodies and forms of men!"
He spake: his eye in lightning rolls!
For the lady was ruthlessly seized; and he kenned
In the beautiful lady the child of his friend!

And now the tears were on his face,
And fondly in his arms he took
Fair Geraldine, who met the embrace,
Prolonging it with joyous look.
Which when she viewed, a vision fell
Upon the soul of Christabel,

The vision of fear, the touch and pain!
She shrunk and shuddered, and saw again —

<63>

(Ah, woe is me! Was it for thee,
Thou gentle maid! such sights to see?)

Again she saw that bosom old,
Again she felt that bosom cold,
And drew in her breath with a hissing sound:
Whereat the Knight turned wildly round,
And nothing saw, but his own sweet maid
With eyes upraised, as one that prayed.

The touch, the sight, had passed away,
And in its stead that vision blest,
Which comforted her after-rest,
While in the lady's arms she lay,
Had put a rapture in her breast,
And on her lips and o'er her eyes
Spread smiles like light!

 With new surprise,
"What ails then my beloved child?"
The Baron said — His daughter mild
Made answer, "All will yet be well!"
I ween, she had no power to tell
Aught else: so mighty was the spell.
Yet he, who saw this Geraldine,
Had deemed her sure a thing divine.
Such sorrow with such grace she blended,
As if she feared she had offended

Sweet Christabel, that gentle maid!
And with such lowly tones she prayed
She might be sent without delay
Home to her father's mansion.

"Nay!
Nay, by my soul!" said Leoline.
"Ho! Bracy the bard, the charge be thine!
Go thou, with music sweet and loud,
And take two steeds with trappings proud,
And take the youth whom thou lov'st best

<64>

To bear thy harp, and learn thy song,
And clothe you both in solemn vest,
And over the mountains haste along,
Lest wandering folk, that are abroad,
Detain you on the valley road.

"And when he has crossed the Irthing flood,
My merry bard! he hastes, he hastes
Up Knorren Moor, through Halegarth Wood,
And reaches soon that castle good
Which stands and threatens Scotland's wastes.

"Bard Bracy! bard Bracy! your horses are fleet,
Ye must ride up the hall, your music so sweet,
More loud than your horses' echoing feet!
And loud and loud to Lord Roland call,
Thy daughter is safe in Langdale hall!
Thy beautiful daughter is safe and free —
Sir Leoline greets thee thus through me.

"He bids thee come without delay
With all thy numerous array;
And take thy lovely daughter home:
And he will meet thee on the way
With all his numerous array
White with their panting palfreys' foam:
And, by mine honour! I will say,
That I repent me of the day
When I spake words of fierce disdain
To Roland de Vaux of Tryermaine! —
— For since that evil hour hath flown,
Many a summer's sun hath shone;
Yet ne'er found I a friend again
Like Roland de Vaux of Tryermaine."

The lady fell, and clasped his knees,
Her face upraised, her eyes o'erflowing;
And Bracy replied, with faltering voice,
His gracious hail on all bestowing;
"Thy words, thou sire of Christabel,

<65>

Are sweeter than my harp can tell;
Yet might I gain a boon of thee,
This day my journey should not be,
So strange a dream hath come to me;
That I had vowed with music loud
To clear yon wood from thing unblest,
Warn'd by a vision in my rest!
For in my sleep I saw that dove,
That gentle bird, whom thou dost love,
And call'st by thy own daughter's name —
Sir Leoline! I saw the same,
Fluttering, and uttering fearful moan,
Among the green herbs in the forest alone.
Which when I saw and when I heard,
I wonder'd what might ail the bird;
For nothing near it could I see,
Save the grass and green herbs underneath the old tree.

"And in my dream, methought, I went
To search out what might there be found;
And what the sweet bird's trouble meant,
That thus lay fluttering on the ground.
I went and peered, and could descry
No cause for her distressful cry;
But yet for her dear lady's sake
I stooped, methought, the dove to take,
When lo! I saw a bright green snake
Coiled around its wings and neck.
Green as the herbs on which it couched,
Close by the dove's its head it crouched;
And with the dove it heaves and stirs,
Swelling its neck as she swelled hers!
I woke; it was the midnight hour,
The clock was echoing in the tower;
But though my slumber was gone by,
This dream it would not pass away —
It seems to live upon my eye!
And thence I vowed this self-same day
With music strong and saintly song

<66>

To wander through the forest bare,
Lest aught unholy loiter there."

Thus Bracy said: the Baron, the while,
Half-listening heard him with a smile;
Then turned to Lady Geraldine,
His eyes made up of wonder and love;
And said in courtly accents fine,
"Sweet maid, Lord Roland's beauteous dove,
With arms more strong than harp or song,
Thy sire and I will crush the snake!"
He kissed her forehead as he spake,
And Geraldine in maiden wise
Casting down her large bright eyes,
With blushing cheek and courtesy fine
She turned her from Sir Leoline;
Softly gathering up her train,
That o'er her right arm fell again;
And folded her arms across her chest,
And couched her head upon her breast,
And looked askance at Christabel —
Jesu, Maria, shield her well!

A snake's small eye blinks dull and shy,
And the lady's eyes they shrunk in her head,
Each shrunk up to a serpent's eye,
And with somewhat of malice, and more of dread,
At Christabel she look'd askance! —
One moment — and the sight was fled!
But Christabel in dizzy trance
Stumbling on the unsteady ground
Shuddered aloud, with a hissing sound;
And Geraldine again turned round,
And like a thing, that sought relief,
Full of wonder and full of grief,
She rolled her large bright eyes divine
Wildly on Sir Leoline.

<67>

The maid, alas! her thoughts are gone,
She nothing sees — no sight but one!
The maid, devoid of guile and sin,
I know not how, in fearful wise,
So deeply had she drunken in
That look, those shrunken serpent eyes,
That all her features were resigned
To this sole image in her mind:
And passively did imitate
That look of dull and treacherous hate!
And thus she stood, in dizzy trance,
Still picturing that look askance
With forced unconscious sympathy
Full before her father's view —
As far as such a look could be
In eyes so innocent and blue!

And when the trance was o'er, the maid
Paused awhile, and inly prayed:
Then falling at the Baron's feet,
"By my mother's soul do I entreat
That thou this woman send away!"
She said: and more she could not say:
For what she knew she could not tell,
O'er-mastered by the mighty spell.

Why is thy cheek so wan and wild,
Sir Leoline? Thy only child
Lies at thy feet, thy joy, thy pride,
So fair, so innocent, so mild;
The same, for whom thy lady died!
O, by the pangs of her dear mother
Think thou no evil of thy child!
For her, and thee, and for no other,
She prayed the moment ere she died:
Prayed that the babe for whom she died,
Might prove her dear lord's joy and pride!
That prayer her deadly pangs beguiled,
Sir Leoline!

<68>

And wouldst thou wrong thy only child,
Her child and thine?

Within the Baron's heart and brain
If thoughts, like these, had any share,
They only swelled his rage and pain,
And did but work confusion there.
His heart was cleft with pain and rage,
His cheeks they quivered, his eyes were wild,
Dishonour'd thus in his old age;
Dishonour'd by his only child,
And all his hospitality
To the insulted daughter of his friend
By more than woman's jealousy
Brought thus to a disgraceful end —
He rolled his eye with stern regard
Upon the gentle minstrel bard,
And said in tones abrupt, austere —
"Why, Bracy! dost thou loiter here?
I bade thee hence!" The bard obeyed;
And turning from his own sweet maid,
The aged knight, Sir Leoline,
Led forth the lady Geraldine!

—1801

THE CONCLUSION TO PART THE SECOND

A little child, a limber elf,
Singing, dancing to itself,
A fairy thing with red round cheeks,
That always finds, and never seeks,
Makes such a vision to the sight
As fills a father's eyes with light;
And pleasures flow in so thick and fast
Upon his heart, that he at last
Must needs express his love's excess
With words of unmeant bitterness.
Perhaps 'tis pretty to force together

<69>

Thoughts so all unlike each other;
To mutter and mock a broken charm,
To dally with wrong that does no harm.
Perhaps 'tis tender too and pretty
At each wild word to feel within
A sweet recoil of love and pity.
And what, if in a world of sin
(O sorrow and shame should this be true!)
Such giddiness of heart and brain
Comes seldom save from rage and pain,
So talks as it's most used to do.

?1801

<70>

Kubla Khan

In Xanadu did Kubla Khan
A stately pleasure-dome decree:
Where Alph, the sacred river, ran
Through caverns measureless to man
     Down to a sunless sea.
So twice five miles of fertile ground
With walls and towers were girdled round:
And here were gardens bright with sinuous rills,
Where blossomed many an incense-bearing tree;
And here were forests ancient as the hills,
Enfolding sunny spots of greenery.

But oh! that deep romantic chasm which slanted
Down the green hill athwart a cedarn cover!
    A savage place! as holy and enchanted
    As e'er beneath a waning moon was haunted
    By woman wailing for her demon-lover!
    And from this chasm, with ceaseless turmoil seething,
    As if this earth in fast thick pants were breathing,
    A mighty fountain momently was forced:
    Amid whose swift half-intermitted burst
    Huge fragments vaulted like rebounding hail,
    Or chaffy grain beneath the thresher's flail:
    And 'mid these dancing rocks at once and ever
    It flung up momently the sacred river.
    Five miles meandering with a mazy motion
    Through wood and dale the sacred river ran,
    Then reached the caverns measureless to man,
    And sank in tumult to a lifeless ocean:
    And 'mid this tumult Kubla heard from far
    Ancestral voices prophesying war!

    The shadow of the dome of pleasure
    Floated midway on the waves;
    Where was heard the mingled measure
    From the fountain and the caves.

<71>

It was a miracle of rare device,
A sunny pleasure-dome with caves of ice!

    A damsel with a dulcimer
    In a vision once I saw:
    It was an Abyssinian maid;
    And on her dulcimer she played,
    Singing of Mount Abora.
    Could I revive within me
    Her symphony and song,
    To such a deep delight 'twould win me,
That with music loud and long,
I would build that dome in air,
That sunny dome! those caves of ice!
And all who heard should see them there,
And all should cry, Beware! Beware!
His flashing eyes, his floating hair!
Weave a circle round him thrice,
And close your eyes with holy dread,
For he on honey-dew hath fed,
And drunk the milk of Paradise.

—1798

<72>

The Two Round Spaces
On the Tombstone

The Devil believes that the Lord will come,
Stealing a march without beat of drum,
About the same time that he came last
On an old Christmas-day in a snowy blast:
Till he bids the trump sound neither body nor soul stirs
For the dead men's heads have slipt under their bolsters.

    Ho! ho! brother Bard, in our churchyard
    Both beds and bolsters are soft and green;
    Save one alone, and that's of stone,
    And under it lies a Counsellor keen.
This tomb would be square, if it were not too long;
And 'tis rail'd round with iron, tall, spear-like, and strong.

This fellow from Aberdeen hither did skip
With a waxy face and a blubber lip,
And a black tooth in front to show in part
What was the colour of his whole heart.
    This Counsellor sweet,
    This Scotchman complete
    (The Devil scotch him for a snake!),
    I trust he lies in his grave awake.
    On the sixth of January,
    When all around is white with snow
    As a Cheshire yeoman's dairy,
    Brother Bard, ho! ho! believe it, or no,
    On that stone tomb to you I'll show
    After sunset, and before cock-crow,
    Two round spaces clear of snow.
I swear by our Knight and his forefathers' souls,
That in size and shape they are just like the holes
    In the large house of privity
    Of that ancient family.
On those two places clear of snow
There have sat in the night for an hour or so,
Before sunrise, and after cock-crow

<73>

(He hicking his heels, she cursing her corns,
All to the tune of the wind in their horns),
    The Devil and his Grannam,
    With the snow-drift to fan 'em;
Expecting and hoping the trumpet to blow;
For they are cock-sure of the fellow below!

—1800

The Devil's Thoughts

From his brimstone bed at break of day
    A walking the DEVIL is gone,
To visit his little snug farm of the earth
    And see how his stock went on.

Over the hill and over the dale,
    And he went over the plain,
And backward and forward he swished his long tail
    As a gentleman swishes his cane.

And how then was the Devil drest?
    Oh! he was in his Sunday's best:
His jacket was red and his breeches were blue,
    And there was a hole where the tail came through.

He saw a LAWYER killing a Viper
    On a dung heap beside his stable,
And the Devil smiled, for it put him in mind
    Of Cain and *his* brother, Abel.

A 'POTHECARY on a white horse
    Rode by on his vocations,
And the Devil thought of his old Friend
    DEATH in the Revelations.

He saw a cottage with a double coach-house,
    A cottage of gentility!
And the Devil did grin, for his darling sin
    Is pride that apes humility.

He went into a rich bookseller's shop,
    Quoth he! we are both of one college,
For I myself sate like a cormorant once
    Fast by the tree of knowledge.

<75>

Down the river there plied, with wind and tide,
 A pig with vast celerity;
And the Devil look'd wise as he saw how the while,
It cut its own throat. "There!" quoth he with a smile,
    "Goes England's commercial prosperity."

As he went through Cold-Bath Fields he saw
    A solitary cell;
And the Devil was pleased, for it gave him a hint
    For improving his prisons in Hell.

     ★   ★   ★   ★   ★   ★

General — — — — — - burning face
    He saw with consternation,
And back to hell his way did he take,
For the Devil thought by a slight mistake
    It was general conflagration.

—1799

<76>

Limbo

The sole true Something — This! In Limbo's Den
It frightens Ghosts, as here Ghosts frighten men.
[For skimming in the wake it mock'd the care
Of the old Boat-God for his farthing fare;
Tho' Iris' Ghost itself he never frown'd blacker on
The skin and skin-pent Druggist cross'd the Acheron,
Styx, and with Periphlegeton Cocytus, —
(The very names, me thinks, might frighten us)
Thence cross'd unseiz'd — and shall some fated hour
Be pulveris'd by Demogorgon's power,
And given as poison to annihilate souls —
Even now it shrinks them — they shrink in as Moles
(Nature's mute monks, live mandrakes of the ground)
Creep back from Light — then listen for its sound; —
See but to dread, and dread they know not why —
The natural alien of their negative eye.

'Tis a strange place, the Limbo! — not a Place,
Yet name it so; where Time and weary Space
Fettered from flight, with night-mare sense of fleeing,
Strive for their last crepuscular half-being; —
Lank Space, and scytheless Time with branny hands
Barren and soundless as the measuring sands,
Not mark'd by flit of Shades, — unmeaning they
As moonlight on the dial of the day!
But that is lovely — looks like Human Time,
An Old Man with a steady look sublime,
That stops his earthly task to watch the skies;
But he is blind — a Statue hath such eyes; —
Yet having moonward turn'd his face by chance,
Gazes the orb with moon-like countenance,
With scant white hairs, with foretop bald and high,
He gazes still, — his eyeless face all eye; —
As 'twere an organ full of silent sight,
His whole face seemeth to rejoice in light!
Lip touching lip, all moveless, bust and limb —
He seems to gaze at that which seems to gaze on him!

<77>

No such sweet sights doth Limbo den immure,
Wall'd round, and made a spirit-jail secure,
By the mere horror of blank Naught-at-all,
Whose circumambience doth these ghosts enthral.
A lurid thought is growthless, dull Privation,
Yet that is but a Purgatory curse;
Hell knows a fear far worse,
A fear — a future state; — 'tis positive Negation!

—*1817*

<78>

The Rash Conjurer

Strong spirit-bidding sounds!
  With deep and hollow voice,
  Twixt Hope and Dread,
   Seven Times I said
    Iohva Mitzoveh
    Vohoeen!
And up came an imp in the shape of a
  Pea-hen!
I saw, I doubted,
And seven times spouted
   Johva Mitzoveh
    Yahóevohäen!
When Anti-Christ starting up, butting
   and baying,
In the shape of a mischievous curly
         black Lamb —
With a vast flock of Devils behind
      and beside,
  And before 'em their Shepherdess
    Lucifer's Dam,
   Riding astride
   On an old black Ram,
With Tartary stirrups, knees up to her chin,
And a sleek chrysom imp to her Dugs muzzled in, —
   "Gee-up, my old Belzy!" (she cried,
    As she sung to her suckling cub)
"Trit-a-trot, trot! we'll go far and wide
Trot, Ram-Devil! Trot! Belzebub!"
Her petticoat fine was of scarlet Brocade,
And soft in her lap her Baby she lay'd
With his pretty Nubs of Horns a-sprouting,
And his pretty little Tail all curly-twirly —
St. Dunstan! and this comes of spouting —
   Of Devils what a Hurly-Burly!

<79>

"Behold we are up! what want'st thou then?" —
"Sirs! only that" — "Say when and what" —
"You'd be so good" — "Say what and when" —
"This moment to get down again!" —
"We do it! we do it! we all get down!
But we take you with us to swim
                        or drown!
Down a down to the grim Engulpher!" —
"O me! I am floundering in Fire and Sulphur!
That the Dragon had scrounched you, squeal
                        and squall
Cabbalists! Conjurers! great and small,
Johva Mitzoveh Evohäen and all!
Had *I* never uttered your jaw-breaking words,
I might now have been sloshing down Junket and Curds,
    Like a Devonshire Christian:
        But now a Philistine!

"Ye Earthmen! be warned by a judgement so tragic,
And wipe yourselves cleanly with all books of magic —
Hark! hark! it is Dives! 'Hold your Bother, you Booby!
I am burnt ashy white, and you yet are but ruby.'"

Epilogue.
We ask and urge (here ends the story)
All Christian Papishes to pray
That this unhappy Conjurer may
Instead of Hell, be but in Purgatory —
For then there's Hope, —
Long live the Pope!
    Catholicus.

                               —?1813-1816

<80>

The Raven

A CHRISTMAS TALE, TOLD BY A SCHOOLBOY
TO HIS LITTLE BROTHERS AND SISTERS

Underneath an old oak tree
There was of swine a huge company,
That grunted as they crunched the mast:
For that was ripe, and fell full fast.
Then they trotted away, for the wind grew high:
One acorn they left, and no more you might spy.
Next came a Raven, that liked not such folly:
He belonged, they would say, to the witch Melancholy!
Blacker was he than blackest jet,
Flew low in the rain, and his feathers not wet.
He picked up the acorn and buried it straight
By the side of a rive both deep and great.
 Where did the Raven go?
 He went high and low,
Over hill, over dale, did the black Raven go.
 Many Autumns, many Springs
 Travelled he with wandering wings:
 Many Summers, many Winters —
 I can't tell half his adventures.

At length he came back, and with him a She,
And the acorn was grown to a tall oak tree.
They built them a nest in the topmost bough,
And young ones they had, and were happy enow.
But soon came a Woodman in leathern guise,
His brow, like a pent-house, hung over his eyes.
He'd an axe in his hand, not a word he spoke,
But with many a hem! and a sturdy stroke,
At length he brought down the poor Raven's own oak.
His young ones were killed; for they could not depart,
And their mother did die of a broken heart.

<81>

The boughs from the trunk the Woodman did sever;
And they floated it down on the course of the river.
They sawed it in planks, and its bark they did strip,
And with this tree and others they made a good ship.
The ship, it was launched; but in sight of the land
Such a storm there did rise as no ship could withstand.
It bulged on a rock, and the waves rush'd in fast:
Round and round flew the Raven, and cawed to the blast.
He heard the last shriek of the perishing souls —
See! see! o'er the topmast the mad water rolls!
     Right glad was the Raven, and off he went fleet,
And Death riding home on a cloud he did meet,
And he thank'd him again and again for this treat:
     They had taken his all, and REVENGE IT WAS SWEET!

1797

<82>

Illustration for *Faust*. Harry Clarke, 1925.

Scene from Goethe's Faust

SCENE — Faust's Study.
Enter FAUST with the DOG.

Faustus soliloquizes, in a tone of feeling and sentiment, on the stillness of the night, calming every passion to repose. He is interrupted at intervals by the growling of the Dog, whom he in vain attempts to pacify. He feels a sudden desire to translate a passage from the New Testament, but cannot determine on an expression in his native language sufficiently comprehensive to express the creating power.

FAUST: "In the beginning was the *Word*," 'tis written;
Here do I stumble: who can help me on?
I cannot estimate "the Word" so highly;
I must translate it otherwise, if rightly
I feel myself enlightened by its spirit.
"In the beginning was the *Mind*," 'tis written:
Repeat this line, and weigh its meaning well,

<83>

Nor let thy pen decide too hastily:
Is it the mind creates and fashions all?
"In the beginning was the *Power*," it should be;
Yet, even while I write the passage down,
It warns me that I have not caught its meaning:
Help me, then, Spirit! With deliberation,
And perfect confidence, I will inscribe,
    At last, "In the beginning was the *Deed*."

*At this juncture the yelling and howling of the Dog increase, and
Faustus again commands him to be quiet, and threatens to expel him.
Suddenly he becomes enlarged to an enormous size, and assumes the
form of a hippopotamus, whilst without, spirits are heard bemoaning the
loss of their comrade. Faustus tries to subdue him with a spell of the four
elements; but, finding that charm inefficient, concludes that he is under
the dominion of a higher power, and has recourse to this stronger
incantation: —*

Art thou one who fell,
Deserter from hell?
Then look at this sign,
Whose virtues incline
The legions of hell to obey it.

*At this potent bidding the Dog reluctantly issues forth from behind the
stove, whither he had retreated, and swells till he appears as large as an
elephant, and nearly fills the room. He at length bursts in a cloud of
smoke, which gradually dissipates, and discovers Mephistopheles dres't
like a travelling student.*

MEPHISTOPHELES: Wherefore this noise?
    what can I do to serve you?

FAUST: This was the kernel then, the dog inclosed;
A traveling student! why, it makes me laugh.

MEPHISTOPHELES: All hail, most learned doctor!
    I salute you:
In truth, I must confess you made me tremble.

<84>

FAUST: What dost thou call thyself?

MEPHISTOPHELES: That question seems
To me a simple one, from him who lately
Despised the Word.
He, however, at length designates himself as
A portion of that power,
Whose wills are evil, but whose actions good.

FAUST: What does this dark enigma signify?

MEPHISTOPHELES: I am the spirit who says 'nay' to all,
And rightly so; for all that have existence
Deserve that they should perish; so 'twere better
That nothing earthly should enjoy existence.
All, therefore, that you mortals mean by Sin,
Destruction, in a word, what you call Evil,
Is my peculiar element.

*The conversation is continued in this strain until Mephistopheles
expresses a wish to depart. Faustus wonders that he should meet with
any impediment, having free access to the window, door, and chimney,
but Mephistopheles explains that there is a slight hindrance, which is no
other than a pentagon on the threshold. He got in, 'tis true, because there
was a little opening left in one corner.*

MEPHISTOPHELES: The dog did nothing note,
        as in he sprung,
But now the case assumes another shape,
The Devil has no means to make an exit.

FAUST: But why not make your exit by the window?

MEPHISTOPHELES: It is a rule with spirits and with devils,
By the same way they enter they depart;
The first is a free choice, the last a law.

FAUST: Hell then, it seems, has laws. I like it well:
With gentry so precise, a solemn compact
May, I presume, be made, and will be kept.

<85>

MEPHISTOPHELES: Whate'er we promise you may
      safely trust to;
We will not bate one jot of the agreement.
But that requires some slight consideration,
So let us speak of it anon more fully;
But, for this time, I beg you earnestly
To let me take my leave.

FAUST: A moment stay,
And answer a few questions ere we part.

MEPHISTOPHELES: Nay, now release me. I will soon return,
You then may as you please interrogate me.

FAUST: I did not drag you here. You freely came
And fell into the trap without a bait.
He who has caught the devil should hold him fast,
He may not light on such a prize again.

*Mephistopheles then begs permission to entertain Faustus with a display
of his art, to which the latter acceeds, provided it be an agreeable one.
Mephistopheles promises to enchant his eyes with delightful visions, his
ears with harmonious sounds, and his sense of smelling with the most
exquisite odours. He summons the spirits over whom he has control, who
obey his commands, and conclude by lulling Faustus with a song into a
deep sleep. Mephistopheles dismisses them with this acknowledgment:—*

MEPHISTOPHELES: He sleeps! 'Tis well.
      Ye tender airy spirits,
Ye have entranc'd him nobly with your songs,
And for this concert bind me still your debtor.
Thou art not yet the man to hold the devil.
Amuse his fancy with some pleasing dream.
And plunge him in a sea of wild conceits,
Whilst I invoke a rat's tooth to gnaw off
The magic obstacle which bars my passage.

<86>

As lord of rats, and mice, and all reptiles, he then summons a rat, by whose aid the angle of the pentagon, being moistened with oil, is at length severed. Mephistopheles then takes leave of his sleeping companion, exclaiming, —

'Tis I.
Come in.
You must
Now, Faustus,
Now dream away, until we meet again.

FAUST (*waking*): Am I then once again deceiv'd? and has
That crowd of hovering spirits all, all vanished?
Methought I saw the devil in my dream,
And lo! a little dog sprang forth and left me.

<87>

THOMAS MOORE

A Ballad: The Lake of the Dismal Swamp

Written at Norfolk, in Virginia

"They made her a grave, too cold and damp
For a soul so warm and true;
And she's gone to the Lake of the Dismal Swamp,
Where, all night long, by a fire-fly lamp,
She paddles her white canoe.

"And her fire-fly lamp I soon shall see,
And her paddle I soon shall hear;
Long and loving our life shall be,
And I'll hide the maid in a cypress tree,
When the footstep of death is near."

Away to the Dismal Swamp he speeds —
His path was rugged and sore,
Through tangled juniper, beds of reeds,
Through many a fen where the serpent feeds,
And man never trod before.

And when on the earth he sunk to sleep,
If slumber his eyelids knew,
He lay where the deadly vine doth weep
Its venomous tear and nightly steep
The flesh with blistering dew!

And near him the she-wolf stirr'd the brake,
And the copper-snake breath'd in his ear,
Till he starting cried, from his dream awake,
"Oh! when shall I see the dusky Lake,
And the white canoe of my dear?"

<88>

He saw the Lake, and a meteor bright
Quick over its surface play'd—
"Welcome," he said, "my dear one's light!"
And the dim shore echoed for many a night
The name of the death-cold maid.

Till he hollow'd a boat of the birchen bark,
Which carried him off from shore;
Far, far he follow'd the meteor spark,
The wind was high and the clouds were dark,
And the boat return'd no more.

But oft, from the Indian hunter's camp,
This lover and maid so true
Are seen at the hour of midnight damp
To cross the Lake by a fire-fly lamp,
And paddle their white canoe!

<89>

GEORGE GORDON, LORD BYRON
(1788 - 1824)

Darkness

I had a dream, which was not all a dream.
The bright sun was extinguish'd, and the stars
Did wander darkling in the eternal space,
Rayless, and pathless, and the icy earth
Swung blind and blackening in the moonless air;
Morn came and went — and came, and brought no day,
And men forgot their passions in the dread
Of this their desolation; and all hearts
Were chill'd into a selfish prayer for light:
And they did live by watchfires — and the thrones,
The palaces of crowned kings — the huts,
The habitations of all things which dwell,
Were burnt for beacons; cities were consumed,
And men were gathered round their blazing homes
To look once more into each other's face;
Happy were those who dwelt within the eye
Of the volcanos, and their mountain-torch:
A fearful hope was all the world contain'd;
Forests were set on fire — but hour by hour
They fell and faded — and the crackling trunks
Extinguish'd with a crash — and all was black.
The brows of men by the despairing light
Wore an unearthly aspect, as by fits
The flashes fell upon them; some lay down
And hid their eyes and wept; and some did rest
Their chins upon their clenched hands, and smiled;
And others hurried to and fro, and fed
Their funeral piles with fuel, and looked up
With mad disquietude on the dull sky,
The pall of a past world; and then again
With curses cast them down upon the dust,
And gnash'd their teeth and howl'd: the wild birds shriek'd,

<90>

And, terrified, did flutter on the ground,
And flap their useless wings; the wildest brutes
Came tame and tremulous; and vipers crawl'd
And twined themselves among the multitude,
Hissing, but stingless — they were slain for food.
And War, which for a moment was no more,
Did glut himself again; — a meal was bought
With blood, and each sate sullenly apart
Gorging himself in gloom: no love was left;
All earth was but one thought — and that was death,
Immediate and inglorious; and the pang
Of famine fed upon all entrails — men
Died, and their bones were tombless as their flesh;
The meagre by the meagre were devoured,
Even dogs assail'd their masters, all save one,
And he was faithful to a corse, and kept
The birds and beasts and famish'd men at bay,
Till hunger clung them, or the dropping dead
Lured their lank jaws; himself sought out no food,
But with a piteous and perpetual moan,
And a quick desolate cry, licking the hand
Which answered not with a caress — he died.
The crowd was famish'd by degrees; but two
Of an enormous city did survive,
And they were enemies: they met beside
The dying embers of an altar-place
Where had been heap'd a mass of holy things
For an unholy usage; they raked up,
And shivering scraped with their cold skeleton hands
The feeble ashes, and their feeble breath
Blew for a little life, and made a flame
Which was a mockery; then they lifted up
Their eyes as it grew lighter, and beheld
Each other's aspects — saw, and shriek'd, and died —
Even of their mutual hideousness they died,
Unknowing who he was upon whose brow
Famine had written Fiend. The world was void,
The populous and the powerful — was a lump,
Seasonless, herbless, treeless, manless, lifeless —

<91>

A lump of death — a chaos of hard clay.
The rivers, lakes, and ocean all stood still,
And nothing stirred within their silent depths;
Ships sailorless lay rotting on the sea,
And their masts fell down piecemeal: as they dropp'd
They slept on the abyss without a surge —
The waves were dead; the tides were in their grave,
The moon their mistress had expir'd before;
The winds were withered in the stagnant air,
And the clouds perish'd; Darkness had no need
Of aid from them — She was the Universe.

—1816

<92>

Manfred

ACT I

SCENE I
MANFRED *alone.* — *Scene, a Gothic Gallery.* — *Time, Midnight.*

MANFRED. The lamp must be replenish'd, but even then
It will not burn so long as I must watch.
My slumbers — if I slumber — are not sleep,
But a continuance of enduring thought,
Which then I can resist not: in my heart
There is a vigil, and these eyes but close
To look within; and yet I live, and bear
The aspect and the form of breathing men.
But grief should be the instructor of the wise;
Sorrow is knowledge: they who know the most
Must mourn the deepest o'er the fatal truth,
The Tree of Knowledge is not that of Life.
Philosophy and science, and the springs
Of wonder, and the wisdom of the world,
I have essay'd, and in my mind there is
A power to make these subject to itself —
But they avail not: I have done men good,
And I have met with good even among men —
But this avail'd not: I have had my foes,
And none have baffled, many fallen before me —
But this avail'd not: Good, or evil, life,
Powers, passions, all I see in other beings,
Have been to me as rain unto the sands,
Since that all-nameless hour. I have no dread,
And feel the curse to have no natural fear
Nor fluttering throb, that beats with hopes or wishes
Or lurking love of something on the earth.
Now to my task. —
                    Mysterious Agency!
Ye spirits of the unbounded Universe,
Whom I have sought in darkness and in light!

<93>

Ye, who do compass earth about, and dwell
In subtler essence! ye, to whom the tops
Of mountains inaccessible are haunts,
And earth's and ocean's caves familiar things —
I call upon ye by the written charm
Which gives me power upon you — Rise! appear! *[A pause.]*
They come not yet. — Now by the voice of him
Who is the first among you; by this sign,
Which makes you tremble; by the claims of him
Who is undying, — Rise! appear! — Appear!   *[A pause.]*
If it be so. — Spirits of earth and air,
Ye shall not thus elude me: by a power,
Deeper than all yet urged, a tyrant-spell,
Which had its birthplace in a star condemn'd,
The burning wreck of a demolish'd world,
A wandering hell in the eternal space;
By the strong curse which is upon my soul,
The thought which is within me and around me,
I do compel ye to my will. Appear!

*[A star is seen at the darker end of the gallery: it is stationary;
and a voice is heard singing.*

FIRST SPIRIT.

Mortal! to thy bidding bow'd,
From my mansion in the cloud,
Which the breath of twilight builds,
And the summer's sunset gilds
With the azure and vermilion
Which is mix'd for my pavilion;
Though thy quest may be forbidden,
On a star-beam I have ridden,
To thine adjuration bow'd;
Mortal — be thy wish avow'd!

<94>

Voice of the **SECOND SPIRIT**.

Mont Blanc is the monarch of mountains;
  They crown'd him long ago
On a throne of rocks, in a robe of clouds,
  With a diadem of snow.
Around his waist are forests braced,
  The Avalanche in his hand;
But ere it fall, that thundering ball
  Must pause for my command.
The Glacier's cold and restless mass
  Moves onward day by day;
But I am he who bids it pass,
  Or with its ice delay.
I am the spirit of the place,
  Could make the mountain bow
And quiver to his cavern'd base —
And what with me wouldst *Thou?*

Voice of the **THIRD SPIRIT**.

In the blue depth of the waters,
  Where the wave hath no strife,
Where the wind is a stranger
  And the sea-snake hath life,
Where the Mermaid is decking
  Her green hair with shells;
Like the storm on the surface
  Came the sound of thy spells;
O'er my calm Hall of Coral
  The deep echo roll'd —
To the Spirit of Ocean
  Thy wishes unfold!

<95>

FOURTH SPIRIT.

Where the slumbering earthquake
   Lies pillow'd on fire,
And the lakes of bitumen
   Rise boilingly higher;
Where the roots of the Andes
   Strike deep in the earth,
As their summits to heaven
   Shoot soaringly forth;
I have quitted my birthplace,
   Thy bidding to bide —
Thy spell hath subdued me,
   Thy will be my guide!

FIFTH SPIRIT.

I am the Rider of the wind,
   The Stirrer of the storm;
The hurricane I left behind
   Is yet with lightning warm;
To speed to thee, o'er shore and sea
   I swept upon the blast:
The fleet I met sail'd well, and yet
   'T will sink ere night be past.

SIXTH SPIRIT.

My dwelling is the shadow of the night,
Why doth thy magic torture me with light?

SEVENTH SPIRIT

The star which rules thy destiny
Was ruled, ere earth began, by me:
It was a world as fresh and fair
As e'er revolved round sun in air;
Its course was free and regular,

<96>

Space bosom'd not a lovelier star.
The hour arrived — and it became
A wandering mass of shapeless flame,
A pathless comet, and a curse,
The menace of the universe;
Still rolling on with innate force,
Without a sphere, without a course,
A bright deformity on high,
The monster of the upper sky!
And thou! beneath its influence born —
Thou worm! whom I obey and scorn —
Forced by a power (which is not thine,
And lent thee but to make thee mine)
For this brief moment to descend,
Where these weak spirits round thee bend
And parley with a thing like thee —
What wouldst thou, Child of Clay! with me?

The SEVEN SPIRITS

Earth, ocean, air, night, mountains, winds, thy star,
Are at thy beck and bidding, Child of Clay!
Before thee at thy quest their spirits are —
What wouldst thou with us, son of mortals — say?

MANFRED. Forgetfulness —

FIRST SPIRIT.   Of what — of whom — and why?

MANFRED. Of that which is within me; read it there —
Ye know it, and I cannot utter it.

SPIRIT. We can but give thee that which we possess:
Ask of us subjects, sovereignty, the power
O'er earth, the whole, or portion, or a sign
Which shall control the elements, whereof
We are the dominators, — each and all,
These shall be thine.

<97>

MANFRED.   Oblivion, self-oblivion —
Can ye not wring from out the hidden realms
Ye offer so profusely what I ask?

SPIRIT. It is not in our essence, in our skill;
But — thou mayst die.

MANFRED.   Will death bestow it on me?

SPIRIT. We are immortal, and do not forget;
We are eternal; and to us the past
Is, as the future, present. Art thou answered?

MANFRED. Ye mock me — but the power
        which brought ye here
Hath made you mine. Slaves, scoff not at my will!
The mind, the spirit, the Promethean spark,
The lightning of my being, is as bright,
Pervading, and far-darting as your own,
And shall not yield to yours, though coop'd in clay!
Answer, or I will teach you what I am.

SPIRIT. We answer as we answer'd; our reply
Is even in thine own words.

MANFRED.   Why say ye so?

SPIRIT. If, as thou say'st, thine essence be as ours,
We have replied in telling thee, the thing
Mortals call death hath nought to do with us.

MANFRED. I then have call'd ye from your realms in vain;
Ye cannot, or ye will not, aid me.

SPIRIT.   Say;
What we possess we offer; it is thine:
Bethink ere thou dismiss us, ask again —
Kingdom, and sway, and strength, and length of days —

MANFRED. Accursèd! what have I to do with days?
They are too long already. — Hence — begone!

<98>

SPIRIT. Yet pause: being here, our will would do thee service;
Bethink thee, is there then no other gift
Which we can make not worthless in thine eyes?

MANFRED. No, none: yet stay — one moment, ere we part —
I would behold ye face to face. I hear
Your voices, sweet and melancholy sounds,
As music on the waters; and I see
The steady aspect of a clear large star;
But nothing more. Approach me as ye are,
Or one, or all, in your accustom'd forms.

SPIRIT. We have no forms, beyond the elements
Of which we are the mind and principle:
But choose a form— in that we will appear.

MANFRED. I have no choice, there is no form on earth
Hideous or beautiful to me. Let him,
Who is most powerful of ye, take such aspect
As unto him may seem most fitting. — Come!

*Seventh spirit (appearing in the shape of a beautiful female
figure)*. Behold!

MANFRED.   Oh God! if it be thus, and thou
Art not a madness and a mockery
I yet might be most happy — I will clasp thee,
And we again will be —   *[The figure vanishes.]*
                My heart is crushed!
                        [MANFRED falls senseless.]

(*A voice is heard in the Incantation which follows.*)

When the moon is on the wave,
And the glow-worm in the grass,
And the meteor on the grave,
And the wisp on the morass;
When the falling stars are shooting,
And the answer'd owls are hooting,
And the silent leaves are still
In the shadow of the hill,

<99>

Shall my soul be upon thine,
With a power and with a sign.

Though thy slumber may be deep,
Yet thy spirit shall not sleep;
There are shades which will not vanish,
There are thoughts thou canst not banish;
By a power to thee unknown,
Thou canst never be alone;
Thou art wrapt as with a shroud,
Thou art gather'd in a cloud;
And forever shalt thou dwell
In the spirit of this spell.

Though thou see'st me not pass by,
Thou shalt feel me with thine eye
As a thing that, though unseen,
Must be near thee, and hath been;
And when in that secret dread
Thou hast turn'd around thy head,
Thou shalt marvel I am not
As thy shadow on the spot,
And the power which thou dost feel
Shall be what thou must conceal.

And a magic voice and verse
Hath baptized thee with a curse;
And a spirit of the air
Hath begirt thee with a snare;
In the wind there is a voice
Shall forbid thee to rejoice;
And to thee shall Night deny
All the quiet of her sky;
And the day shall have a sun,
Which shall make thee wish it done.

From thy false tears I did distil
An essence which hath strength to kill;
From thy own heart I then did wring
The black blood in its blackest spring;

<100>

From thy own smile I snatch'd the snake,
For there it coil'd as in a brake;
From thy own lip I drew the charm
Which gave all these their chiefest harm;
In proving every poison known,
I found the strongest was thine own.
By thy cold breast and serpent smile,
By thy unfathom'd gulfs of guile,
By that most seeming virtuous eye,
By thy shut soul's hypocrisy;
By the perfection of thine art
Which pass'd for human thine own heart;
By thy delight in others' pain,
And by thy brotherhood of Cain,
I call upon thee! and compel
Thyself to be thy proper Hell!

And on thy head I pour the vial
Which doth devote thee to this trial;
Nor to slumber, nor to die,
Shall be in thy destiny;
Though thy death shall still seem near
To thy wish, but as a fear;
Lo! the spell now works around thee,
And the clankless chain hath bound thee;
O'er thy heart and brain together
Hath the word been pass'd — now wither!

<101>

PERCY BYSSHE SHELLEY (1792-1822)

The Witches' Sabbath

FROM GOETHE'S *FAUST*, PART I
SCENE 2. — MAY-DAY NIGHT.

THE HARTZ MOUNTAIN, A DESOLATE COUNTRY.

MEPHISTOPHELES. Would you not like a broomstick?
    As for me
I wish I had a good stout ram to ride;
For we are still far from the appointed place.

FAUST. This knotted staff is help enough for me,
Whilst I feel fresh upon my legs. What good
Is there in making short a pleasant way?
To creep along the labyrinths of the vales,
And climb those rocks, where ever-babbling springs,
Precipitate themselves in waterfalls,
Is the true sport that seasons such a path.
Already Spring kindles the birchen spray,
And the hoar pines already feel her breath:
Shall she not work also within our limbs?

MEPHISTOPHELES. Nothing of such an influence do I feel.
My body is all wintry, and I wish
The flowers upon our path were frost and snow.
But see how melancholy rises now,
Dimly uplifting her belated beam,
The blank unwelcome round of the red moon,
And gives so bad a light, that every step
One stumbles 'gainst some crag. With your permission,
I'll call on *Ignis-fatuus* to our aid:
I see one yonder burning jollily.
Halloo, my friend! may I request that you
Would favour us with your bright company?
Why should you blaze away there to no purpose?
Pray be so good as light us up this way.

<102>

IGNIS-FATUUS. With reverence be it spoken, I will try
To overcome the lightness of my nature;
Our course, you know, is generally zigzag.

MEPHISTOPHELES. Ha, ha! your worship thinks
    you have to deal
With men. Go straight on, in the Devil's name,
Or I shall puff your flickering life out.

<103>

IGNIS-FATUUS. Well,
I see you are the master of the house;
I will accommodate myself to you.
Only consider that to-night this mountain
Is all enchanted, and if Jack-a-lantern
Shows you his way, though you should miss your own,
You ought not to be too exact with him.

FAUST, MEPHISTOPHELES, & IGNIS-FATUUS
  (in alternate chorus).
The limits of the sphere of dream,
The bounds of true and false, are past.
Lead us on, thou wandering Gleam,
Lead us onward, far and fast,
To the wide, the desert waste.

But see, how swift advance and shift
Trees behind trees, row by row, —
How, clift by clift, rocks bend and lift
Their frowning foreheads as we go.
The giant-snouted crags, ho! ho!
How they snort, and how they blow!

Through the mossy sods and stones,
Stream and streamlet hurry down —
A rushing throng! A sound of song
Beneath the vault of Heaven is blown!
Sweet notes of love, the speaking tones
Of this bright day, sent down to say
That Paradise on Earth is known,
Resound around, beneath, above.
All we hope and all we love
Finds a voice in this blithe strain,
Which wakens hill and wood and rill,
And vibrates far o'er field and vale,
And which Echo, like the tale
Of old times, repeats again.

<104>

To-whoo! to-whoo! near, nearer now
The sound of song, the rushing throng!
Are the screech, the lapwing, and the jay,
All awake as if 'twere day?
See, with long legs and belly wide,
A salamander in the brake!
Every root is like a snake,
And along the loose hillside,
With strange contortions through the night,
Curls, to seize or to affright;
And, animated, strong, and many,
They dart forth polypus-antennae,

<105>

To blister with their poison spume
The wanderer. Through the dazzling gloom
The many-coloured mice, that thread
The dewy turf beneath our tread,
In troops each other's motions cross,
Through the heath and through the moss;
And, in legions intertangled,
The fire-flies flit, and swarm, and throng,
Till all the mountain depths are spangled.

Tell me, shall we go or stay?
Shall we onward? Come along!
Everything around is swept
Forward, onward, far away!
Trees and masses intercept
The sight, and wisps on every side
Are puffed up and multiplied.

MEPHISTOPHELES. Now vigorously seize my skirt, and gain
This pinnacle of isolated crag.
One may observe with wonder from this point,
How Mammon glows among the mountains.

FAUST. Ay —
And strangely through the solid depth below
A melancholy light, like the red dawn,
Shoots from the lowest gorge of the abyss
Of mountains, lightning hitherward: there rise
Pillars of smoke, here clouds float gently by;
Here the light burns soft as the enkindled air,
Or the illumined dust of golden flowers;
And now it glides like tender colours spreading;
And now bursts forth in fountains from the earth;
And now it winds, one torrent of broad light,
Through the far valley with a hundred veins;
And now once more within that narrow corner
Masses itself into intensest splendour.
And near us, see, sparks spring out of the ground,
Like golden sand scattered upon the darkness;

<106>

The pinnacles of that black wall of mountains
That hems us in are kindled.

MEPHISTOPHELES. Rare: in faith!
Does not Sir Mammon gloriously illuminate
His palace for this festival? — it is
A pleasure which you had not known before.
I spy the boisterous guests already.

FAUST. How
The children of the wind rage in the air!
With what fierce strokes they fall upon my neck!

MEPHISTOPHELES. Cling tightly to the old ribs of the crag.
Beware! for if with them thou warrest
In their fierce flight towards the wilderness,
Their breath will sweep thee into dust, and drag
Thy body to a grave in the abyss.
A cloud thickens the night.
Hark! how the tempest crashes through the forest!
The owls fly out in strange affright;
The columns of the evergreen palaces
Are split and shattered;
The roots creak, and stretch, and groan;
And ruinously overthrown,
The trunks are crushed and shattered
By the fierce blast's unconquerable stress.
Over each other crack and crash they all
In terrible and intertangled fall;
And through the ruins of the shaken mountain
The airs hiss and howl —
It is not the voice of the fountain,
Nor the wolf in his midnight prowl.
Dost thou not hear?
Strange accents are ringing
Aloft, afar, anear?
The witches are singing!
The torrent of a raging wizard song
Streams the whole mountain along.

<107>

CHORUS OF WITCHES.
The stubble is yellow, the corn is green,
Now to the Brocken the witches go;
The mighty multitude here may be seen
Gathering, wizard and witch, below.
Sir Urian is sitting aloft in the air;
Hey over stock! and hey over stone!
'Twixt witches and incubi, what shall be done?
Tell it who dare! tell it who dare!

A VOICE. Upon a sow-swine, whose farrows were nine,
Old Baubo rideth alone.

CHORUS.
Honour her, to whom honour is due,
Old mother Baubo, honour to you!
An able sow, with old Baubo upon her,
Is worthy of glory, and worthy of honour!
The legion of witches is coming behind,
Darkening the night, and outspeeding the wind —

A VOICE. Which way comest thou?

[ANOTHER] VOICE. Over Ilsenstein;
The owl was awake in the white moonshine;
I saw her at rest in her downy nest,
And she stared at me with her broad, bright eyne.

VOICES.
And you may now as well take your course on to Hell,
Since you ride by so fast on the headlong blast.

A VOICE. She dropped poison upon me as I passed.
Here are the wounds —

CHORUS OF WITCHES.
Come away! come along!
The way is wide, the way is long,
But what is that for a Bedlam throng?
Stick with the prong, and scratch with the broom.

<108>

The child in the cradle lies strangled at home,
And the mother is clapping her hands. —

SEMICHORUS OF WIZARDS 1.
We glide in
Like snails when the women are all away;
And from a house once given over to sin
Woman has a thousand steps to stray.

SEMICHORUS 2.
A thousand steps must a woman take,
Where a man but a single spring will make.

VOICES ABOVE.
Come with us, come with us, from Felsensee.

VOICES BELOW.
With what joy would we fly through the upper sky!
We are washed, we are 'nointed, stark naked are we;
But our toil and our pain are forever in vain.

BOTH CHORUSES.
The wind is still, the stars are fled,
The melancholy moon is dead;
The magic notes, like spark on spark,
Drizzle, whistling through the dark. Come away!

VOICES BELOW. Stay, Oh, stay!

VOICES ABOVE. Out of the crannies of the rocks
Who calls?

VOICES BELOW. Oh, let me join your flocks!
I, three hundred years have striven
To catch your skirt and mount to Heaven, —
And still in vain. Oh, might I be
With company akin to me!

BOTH CHORUSES.
Some on a ram and some on a prong,[1]

---
[1] *Prong.* A pitchfork or hay-fork.

<109>

On poles and on broomsticks we flutter along;
Forlorn is the wight who can rise not to-night.

A HALF-WITCH BELOW.
I have been tripping this many an hour:
Are the others already so far before?
No quiet at home, and no peace abroad!
And less methinks is found by the road.

CHORUS OF WITCHES.
Come onward, away! aroint thee, aroint!
A witch to be strong must anoint — anoint —
Then every trough will be boat enough;
With a rag for a sail we can sweep through the sky,
Who flies not to-night, when means he to fly?

BOTH CHORUSES.
We cling to the skirt,[2] and we strike on the ground;
Witch-legions thicken around and around;
Wizard-swarms cover the heath all over.

[They descend.]

MEPHISTOPHELES. What thronging, dashing,
        raging, rustling;
What whispering, babbling, hissing, bustling;
What glimmering, spurting, stinking, burning,
As Heaven and Earth were overturning.
There is a true witch element about us;
Take hold on me, or we shall be divided: —
Where are you?

FAUST *(from a distance)* Here!

MEPHISTOPHELES.   What!
I must exert my authority in the house.
Place for young Voland! pray make way, good people.
Take hold on me, doctor, and with one step
Let us escape from this unpleasant crowd:
They are too mad for people of my sort.

----
[2] *Skirt.* Flap of a saddle.

<110>

Just there shines a peculiar kind of light —
Something attracts me in those bushes. Come
This way: we shall slip down there in a minute.

FAUST. Spirit of Contradiction! Well, lead on —
'Twere a wise feat indeed to wander out
Into the Brocken[3] upon May-day night,[4]
And then to isolate oneself in scorn,
Disgusted with the humours of the time.

MEPHISTOPHELES. See yonder, round a many-coloured flame
A merry club is huddled altogether:
Even with such little people as sit there
One would not be alone.

FAUST.   Would that I were
Up yonder in the glow and whirling smoke,
Where the blind million rush impetuously
To meet the evil ones; there might I solve
Many a riddle that torments me.

MEPHISTOPHELES.   Yet
Many a riddle there is tied anew
Inextricably. Let the great world rage!
We will stay here safe in the quiet dwellings.
'Tis an old custom. Men have ever built
Their own small world in the great world of all.
I see young witches naked there, and old ones
Wisely attired with greater decency.
Be guided now by me, and you shall buy
A pound of pleasure with a dram of trouble.
I hear them tune their instruments — one must
Get used to this damned scraping. Come, I'll lead you
Among them; and what there you do and see,
As a fresh compact 'twixt us two shall be.
How say you now? this space is wide enough —
Look forth, you cannot see the end of it —
An hundred bonfires burn in rows, and they

---

[3] *Brocken*. Highest point in the Harz Mountains, where climbers can see a
"spectre" in the mist, an optical illusion caused by the shadows of the climbers.
[4] *May-day night*. May Eve, April 30, a cardinal holiday of the pagan calendar.

<111>

Who throng around them seem innumerable:
Dancing and drinking, jabbering, making love,
And cooking, are at work. Now tell me, friend,
What is there better in the world than this?

FAUST. In introducing us, do you assume
The character of Wizard or of Devil?

MEPHISTOPHELES. In truth, I generally go about
In strict incognito; and yet one likes
To wear one's orders upon gala days.
I have no ribbon at my knee; but here
At home, the cloven foot is honourable.
See you that snail there? — she comes creeping up,
And with her feeling eyes hath smelt out something.
I could not, if I would, mask myself here.
Come now, we'll go about from fire to fire:
I'll be the Pimp, and you shall be the Lover.

[To some old women, who are sitting on a heap of glimmering coals.]
Old gentlewomen, what do you do out here?
You ought to be with the young rioters
Right in the thickest of the revelry —
But every one is best content at home.

GENERAL. Who dare confide in right or a just claim?
So much as I had done for them! and now —
With women and the people 'tis the same,
Youth will stand foremost ever, — age may go
To the dark grave unhonoured.

MINISTER.   Nowadays
People assert their rights: they go too far;
But as for me, the good old times I praise;
Then we were all in all — 'twas something worth
One's while to be in place and wear a star;
That was indeed the golden age on earth.

PARVENU. We too are active, and we did and do
What we ought not, perhaps; and yet we now

<112>

Will seize, whilst all things are whirled round and round,
A spoke of Fortune's wheel, and keep our ground.

AUTHOR. Who now can taste a treatise of deep sense
And ponderous volume? 'tis impertinence
To write what none will read, therefore will I
To please the young and thoughtless people try.

MEPHISTOPHELES
(who at once appears to have grown very old).
I find the people ripe for the last day,
Since I last came up to the wizard mountain;
And as my little cask runs turbid now,
So is the world drained to the dregs.

PEDLAR-WITCH. Look here,
Gentlemen; do not hurry on so fast;
And lose the chance of a good pennyworth.
I have a pack full of the choicest wares
Of every sort, and yet in all my bundle
Is nothing like what may be found on earth;
Nothing that in a moment will make rich
Men and the world with fine malicious mischief —
There is no dagger drunk with blood; no bowl
From which consuming poison may be drained
By innocent and healthy lips; no jewel,
The price of an abandoned maiden's shame;
No sword which cuts the bond it cannot loose,
Or stabs the wearer's enemy in the back;
No —

MEPHISTOPHELES. Gossip, you know little of these times.
What has been, has been; what is done, is past,
They shape themselves into the innovations
They breed, and innovation drags us with it.
The torrent of the crowd sweeps over us:
You think to impel, and are yourself impelled.

<113>

FAUST. What is that yonder?

MEPHISTOPHELES: Mark her well. It is
Lilith.

FAUST. Who?

MEPHISTOPHELES. Lilith, the first wife of Adam.
Beware of her fair hair, for she excels
All women in the magic of her locks;
And when she winds them round a young man's neck,
She will not ever set him free again.

<114>

FAUST. There sit a girl and an old woman — they
Seem to be tired with pleasure and with play.

MEPHISTOPHELES. There is no rest to-night for any one:
When one dance ends another is begun;
Come, let us to it. We shall have rare fun.

[Faust dances and sings with a girl, and Mephistopheles with an old woman.]

FAUST. I had once a lovely dream
In which I saw an apple-tree,
Where two fair apples with their gleam
To climb and taste attracted me.

THE GIRL. She with apples you desired
From Paradise came long ago:
With you I feel that if required,
Such still within my garden grow.

. . .

PROCTO-PHANTASMIST.[5]
What is this cursed multitude about?
Have we not long since proved to demonstration
That ghosts move not on ordinary feet?
But these are dancing just like men and women.

THE GIRL. What does he want then at our ball?

FAUST.   Oh! he
Is far above us all in his conceit:
Whilst we enjoy, he reasons of enjoyment;
And any step which in our dance we tread,
If it be left out of his reckoning,
Is not to be considered as a step.

---

[5] *Procto-Phantasmist*. An obscene name meaning "Anus-Ghost-Believer,"
probably an insult aimed at one of Goethe's literary enemies, Friedrich Nicolai,
who ridiculed the idea of ghosts. Walter Kaufmann tracked down the origin of
Goethe's nickname, noting that Nicolai, "declared publicly ... that he, too, had
once been plagued by ghosts, but that he had got rid of them by applying leeches
to his rump." (28) This is rendered as "Brocto-Phantasmist" in some editions.

<115>

There are few things that scandalize him not:
And when you whirl round in the circle now,
As he went round the wheel in his old mill,
He says that you go wrong in all respects,
Especially if you congratulate him
Upon the strength of the resemblance.

PROCTO-PHANTASMIST.   Fly!
Vanish! Unheard-of impudence! What, still there!
In this enlightened age too, since you have been
Proved not to exist! — But this infernal brood
Will hear no reason and endure no rule.
Are we so wise, and is the *pond* still haunted?
How long have I been sweeping out this rubbish
Of superstition, and the world will not
Come clean with all my pains! — it is a case
Unheard of!

THE GIRL. Then leave off teasing us so.

PROCTO-PHANTASMIST.
I tell you, spirits, to your faces now,
That I should not regret this despotism
Of spirits, but that mine can wield it not.
To-night I shall make poor work of it,
Yet I will take a round with you, and hope
Before my last step in the living dance
To beat the poet and the devil together.

MEPHISTOPHELES. At last he will sit down
     in some foul puddle;
That is his way of solacing himself;
Until some leech, diverted with his gravity,
Cures him of spirits and the spirit together.
[To Faust, who has seceded from the dance.]
Why do you let that fair girl pass from you,
Who sung so sweetly to you in the dance?

FAUST. A red mouse in the middle of her singing
Sprung from her mouth.

<116>

MEPHISTOPHELES. That was all right, my friend:
Be it enough that the mouse was not gray.
Do not disturb your hour of happiness
With close consideration of such trifles.

FAUST. Then saw I —

MEPHISTOPHELES. What?

FAUST. Seest thou not a pale,
Fair girl, standing alone, far, far away?
She drags herself now forward with slow steps,
And seems as if she moved with shackled feet:
I cannot overcome the thought that she
Is like poor Margaret.

MEPHISTOPHELES. Let it be — pass on —
No good can come of it — it is not well
To meet it — it is an enchanted phantom,
A lifeless idol; with its numbing look,
It freezes up the blood of man; and they
Who meet its ghastly stare are turned to stone,
Like those who saw Medusa.

FAUST.   Oh, too true!
Her eyes are like the eyes of a fresh corpse
Which no beloved hand has closed, alas!
That is the breast which Margaret yielded to me —
Those are the lovely limbs which I enjoyed!

MEPHISTOPHELES. It is all magic, poor deluded fool!
She looks to every one like his first love.

FAUST. Oh, what delight! what woe! I cannot turn
My looks from her sweet piteous countenance.
How strangely does a single blood-red line,
Not broader than the sharp edge of a knife,
Adorn her lovely neck!

MEPHISTOPHELES. Ay, she can carry
Her head under her arm upon occasion;

<117>

Perseus has cut it off for her. These pleasures
End in delusion. — Gain this rising ground,
It is as airy here as in the Prater.[6]
And if I am not mightily deceived,
I see a theatre. — What may this mean?

ATTENDANT. Quite a new piece, the last of seven, for 'tis
The custom now to represent that number.
'Tis written by a Dilettante, and
The actors who perform are Dilettanti;
Excuse me, gentlemen; but I must vanish.
I am a Dilettante curtain-lifter.

—1822

[Shelley translated two scenes from *Faust* in 1822, while in the company of Lord Byron. The Walpurgis Night scene was not widely available in English, and Shelley admitted that parts of it were incomprehensible to him until he examined the engravings for Faust by Friedrich Retzsch (1779-1857), whose 26 engraved plates to Faust were admired by Goethe. Shelley wrote, in April 1822: "I have been reading over & over again Faust, & always with sensations that no other composition excites. It deepens the gloom & augments the rapidity of the ideas, & would therefore seem to be an unfit study for any person who is a prey to the reproaches of memory, & the delusions of an imagination not to be restrained."[7] In one of those ghastly coincidences of publishing, Shelley's Faust scene was published in 1834, along with "outlines" of Retzsch's engravings, and with the anonymous *Faust* excerpts by Coleridge, the one poet for whom Shelley held the highest scorn.]

---

[6] *Prater.* Public park in Vienna.
[7] Letter quoted in *The Journals of Claire Clairmont* (245). Claire was working at this time on her own translation of *Faust,* of which no trace has survived.

<118>

On the Medusa of Leonardo Da Vinci[8]
In The Florentine Gallery

1.

It lieth, gazing on the midnight sky,
Upon the cloudy mountain-peak supine;
Below, far lands are seen tremblingly;
Its horror and its beauty are divine.
Upon its lips and eyelids seems to lie
Loveliness like a shadow, from which shine,
Fiery and lurid, struggling underneath,
The agonies of anguish and of death.

2.

Yet it is less the horror than the grace
Which turns the gazer's spirit into stone,
Whereon the lineaments of that dead face
Are graven, till the characters be grown
Into itself, and thought no more can trace;
'Tis the melodious hue of beauty thrown
Athwart the darkness and the glare of pain,
Which humanize and harmonize the strain.

3.

And from its head as from one body grow,
As [   ][9] grass out of a watery rock,
Hairs which are vipers, and they curl and flow
And their long tangles in each other lock,
And with unending involutions show
Their mailed radiance, as it were to mock
The torture and the death within, and saw
The solid air with many a ragged jaw.

---

[8] Leonardo Da Vinci's *Medusa*, now lost, was a work of the artist's youth. Vasari claimed that the work so horrified Leonardo's father, that he sold it. The painting seen by Shelley, shown on the following page, is now attributed to an unknown Flemish artist, circa 1600 CE. (Uffizi Gallery).
[9] Shelley leaves a blank space for a word here.

<119>

4.

And, from a stone beside, a poisonous eft
Peeps idly into those Gorgonian eyes;
Whilst in the air a ghastly bat, bereft
Of sense, has flitted with a mad surprise
Out of the cave this hideous light had cleft,
And he comes hastening like a moth that hies
After a taper; and the midnight sky
Flares, a light more dread than obscurity.

5.

'Tis the tempestuous loveliness of terror;
For from the serpents gleams a brazen glare
Kindled by that inextricable error,
Which makes a thrilling vapour of the air
Become a [   ]10 and ever-shifting mirror
Of all the beauty and the terror there —
A woman's countenance, with serpent-locks,
Gazing in death on Heaven from those wet rocks.

---

10 Shelley leaves a blank space where a single-syllable word should be. I find the
word "cold" acceptable here. Mrs. Shelley published this nearly-complete poem
in Shelley's *Posthumous Poems* in 1824.

<120>

Saint Edmond's Eve

Oh! did you observe the Black Canon pass,
And did you observe his frown?
He goeth to say the midnight mass,
In holy St. Edmond's town.[11]

He goeth to sing the burial chaunt,
And to lay the wandering sprite,
Whose shadowy, restless form doth haunt,
The Abbey's drear aisle this night.[12]

It saith it will not its wailing cease,
'Till that holy man come near,
'Till he pour o'er its grave the prayer of peace,
And sprinkle the hallowed tear.

The Canon's horse is stout and strong
The road is plain and fair,
But the Canon slowly wends along,
And his brow is gloomed with care.

Who is it thus late at the Abbey-gate?
Sullen echoes the portal bell,
It sounds like the whispering voice of fate,
It sounds like a funeral knell.

The Canon his faltering knee thrice bowed,
And his frame was convulsed with fear,
When a voice was heard distinct and loud,
"Prepare! for thy hour is near."

---

[11] Bury St. Edmunds, named for the Anglo-Saxon martyr-king, killed by the
Danes in 869 CE.
[12] Abbey of Bury St. Edmunds (Suffolk) was a Benedictine monastery until its
dissolution in 1539. The monks of this abbey were under the supervision of the
Bishop of Elmham and Dunwich. The abbey was so hated by the local
inhabitants that it was the site of riots, as well as armed struggles between monks
and townspeople. Several churches built on the site were burned and destroyed.
The ruins are shown on the following page.

<121>

He crosses his breast, he mutters a prayer,
To Heaven he lifts his eye,
He heeds not the Abbot's gazing stare,
Nor the dark Monks who murmured by.

Bare-headed he worships the sculptured saints
That frown on the sacred walls,
His face it grows pale, — he trembles, he faints,
At the Abbot's feet he falls.

And straight the father's robe he kissed,
Who cried, "Grace dwells with thee,
The spirit will fade like the morning mist,
At your *benedicite*.

"Now haste within! the board is spread,
Keen blows the air, and cold,
The spectre sleeps in its earthy bed,
'Till St. Edmond's bell hath tolled, —

"Yet rest your wearied limbs to-night,
You've journeyed many a mile,
To-morrow lay the wailing sprite,
That shrieks in the moonlight aisle.

<122>

"Oh! faint are my limbs and my bosom is cold,
Yet to-night must the sprite be laid,
Yet to-night when the hour of horror's told,
Must I meet the wandering shade.

"Nor food, nor rest may now delay, —
For hark! the echoing pile,
A bell loud shakes! — Oh haste away,
O lead to the haunted aisle."

The torches slowly move before,
The cross is raised on high,
A smile of peace the Canon wore,
But horror dimmed his eye —

And now they climb the footworn stair,
The chapel gates unclose,
Now each breathed low a fervent prayer,
And fear each bosom froze —

Now paused awhile the doubtful band
And viewed the solemn scene, —
Full dark the clustered columns stand,
The moon gleams pale between —

"Say father, say, what cloisters' gloom
Conceals the unquiet shade,
Within what dark unhallowed tomb,
The corse unblessed was laid." —

"Through yonder drear aisle alone it walks,
And murmurs a mournful plaint,
Of thee! Black Canon, it wildly talks,
And call on thy patron saint —

"The pilgrim this night with wondering eyes,
As he prayed at St. Edmond's shrine,[13]
From a black marble tomb hath seen it rise,
And under yon arch recline." —

---

[13] St. Edmund's shrine stood behind the high altar.

<123>

"Oh! say upon that black marble tomb,
What memorial sad appears." —
"Undistinguished it lies in the chancel's gloom,
No memorial sad it bears" —

The Canon his paternoster reads,
His rosary hung by his side,
Now swift to the chancel doors he leads,
And untouched they open wide,

Resistless, strange sounds his steps impel,
To approach to the black marble tomb,
"Oh! enter, Black Canon," a whisper fell,
"Oh! enter, thy hour is come."

He paused, told his beads, and the threshold passed.
Oh! horror, the chancel doors close,
A loud yell was borne on the rising blast,
And a deep, dying groan arose.

The Monks in amazement shuddering stand,
They burst through the chancel's gloom,
From St. Edmond's shrine, lo! a skeleton's hand,
Points to the black marble tomb.

Lo! deeply engraved, an inscription blood red,
In characters fresh and clear —
"The guilty Black Canon of Elmham's dead,
And his wife lies buried here!"

In Elmham's[14] tower he wedded a Nun,
To St. Edmond's his bride he bore,
On this eve her noviciate here was begun,
And a Monk's gray weeds she wore; —

O! deep was her conscience dyed with guilt,
Remorse she full oft revealed,
Her blood by the ruthless Black Canon was spilt,
And in death her lips he sealed;

---

14 North Elmham, Norfolk, was the site of a cathedral, seat of the Bishop of
Elmham until 1075 CE. The ruins of the cathedral remain.

<124>

Her spirit to penance this night was doomed,
'Till the Canon atoned the deed,
Here together they now shall rest entombed,
'Till their bodies from dust are freed —

Hark! a loud peal of thunder shakes the roof,
Round the altar bright lightnings play,
Speechless with horror the Monks stand aloof,
And the storm dies sudden away —

The inscription was gone! a cross on the ground,
And a rosary shone through the gloom,
But never again was the Canon there found,
Or the Ghost on the black marble tomb.

<125>

Revenge

"Ah! quit me not yet, for the wind whistles shrill,
Its blast wanders mournfully over the hill,
The thunder's wild voice rattles madly above,
You will not then, cannot then, leave me my love. —

"I must dearest Agnes, the night is far gone —
I must wander this evening to Strasburg alone,
I must seek the drear tomb of my ancestors' bones,
And must dig their remains from beneath the cold stones.

"For the spirit of Conrad there meets me this night,
And we quit not the tomb 'till dawn of the light,
And Conrad's been dead just a month and a day!
So farewell dearest Agnes for I must away, —

"He bid me bring with me what most I held dear,
Or a month from that time should I lie on my bier,
And I'd sooner resign this false fluttering breath,
Than my Agnes should dread either danger or death,

"And I love you to madness my Agnes I love,
My constant affection this night will I prove,
This night will I go to the sepulchre's jaw
Alone will I glut its all conquering maw" —

"No! no loved Adolphus thy Agnes will share,
In the tomb all the dangers that wait for you there,
I fear not the spirit, — I fear not the grave,
My dearest Adolphus I'd perish to save" —

"Nay seek not to say that thy love shall not go,
But spare me those ages of horror and woe,
For I swear to thee here that I'll perish ere day,
If you go unattended by Agnes away" —

<126>

The night it was bleak the fierce storm raged around,
The lightning's blue fire-light flashed on the ground,
Strange forms seemed to flit, — and howl tidings of fate,
As Agnes advanced to the sepulchre gate. —

The youth struck the portal, — the echoing sound
Was fearfully rolled midst the tombstones around,
The blue lightning gleamed o'er the dark chapel spire,
And tinged were the storm clouds with sulphurous fire.

Still they gazed on the tombstone where Conrad reclined,
Yet they shrank at the cold chilling blast of the wind,
When a strange silver brilliance pervaded the scene,
And a figure advanced — tall in form — fierce in mien.

A mantle encircled his shadowy form,
As light as a gossamer borne on the storm,
Celestial terror sat throned in his gaze,
Like the midnight pestiferous meteor's blaze. —

SPIRIT:
"Thy father, Adolphus! was false, false as hell,
And Conrad has cause to remember it well,
He ruined my Mother, despised me his son,
I quitted the world ere my vengeance was done.

"I was nearly expiring — 'twas close of the day, —
A demon advanced to the bed where I lay,
He gave me the power from whence I was hurled,
To return to revenge, to return to the world, —

"Now Adolphus I'll seize thy best loved in my arms,
I'll drag her to Hades all blooming in charms,
On the black whirlwind's thundering pinion I'll ride,
And fierce yelling fiends shall exult o'er thy bride" —

<127>

He spoke, and extending his ghastly arms wide,
Majestic advanced with a swift noiseless stride,
He clasped the fair Agnes — he raised her on high,
And cleaving the roof sped his way to the sky —

All was now silent, — and over the tomb,
Thicker, deeper, was swiftly extended a gloom,
Adolphus in horror sank down on the stone,
And his fleeting soul fled with a harrowing groan.

—December 1809

<128>

Ghasta, or The Avenging Demon

The idea of the following tale was taken from a few unconnected German Stanzas. — The principal Character is evidently the Wandering Jew, and although not mentioned by name, the burning Cross on his forehead undoubtedly alludes to that superstition, so prevalent in the part of Germany called the Black Forest, where this scene is supposed to lie.

Hark! the owlet flaps her wing,
In the pathless dell beneath,
Hark! night ravens loudly sing,
Tidings of despair and death. —

Horror covers all the sky,
Clouds of darkness blot the moon,
Prepare! for mortal thou must die,
Prepare to yield thy soul up soon —

Fierce the tempest raves around,
Fierce the volleyed lightnings fly,
Crashing thunder shakes the ground,
Fire and tumult fill the sky. —

Hark! the tolling village bell,
Tells the hour of midnight come,
Now can blast the powers of Hell,
Fiend-like goblins now can roam —

See! his crest all stained with rain,
A warrior hastening speeds his way,
He starts, looks round him, starts again,
And sighs for the approach of day.

See! his frantic steed he reins,
See! he lifts his hands on high,
Implores a respite to his pains,
From the powers of the sky. —

<129>

He seeks an Inn, for faint from toil,
Fatigue had bent his lofty form,
To rest his wearied limbs awhile,
Fatigued with wandering and the storm.

. . . . . .

Slow the door is opened wide —
With trackless tread a stranger came,
His form Majestic, slow his stride,
He sate, nor spake, — nor told his name —

Terror blanched the warrior's cheek,
Cold sweat from his forehead ran,
In vain his tongue essayed to speak, —
At last the stranger thus began:

"Mortal! thou that saw'st the sprite,
Tell me what I wish to know,
Or come with me before 'tis light,
Where cypress trees and mandrakes grow.

"Fierce the avenging Demon's ire,
Fiercer than the wintry blast,
Fiercer than the lightning's fire,
When the hour of twilight's past" —

The warrior raised his sunken eye.
It met the stranger's sullen scowl,
"Mortal! Mortal! thou must die,"
In burning letters chilled his soul.

WARRIOR:
Stranger! whoso'er you are,
I feel impelled my tale to tell —
Horrors stranger shalt thou hear,
Horrors drear as those of Hell.

<130>

O'er my Castle silence reigned,
Late the night and drear the hour,
When on the terrace I observed,
A fleeting shadowy mist to lower. —

Light the cloud as summer fog,
Which transient shuns the morning beam;
Fleeting as the cloud on bog,
That hangs or on the mountain stream. —

Horror seized my shuddering brain,
Horror dimmed my starting eye.
In vain I tried to speak, — In vain
My limbs essayed the spot to fly —

At last the thin and shadowy form,
With noiseless, trackless footsteps came, —
Its light robe floated on the storm,
Its head was bound with lambent flame.

In chilling voice drear as the breeze
Which sweeps along th' autumnal ground,
Which wanders through the leafless trees,
Or the mandrake's groan which floats around.

"Thou art mine and I am thine,
Till the sinking of the world,
I am thine and thou art mine,
'Till in ruin death is hurled —

"Strong the power and dire the fate,
Which drags me from the depths of Hell,
Breaks the tomb's eternal gate,
Where fiendish shapes and dead men yell,

"Haply I might ne'er have shrank
From flames that rack the guilty dead,
Haply I might ne'er have sank
On pleasure's flowery, thorny bed —

<131>

"But stay! no more I dare disclose,
Of the tale I wish to tell,
On Earth relentless were my woes,
But fiercer are my pangs in Hell —

"Now I claim thee as my love,
Lay aside all chilling fear,
My affection will I prove,
Where sheeted ghosts and spectres are!

"For thou art mine, and I am thine,
'Till the dreaded judgement day,
I am thine, and thou art mine —
Night is past — I must away."

Still I gazed, and still the form
Pressed upon my aching sight,
Still I braved the howling storm,
When the ghost dissolved in night. —

Restless, sleepless fled the night,
Sleepless as a sick man's bed,
When he sighs for morning light,
When he turns his aching head, —

Slow and painful passed the day.
Melancholy seized my brain,
Lingering fled the hours away,
Lingering to a wretch in pain. —

At last came night, ah! horrid hour,
Ah! chilling time that wakes the dead,
When demons ride the clouds that lower,
— The phantom sat upon my bed.

In hollow voice, low as the sound
Which in some charnel makes its moan,
What floats along the burying ground,
The phantom claimed me as her own.

<132>

Her chilling finger on my head,
With coldest touch congealed my soul —
Cold as the finger of the dead,
Or damps which round a tombstone roll —

Months are passed in lingering round,
Every night the spectre comes,
With thrilling step it shakes the ground,
With thrilling step it round me roams —

Stranger! I have told to thee,
All the tale I have to tell —
Stranger! canst thou tell to me,
How to 'scape the powers of Hell? —

STRANGER:
"Warrior! I can ease thy woes,
Wilt thou, wilt thou, come with me —
Warrior! I can all disclose,
Follow, follow, follow me.

Yet the tempest's duskiest wing,
Its mantle stretches o'er the sky,
Yet the midnight ravens sing,
'Mortal! Mortal! thou must die.'"

At last they saw a river clear,
That crossed the heathy path they trod,
The Stranger's look was wild and drear,
The firm Earth shook beneath his nod —

He raised a wand above his head,
He traced a circle on the plain,
In a wild verse he called the dead,
The dead with silent footsteps came.

A burning brilliance on his head,
Flaming filled the stormy air,
In a wild verse he called the dead,
The dead in motley crowd were there. —

<133>

"Ghasta! Ghasta! come along,
Bring thy fiendish crowd with thee,
Quickly raise th' avenging Song,
Ghasta! Ghasta! come to me."

Horrid shapes in mantles gray,
Flit athwart the stormy night,
"Ghasta! Ghasta! come away,
Come away before 'tis light."

See! the sheeted Ghost they bring,
Yelling dreadful o'er the heath,
Hark! the deadly verse they sing,
Tidings of despair and death!

The yelling Ghost before him stands,
See! she rolls her eyes around,
Now she lifts her bony hands,
Now her footsteps shake the ground.

STRANGER:
Phantom of Theresa say,
Why to earth again you came,
Quickly speak, I must away!
Or you must bleach for aye in flame, —

PHANTOM:
Mighty one I know thee now,
Mightiest power of the sky,
Know thee by thy flaming brow,
Know thee by thy sparkling eye.

That fire is scorching! Oh! I came,
From the caverned depth of Hell,
My fleeting false Rodolph to claim,
Mighty one! I know thee well. —

<134>

STRANGER

Ghasta! seize yon wandering sprite,
Drag her to the depth beneath,
Take her swift, before 'tis light,
Take her to the cells of death!

Thou that heardst the trackless dead,
In the mouldering tomb must lie,
Mortal! look upon my head,
Mortal! Mortal! thou must die.

Of glowing flame a cross was there,
Which threw a light around his form,
Whilst his lank and raven hair,
Floated wild upon the storm. —

The warrior upwards turned his eyes,
Gazed upon the cross of fire,
There sat horror and surprise,
There sat God's eternal ire. —

A shivering through the Warrior flew,
Colder than the nightly blast,
Colder than the evening dew,
When the hour of twilight's past. —

Thunder shakes th' expansive sky,
Shakes the bosom of the heath,
Mortal! Mortal! thou must die —
The warrior sank convulsed in death.

January, 1810.

<135>

JOHN KEATS

La Belle Dame Sans Merci: A Ballad

O, what can ail thee, knight-at-arms,
    Alone and palely loitering?
The sedge has withered from the lake,
    And no birds sing.

O what can ail thee, knight-at-arms,
    So haggard and so woe-begone?
The squirrel's granary is full,
    And the harvest's done.

I see a lily on thy brow,
    With anguish moist and fever-dew,
And on thy cheeks a fading rose
    Fast withereth too.

I met a lady in the meads
    Full beautiful — a faery's child,
Her hair was long, her foot was light,
    And her eyes were wild.

I made a garland for her head,
    And bracelets too, and fragrant zone;
She looked at me as she did love,
    And made sweet moan.

I set her on my pacing steed,
    And nothing else saw all day long,
For sidelong would she bend, and sing
    A faery's song.

<136>

She found me roots of relish sweet,
    And honey wild, and manna-dew,
And sure in language strange she said —
    "I love thee true."

She took me to her elfin grot,
    And there she wept and sighed full sore,
And there I shut her wild wild eyes
    With kisses four.

And there she lullèd me asleep,
    And there I dreamed — Ah! woe betide! —
The latest dream I ever dreamt
    On the cold hill side.

I saw pale kings and princes too,
    Pale warriors, death-pale were they all;
They cried — "La Belle Dame sans Merci
    Thee hath in thrall!"

I saw their starved lips in the gloam,
    With horrid warning gapèd wide,
And I awoke and found me here,
    On the cold hill's side.

And this is why I sojourn here,
    Alone and palely loitering,
Though the sedge is withered from the lake,
    And no birds sing.

<137>

LEIGH HUNT (1784-1859)

Song of fairies Robbing an Orchard

We, the Fairies, blithe and antic,
Of dimensions not gigantic,
Though the moonshine mostly keep us,
Oft in orchards frisk and peep us.

Stolen sweets are always sweeter,
Stolen kisses much completer,
Stolen looks are nice in chapels,
Stolen, stolen, be your apples.

When to bed the world are bobbing,
Then's the time for orchard-robbing;
Yet the fruit were scarce worth peeling,
Were it not for stealing, stealing.

<138>

GEORGE DARLEY (1795-1846)

Dead Man's Dirge

Prayer unsaid, and mass unsung
Deadman's dirge must now be rung
Dingle-dong the dead bells sound
Mermen chant his dirge around

Wash him bloodless,
smooth him fair,
Stretch his limbs and sleek his hair:
Dingle-dong the dead bells go
Mermen swing them to and fro.

In the wormless sand shall he
Feast for no foul glutton be
Dingle-dong the dead bells chime!
Mermen keep the tone and time!

We must with a tombstone brave
Shut the shark out from his grave:
Dingle-dong the dead bells toll!
Mermen dirgers ring his knoll!

Such a slab will we lay o'er him,
All the dead shall rise before him;
Dingle-dong the dead bells boom;
Mermen lay him in his tomb.

<139>

SARAH HELEN WHITMAN (1803-1878)

The Raven

Raven, from the dim dominions
   On the Night's Plutonian shore,
Oft I hear thy dusky pinions
   Wave and flutter round my door —
See the shadow of thy pinions
   Float along the moon-lit floor;

Often, from the oak-woods glooming
   Round some dim ancestral tower,
In the lurid distance looming —
   Some high solitary tower —
I can hear thy storm-cry booming
   Through the lonely midnight hour.

When the moon is at the zenith,
   Thou dost haunt the moated hall,
Where the marish flower greeneth
   O'er the waters, like a pall —
Where the House of Usher leaneth,
   Darkly nodding to its fall:

There I see thee, dimly gliding —
   See thy black plumes waving slow —
In its hollow casements hiding,
   When their shadow yawns below,
To the sullen tarn confiding
   The dark secrets of their woe: —

See thee, when the stars are burning
   In their cressets, silver clear —
When Ligeia's spirit yearning
   For the earth-life, wanders near —
When Morella's soul returning,
   Weirdly whispers "I am here."

<140>

Once, within a realm enchanted,
    On a far isle of the seas,
By unearthly visions haunted,
    By unearthly melodies,
Where the evening sunlight slanted
    Golden through the garden trees —

Where the dreamy moonlight dozes,
    Where the early violets dwell,
Listening to the silver closes
    Of a lyric loved too well,
Suddenly, among the roses,
    Like a cloud, thy shadow fell.

Once, where Ulalume lies sleeping,
    Hard by Auber's haunted mere,
With the ghouls a vigil keeping,
    On that night of all the year,
Came thy sounding pinions, sweeping
    Through the leafless woods of Weir!

Oft, with Proserpine I wander
    On the Night's Plutonian shore,
Hoping, fearing, while I ponder
    On thy loved and lost Lenore —
On the demon doubts that sunder
    Soul from soul forevermore;
Trusting, though with sorrow laden,
    That when life's dark dream is o'er,
By whatever name the maiden
    Lives within thy mystic lore,
Eiros, in that distant Aidenn,
    Shall his Charmion meet once more.

<141>

HENRY WADSWORTH LONGFELLOW
(1807-1882)

The Hungry Ghosts

Canto XIX of *The Song of Hiawatha*

Never stoops the soaring vulture
On his quarry in the desert,
On the sick or wounded bison,
But another vulture, watching
From his high aerial look-out,
Sees the downward plunge, and follows;
And a third pursues the second,
Coming from the invisible ether,
First a speck, and then a vulture,
Till the air is dark with pinions.

So disasters come not singly;
But as if they watched and waited,
Scanning one another's motions,
When the first descends, the others
Follow, follow, gathering flock-wise
Round their victim, sick and wounded,
First a shadow, then a sorrow,
Till the air is dark with anguish.

Now, o'er all the dreary North-land,
Mighty Peboan, the Winter,
Breathing on the lakes and rivers,
Into stone had changed their waters.
From his hair he shook the snow-flakes,
Till the plains were strewn with whiteness,
One uninterrupted level,
As if, stooping, the Creator
With his hand had smoothed them over.

<142>

Through the forest, wide and wailing,
Roamed the hunter on his snow-shoes;
In the village worked the women,
Pounded maize, or dressed the deer-skin;
And the young men played together
On the ice the noisy ball-play,
On the plain the dance of snow-shoes.

One dark evening, after sundown,
In her wigwam Laughing Water
Sat with old Nokomis, waiting
For the steps of Hiawatha
Homeward from the hunt returning.

On their faces gleamed the firelight,
Painting them with streaks of crimson,
In the eyes of old Nokomis
Glimmered like the watery moonlight,
In the eyes of Laughing Water
Glistened like the sun in water;
And behind them crouched their shadows
In the corners of the wigwam,
And the smoke in wreaths above them
Climbed and crowded through the smoke-flue.

Then the curtain of the doorway
From without was slowly lifted;
Brighter glowed the fire a moment,
And a moment swerved the smoke-wreath,
As two women entered softly,
Passed the doorway uninvited,
Without word of salutation,
Without sign of recognition,
Sat down in the farthest corner,
Crouching low among the shadows.

<143>

From their aspect and their garments,
Strangers seemed they in the village;
Very pale and haggard were they,
As they sat there sad and silent,
Trembling, cowering with the shadows.

Was it the wind above the smoke-flue,
Muttering down into the wigwam?
Was it the owl, the Koko-koho,
Hooting from the dismal forest?
Sure a voice said in the silence:
"These are corpses clad in garments,
These are ghosts that come to haunt you,
From the kingdom of Ponemah,
From the land of the Hereafter!"

Homeward now came Hiawatha
From his hunting in the forest,
With the snow upon his tresses,
And the red deer on his shoulders.
At the feet of Laughing Water
Down he threw his lifeless burden;
Nobler, handsomer she thought him,
Than when first he came to woo her,
First threw down the deer before her,
As a token of his wishes,
As a promise of the future.

Then he turned and saw the strangers,
Cowering, crouching with the shadows;
Said within himself, "Who are they?
What strange guests has Minnehaha?"
But he questioned not the strangers,
Only spake to bid them welcome
To his lodge, his food, his fireside.

<144>

When the evening meal was ready,
And the deer had been divided,
Both the pallid guests, the strangers,
Springing from among the shadows,
Seized upon the choicest portions,
Seized the white fat of the roebuck,
Set apart for Laughing Water,
For the wife of Hiawatha;
Without asking, without thanking,
Eagerly devoured the morsels,
Flitted back among the shadows
In the corner of the wigwam.

Not a word spake Hiawatha,
Not a motion made Nokomis,
Not a gesture Laughing Water;
Not a change came o'er their features;
Only Minnehaha softly
Whispered, saying, "They are famished;
Let them do what best delights them;
Let them eat, for they are famished."

Many a daylight dawned and darkened,
Many a night shook off the daylight
As the pine shakes off the snow-flakes
From the midnight of its branches;
Day by day the guests unmoving
Sat there silent in the wigwam;
But by night, in storm or starlight,
Forth they went into the forest,
Bringing fire-wood to the wigwam,
Bringing pine-cones for the burning,
Always sad and always silent.

<145>

And whenever Hiawatha
Came from fishing or from hunting,
When the evening meal was ready,
And the food had been divided,
Gliding from their darksome corner,
Came the pallid guests, the strangers,
Seized upon the choicest portions
Set aside for Laughing Water,
And without rebuke or question
Flitted back among the shadows.

Never once had Hiawatha
By a word or look reproved them;
Never once had old Nokomis
Made a gesture of impatience;
Never once had Laughing Water
Shown resentment at the outrage.
All had they endured in silence,
That the rights of guest and stranger,
That the virtue of free-giving,
By a look might not be lessened,
By a word might not be broken.

Once at midnight Hiawatha,
Ever wakeful, ever watchful,
In the wigwam, dimly lighted
By the brands that still were burning,
By the glimmering, flickering firelight
Heard a sighing, oft repeated,
Heard a sobbing, as of sorrow.

From his couch rose Hiawatha,
From his shaggy hides of bison,
Pushed aside the deer-skin curtain,
Saw the pallid guests, the shadows,
Sitting upright on their couches,
Weeping in the silent midnight.

<146>

And he said: "O guests! why is it
That your hearts are so afflicted,
That you sob so in the midnight?
Has perchance the old Nokomis,
Has my wife, my Minnehaha,
Wronged or grieved you by unkindness,
Failed in hospitable duties?"

Then the shadows ceased from weeping,
Ceased from sobbing and lamenting,
And they said, with gentle voices:
"We are ghosts of the departed,
Souls of those who once were with you.
From the realms of Chibiabos
Hither have we come to try you,
Hither have we come to warn you.

"Cries of grief and lamentation
Reach us in the Blessed Islands;
Cries of anguish from the living,
Calling back their friends departed,
Sadden us with useless sorrow.
Therefore have we come to try you;
No one knows us, no one heeds us.
We are but a burden to you,
And we see that the departed
Have no place among the living.

"Think of this, O Hiawatha!
Speak of it to all the people,
That henceforward and forever
They no more with lamentations
Sadden the souls of the departed
In the Islands of the Blessed.

<147>

"Do not lay such heavy burdens
In the graves of those you bury,
Not such weight of furs and wampum,
Not such weight of pots and kettles,
For the spirits faint beneath them.
Only give them food to carry,
Only give them fire to light them.

"Four days is the spirit's journey
To the land of ghosts and shadows,
Four its lonely night encampments;
Four times must their fires be lighted.
Therefore, when the dead are buried,
Let a fire, as night approaches,
Four times on the grave be kindled,
That the soul upon its journey
May not lack the cheerful firelight,
May not grope about in darkness.

"Farewell, noble Hiawatha!
We have put you to the trial,
To the proof have put your patience,
By the insult of our presence,
By the outrage of our actions.
We have found you great and noble.
Fail not in the greater trial,
Faint not in the harder struggle."

<148>

When they ceased, a sudden darkness
Fell and filled the silent wigwam.
Hiawatha heard a rustle
As of garments trailing by him,
Heard the curtain of the doorway
Lifted by a hand he saw not,
Felt the cold breath of the night air,
For a moment saw the starlight;
But he saw the ghosts no longer,
Saw no more the wandering spirits
From the kingdom of Ponemah,
From the land of the Hereafter.

<149>

The Saga of King Olaf

Selections from *Tales of a Wayside Inn*

THE CHALLENGE OF THOR

I am the God Thor,
I am the War God,
I am the Thunderer!
Here in my Northland,
My fastness and fortress,
Reign I forever!

Here amid icebergs
Rule I the nations;
This is my hammer,
Miölner[1] the mighty;
Giants and sorcerers
Cannot withstand it!

These are the gauntlets[2]
Wherewith I wield it,
And hurl it afar off;
This is my girdle;
Whenever I brace it,
Strength is redoubled!

The light thou beholdest
Stream through the heavens.
In flashes of crimson,
Is but my red beard
Blown by the night-wind,
Affrighting the nations!

---

[1] *Miölner.* Mjolnir, "The Crusher."
[2] *Gauntlets.* Iron gloves.

<150>

Jove is my brother;
Mine eyes are the lightning;
The wheels of my chariot
Roll in the thunder.
The blows of my hammer
Ring in the earthquake!

Force rules the world still,
Has ruled it, shall rule it;
Meekness is weakness,
Strength is triumphant.
Over the whole earth
Still is it Thor's-Day!

Thou art a God too,
O Galilean!
And thus, single-handed
Unto the combat,
Gauntlet or Gospel,
Here I defy thee!

QUEEN SIGRID THE HAUGHTY

Queen Sigrid the Haughty[3] sat proud and aloft
In her chamber, that looked over meadow and croft.
   Heart's dearest,
   Why dost thou sorrow so?[4]

The floor with tassels of fir was besprent,
Filling the room with their fragrant scent.

She heard the birds sing, she saw the sun shine,
The air of summer was sweeter than wine.

---

[3] Sigrid, Queen of Sweden.
[4] *Heart's dearest...* These refrain lines appear to have nothing to do with the poem's narrative.

<151>

Like a sword without scabbard the bright river lay
Between her own kingdom and Norroway.

But Olaf the King[5] had sued for her hand,
The sword would be sheathed, the river be spanned.

Her maidens were seated around her knee,
Working bright figures in tapestry.

And one was singing the ancient rune
Of Brynhilda's love and the wrath of Gudrun.[6]

And through it, and round it, and over it all
Sounded incessant the waterfall.

The Queen in her hand held a ring of gold,
From the door of Ladé's Temple old.

King Olaf had sent her this wedding gift,
But her thoughts as arrows were keen and swift.

She had given the ring to her goldsmiths twain,
Who smiled, as they handed it back again.

And Sigrid the Queen, in her haughty way,
Said, "Why do you smile, my goldsmiths, say?"

And they answered: "O Queen! if the truth must be told,
The ring is of copper, and not of gold!"

The lightning flashed o'er her forehead and cheek,
She only murmured, she did not speak:

"If in his gifts he can faithless be,
There will be no gold in his love to me."

---

[5] *Olaf the King.* Olaf Tryggvesson (956-1000 CE), a convert who Christianized many Norwegians by fire and sword.
[6] *Brynhilda and Gudrun.* Tales of Siegfried/Sigurd and his two women are common to both Norse and Germanic lore, culminating in Siegfried, Brunhilde and Gutrune in Wagner's *Ring of the Nibelung.*

<152>

A footstep was heard on the outer stair,
And in strode King Olaf with royal air.

He kissed the Queen's hand, and he whispered of love,
And swore to be true as the stars are above.

But she smiled with contempt as she answered: "O King,
Will you swear it, as Odin once swore, on the ring?"

And the King: "O speak not of Odin to me,
The wife of King Olaf a Christian must be."

Looking straight at the King, with her level brows,
She said, "I keep true to my faith and my vows."

Then the face of King Olaf was darkened with gloom,
He rose in his anger and strode through the room.

"Why, then, should I care to have thee?" he said,
"A faded old woman, a heathenish jade!"

His zeal was stronger than fear or love,
And he struck the Queen in the face with his glove.

Then forth from the chamber in anger he fled,
And the wooden stairway shook with his tread.

Queen Sigrid the Haughty said under her breath,
"This insult, King Olaf, shall be thy death!"
  Heart's dearest,
  Why dost thou sorrow so?

<153>

THE SKERRY OF SHRIEKS

Now from all King Olaf's farms
  His men-at-arms
Gathered on the Eve of Easter;
To his house at Angvaldsness[7]
  Fast they press,
Drinking with the royal feaster.
Loudly through the wide-flung door
  Came the roar
Of the sea upon the Skerry;[8]
And its thunder loud and near
  Reached the ear,
Mingling with their voices merry.

"Hark!" said Olaf to his Scald,
  Halfred the Bald,
"Listen to that song, and learn it!
Half my kingdom would I give,
  As I live,
If by such songs you would earn it!

"For of all the runes and rhymes
  Of all times,
Best I like the ocean's dirges,
When the old harper heaves and rocks,
  His hoary locks
Flowing and flashing in the surges!" —

Halfred answered: "I am called
  The Unappalled!
Nothing hinders me or daunts me.
Hearken to me, then, O King,
  While I sing
The great Ocean Song that haunts me." —

---

[7] *Angvaldsness.* A village on the Norwegian island of Karmt.
[8] *Skerry.* Scottish word for a reef.

<154>

"I will hear your song sublime
      Some other time,"
Says the drowsy monarch, yawning,
And retires; each laughing guest
      Applauds the jest;
Then they sleep till day is dawning.

Pacing up and down the yard,
      King Olaf's guard
Saw the sea-mist slowly creeping
O'er the sands, and up the hill,
      Gathering still
Round the house where they were sleeping.

It was not the fog he saw,
      Nor misty flaw,
That above the landscape brooded;
It was Eyvind Kallda's crew
      Of warlocks blue,
With their caps of darkness hooded!

Round and round the house they go,
      Weaving slow
Magic circles to encumber
And imprison in their ring
      Olaf the King,
As he helpless lies in slumber.

Then athwart the vapors dun
      The Easter sun
Streamed with one broad track of splendor!
In their real forms appeared
      The warlocks weird,
Awful as the Witch of Endor.[9]

---

[9] *Witch of Endor.* A witch and necromancer visited by King Saul in the Old Testament (*Samuel* vvxiii. 7-25).

<155>

Blinded by the light that glared,
        They groped and stared
Round about with steps unsteady;
From his window Olaf gazed,
        And, amazed,
"Who are these strange people?" said he. —

"Eyvind Kellda and his men!"
        Answered then
From the yard a sturdy farmer;
While the men-at-arms apace
        Filled the place,
Busily buckling on their armor.

From the gates they sallied forth,
        South and north,
Scoured the island coast around them,
Seizing all the warlock band,
        Foot and hand
On the Skerry's rocks they bound them.

And at eve the king again
        Called his train,
And, with all the candles burning,
Silent sat and heard once more
        The sullen roar
Of the ocean tides returning.

Shrieks and cries of wild despair
        Filled the air,
Growing fainter as they listened;
Then the bursting surge alone
        Sounded on; —
Thus the sorcerers were christened![10]

---

[10] *Christened,* i.e., drowned on the reef when the tide rose.

<156>

"Sing, O Scald, your song sublime,
    Your ocean-rhyme,"
Cried King Olaf: "It will cheer me!" —
Said the Scald, with pallid cheeks,
    "The Skerry of Shrieks
Sings too loud for you to hear me!"

THE WRAITH OF ODIN

The guests were loud, the ale was strong,
King Olaf feasted late and long;
The hoary Scalds together sang;
O'erhead the smoky rafters rang.
    Dead rides Sir Morten of Fogelsang.[11]

The door swung wide, with creak and din;
A blast of cold night-air came in,
And on the threshold shivering stood
A one-eyed guest, with cloak and hood.
    Dead rides Sir Morten of Fogelsang.

The King exclaimed, "O graybeard pale!
Come warm thee with this cup of ale."
The foaming draught the old man quaffed,
The noisy guests looked on and laughed.
    Dead rides Sir Morten of Fogelsang.

Then spake the King: "Be not afraid;
Sit here by me." The guest obeyed,
And, seated at the table, told
Tales of the sea, and Sagas old.
    Dead rides Sir Morten of Fogelsang.

---

[11] *Dead rides Sir Morten...* The refrain of the poem has nothing to do with the narrative. This sometimes occurs inexplicably in old ballads, suggesting that a newer ballad retained the meter and melody of an older one, leaving the old refrain as a reminder.

<157>

And ever, when the tale was o'er,
The King demanded yet one more;
Till Sigurd the Bishop smiling said,
" 'Tis late, O King, and time for bed."
 Dead rides Sir Morten of Fogelsang.

The King retired; the stranger guest
Followed and entered with the rest;
The lights were out, the pages gone,
But still the garrulous guest spake on.
 Dead rides Sir Morten of Fogelsang.

As one who from a volume reads,
He spake of heroes and their deeds,
Of lands and cities he had seen,
And stormy gulfs that tossed between.
 Dead rides Sir Morten of Fogelsang.

Then from his lips in music rolled
The Havamal[12] of Odin old,
With sounds mysterious as the roar
Of billows on a distant shore.
 Dead rides Sir Morten of Fogelsang.

"Do we not learn from runes and rhymes
Made by the gods in elder times,
And do not still the great Scalds teach
That silence better is than speech?"
 Dead rides Sir Morten of Fogelsang.

Smiling at this, the King replied,
"Thy lore is by thy tongue belied;
For never was I so enthralled
Either by Saga-man or Scald."
 Dead rides Sir Morten of Fogelsang.

---

[12] *Havamal.* A triumphal song attributed to Odin.

<158>

The Bishop said, "Late hours we keep!
Night wanes, O King! 'tis time for sleep!"
Then slept the King, and when he woke
The guest was gone, the morning broke.
    Dead rides Sir Morten of Fogelsang.

They found the doors securely barred,
They found the watch-dog in the yard,
There was no footprint in the grass,
And none had seen the stranger pass.
    Dead rides Sir Morten of Fogelsang.

King Olaf crossed himself and said:
"I know that Odin the Great is dead;
Sure is the triumph of our Faith,
The one-eyed stranger was his wraith."
    Dead rides Sir Morten of Fogelsang.

—1863

<159>

Torquemada

In the heroic days when Ferdinand
And Isabella ruled the Spanish land,
And Torquemada,[13] with his subtle brain,
Ruled them, as Grand Inquisitor of Spain,
In a great castle near Valladolid,
Moated and high and by fair woodlands hid,
There dwelt, as from the chronicles we learn,[14]
An old Hidalgo proud and taciturn,
Whose name has perished, with his towers of stone,
And all his actions save this one alone;

[13] Tomás de Torquemada (1420-1498), the first Grand Inquisitor of the Spanish Inquisition. He held this office from 1483 until his death in 1498. The Inquisition continued, with only small interruptions, until 1836.
[14] *From the chronicles.* The poem is based on an episode from 1581, related in Adolfo De Castro's *La Historia de los Protestantes Españoles y de su Persecución por Felipe II*, published in Cadiz in 1851. Longfellow most likely read Thomas Parker's English translation, published in London the same year. Since the events in the narrative occurred in 1581 in the reign of King Philip II, Longfellow has taken a great poetic liberty in backdating this story.

<160>

This one, so terrible, perhaps 'twere best
If it, too, were forgotten with the rest;
Unless, perchance, our eyes can see therein
The martyrdom triumphant o'er the sin;
A double picture, with its gloom and glow,
The splendor overhead, the death below.

This sombre man counted each day as lost
On which his feet no sacred threshold crossed;
And when he chanced the passing Host to meet,
He knelt and prayed devoutly in the street;
Oft he confessed; and with each mutinous thought,
As with wild beasts at Ephesus[15], he fought.
In deep contrition scourged himself in Lent,
Walked in processions, with his head down bent,
At plays of Corpus Christi oft was seen,
And on Palm Sunday bore his bough of green.
His only pastime was to hunt the boar
Through tangled thickets of the forest hoar,
Or with his jingling mules to hurry down
To some grand bull-fight in the neighboring town,
Or in the crowd with lighted taper stand,
When Jews were burned, or banished from the land.
Then stirred within him a tumultuous joy;
The demon whose delight is to destroy
Shook him, and shouted with a trumpet tone,
"Kill! kill! and let the Lord find out his own!"

And now, in that old castle in the wood,
His daughters, in the dawn of womanhood,
Returning from their convent school, had made
Resplendent with their bloom the forest shade,
Reminding him of their dead mother's face,
When first she came into that gloomy place,—
A memory in his heart as dim and sweet
As moonlight in a solitary street,
Where the same rays, that lift the sea, are thrown
Lovely but powerless upon walls of stone.

---

[15] *Ephesus*. City in Asia Minor, site of animal fights and gladiator events in Roman times.

<161>

These two fair daughters of a mother dead
Were all the dream had left him as it fled.
A joy at first, and then a growing care,
As if a voice within him cried, "Beware!"
A vague presentiment of impending doom,
Like ghostly footsteps in a vacant room,
Haunted him day and night; a formless fear
That death to some one of his house was near,
With dark surmises of a hidden crime,
Made life itself a death before its time.
Jealous, suspicious, with no sense of shame,
A spy upon his daughters he became;
With velvet slippers, noiseless on the floors,
He glided softly through half-open doors;
Now in the room, and now upon the stair,
He stood beside them ere they were aware;
He listened in the passage when they talked,
He watched them from the casement when they walked,
He saw the gypsy haunt the river's side,
He saw the monk among the cork-trees glide;
And, tortured by the mystery and the doubt
Of some dark secret, past his finding out,
Baffled he paused; then reassured again
Pursued the flying phantom of his brain.
He watched them even when they knelt in church;
And then, descending lower in his search,
Questioned the servants, and with eager eyes
Listened incredulous to their replies;
The gypsy? none had seen her in the wood!
The monk? a mendicant in search of food!
At length the awful revelation came,
Crushing at once his pride of birth and name,
The hopes his yearning bosom forward cast,
And the ancestral glories of the past;
All fell together, crumbling in disgrace,
A turret rent from battlement to base.

<162>

His daughters talking in the dead of night
In their own chamber, and without a light,
Listening, as he was wont, he overheard,
And learned the dreadful secret, word by word;
And hurrying from his castle, with a cry
He raised his hands to the unpitying sky,
Repeating one dread word, till bush and tree
Caught it, and shuddering answered, "Heresy!"[16]
Wrapped in his cloak, his hat drawn o'er his face,
Now hurrying forward, now with lingering pace,
He walked all night the alleys of his park,
With one unseen companion in the dark,
The Demon who within him lay in wait,
And by his presence turned his love to hate,
Forever muttering in an undertone,
"Kill! kill! and let the Lord find out his own!"
Upon the morrow, after early Mass,
While yet the dew was glistening on the grass,
And all the woods were musical with birds,
The old Hidalgo, uttering fearful words,
Walked homeward with the Priest, and in his room
Summoned his trembling daughters to their doom.

When questioned, with brief answers they replied,
Nor when accused evaded or denied;
Expostulations, passionate appeals,
All that the human heart most fears or feels,
In vain the Priest with earnest voice essayed,
In vain the father threatened, wept, and prayed;
Until at last he said, with haughty mien,
"The Holy Office, then, must intervene!"

And now the Grand Inquisitor of Spain,
With all the fifty horsemen of his train,
His awful name resounding, like the blast
Of funeral trumpets, as he onward passed,
Came to Valladolid, and there began

---

[16] The "heresy" of the daughters is unnamed here, perhaps to preserve the pre-Luther period of Torquemada. In DeCastro, the daughters are "professors of the reformed religion" (De Castro/Parker 269).

<163>

To harry the rich Jews with fire and ban.
To him the Hidalgo went, and at the gate
Demanded audience on affairs of state,
And in a secret chamber stood before
A venerable graybeard of fourscore,
Dressed in the hood and habit of a friar;
Out of his eyes flashed a consuming fire,
And in his hand the mystic horn he held,
Which poison and all noxious charms dispelled.[17]
He heard in silence the Hidalgo's tale,
Then answered in a voice that made him quail:
"Son of the Church! when Abraham of old
To sacrifice his only son was told,[18]
He did not pause to parley nor protest,
But hastened to obey the Lord's behest.
In him it was accounted righteousness;
The Holy Church expects of thee no less!"
A sacred frenzy seized the father's brain,
And Mercy from that hour implored in vain.
Ah! who will e'er believe the words I say?
His daughters he accused, and the same day
They both were cast into the dungeon's gloom,
That dismal antechamber of the tomb,
Arraigned, condemned, and sentenced to the flame,
The secret torture and the public shame.
Then to the Grand Inquisitor once more
The Hidalgo went, more eager than before,
And said: "When Abraham offered up his son,
He clave the wood wherewith it might be done.
By his example taught, let me too bring
Wood from the forest for my offering!"
And the deep voice, without a pause, replied:
"Son of the Church! by faith now justified,
Complete thy sacrifice, even as thou wilt;
The Church absolves thy conscience from all guilt!"
Then this most wretched father went his way

---

[17] *Mystic horn.* Torquemada owned what he thought was a unicorn's horn, which was believed to protect him from poisoners.
[18] *Abraham of old.* See the story of Abraham and Isaac in the Old Testament (*Genesis* xxii).

<164>

Into the woods, that round his castle lay,
Where once his daughters in their childhood played
With their young mother in the sun and shade.

Now all the leaves had fallen; the branches bare
Made a perpetual moaning in the air,
And screaming from their eyries overhead
The ravens sailed athwart the sky of lead.
With his own hands he lopped the boughs and bound
Fagots, that crackled with foreboding sound,
And on his mules, caparisoned and gay
With bells and tassels, sent them on their way.

Then with his mind on one dark purpose bent,
Again to the Inquisitor he went,
And said: "Behold, the fagots I have brought,
And now, lest my atonement be as naught,
Grant me one more request, one last desire,—

<165>

With my own hand to light the funeral fire!"
And Torquemada answered from his seat,
"Son of the Church! Thine offering is complete;
Her servants through all ages shall not cease
To magnify thy deed. Depart in peace!"

Upon the market-place, builded of stone
The scaffold rose, whereon Death claimed his own.
At the four corners, in stern attitude,
Four statues of the Hebrew Prophets stood,
Gazing with calm indifference in their eyes
Upon this place of human sacrifice,
Round which was gathering fast the eager crowd,
With clamor of voices dissonant and loud,
And every roof and window was alive
With restless gazers, swarming like a hive.
The church-bells tolled, the chant of monks drew near,
Loud trumpets stammered forth their notes of fear,
A line of torches smoked along the street,
There was a stir, a rush, a tramp of feet,
And, with its banners floating in the air,
Slowly the long procession crossed the square,
And, to the statues of the Prophets bound,
The victims stood, with fagots piled around.
Then all the air a blast of trumpets shook,
And louder sang the monks with bell and book,
And the Hidalgo, lofty, stern, and proud,
Lifted his torch, and, bursting through the crowd,
Lighted in haste the fagots, and then fled,
Lest those imploring eyes should strike him dead![19]

---

[19] As De Castro tells it, "After becoming his own enemy and throwing his
daughters into the loathsome cells of the Inquisition, nay, bringing his own
wood to construct the burning pile, he asked permission of the inquisitors, to set
light, with his own hand, in a public auto-de-fe, to that same heap which was to
reduce to ashes the delicate frames of these his unhappy girls, unhappier still in
having known such a father.

"The inquisitors who saw in this barbarous wretch a model of slaves, received
most graciously his petition; and in order to the exaltation of the Catholic faith,
proclaimed with cymbals and trumpets, not only the inhuman demand, but their
permission to comply with it.

"The two unfortunate girls accordingly perished at Valladolid in 1581." (271)

<166>

O pitiless skies! why did your clouds retain
For peasants' fields their floods of hoarded rain?
O pitiless earth! why opened no abyss
To bury in its chasm a crime like this?
That night, a mingled column of fire and smoke
From the dark thickets of the forest broke,
And, glaring o'er the landscape leagues away,
Made all the fields and hamlets bright as day.
Wrapped in a sheet of flame the castle blazed,
And as the villagers in terror gazed,

They saw the figure of that cruel knight
Lean from a window in the turret's height,
His ghastly face illumined with the glare,
His hands upraised above his head in prayer,
Till the floor sank beneath him, and he fell
Down the black hollow of that burning well.

Three centuries and more above his bones
Have piled the oblivious years like funeral stones;
His name has perished with him, and no trace
Remains on earth of his afflicted race;
But Torquemada's name, with clouds o'ercast,
Looms in the distant landscape of the Past,
Like a burnt tower upon a blackened heath,
Lit by the fires of burning woods beneath![20]

---

[20] Even in Longfellow's time, the Spanish government imprisoned, tortured, and sentenced to hard labor, not only those preaching Protestantism, but Protestant believers, and anyone who converted from Catholicism to Protestantism. The case of Manuel Matamoros and other imprisoned Protestants created an international scandal in the 1860s. See William Greene's *Manuel Matamoros and His Fellow Prisoners* (1863).

<167>

Enceladus

Under Mount Etna[21] he lies,
It is slumber, it is not death;
For he struggles at times to arise,
And above him the lurid skies
Are hot with his fiery breath.
The crags are piled on his breast,
The earth is heaped on his head;
But the groans of his wild unrest,
Though smothered and half suppressed,
Are heard, and he is not dead.
And the nations far away
Are watching with eager eyes;
They talk together and say,
"To-morrow, perhaps to-day,
Enceladus will arise!"[22]
And the old gods, the austere
Oppressors in their strength,[23]
Stand aghast and white with fear
At the ominous sounds they hear,
And tremble, and mutter, "At length!"
Ah me! for the land that is sown
With the harvest of despair!
Where the burning cinders, blown
From the lips of the overthrown
Enceladus, fill the air.

---

[21] *Mount Etna.* The tallest active volcano on the European continent, Etna looms over the Sicilian landscape.

[22] *Enceladus.* Longfellow here associates the volcano with the Titan Enceladus, who, during the battle between Titans and Olympians, was hit by a "missile" (probably a boulder or entire mountain) hurled by Athena. The Titan was flattened, forming the island of Sicily (Graves, 35.f). Longfellow might have better employed the monster Typhon, who was imprisoned under the mountain by Zeus. The forges of Hephaestus were also rumored to be under the volcano.

[23] *Oppressors in their strength.* These lines reveal that Longfellow may be using the poem to symbolize the 1860 events of the *Risorgimento,* which freed Sicily and launched the capture of Southern Italy by Garibaldi. Sicily became part of the new Kingdom of Italy in 1861. This makes clear why the poet seems to wish for the rebirth of the seemingly destructive monster, and why he chose Enceladus, symbolic of the entire island, instead of the volcano monster Typhon.

<168>

Where ashes are heaped in drifts
Over vineyard and field and town,
Whenever he starts and lifts
His head through the blackened rifts
Of the crags that keep him down.
See, see! the red light shines!
'Tis the glare of his awful eyes!
And the storm-wind shouts through the pines
Of Alps and of Apennines,
"Enceladus, arise!"

<169>

FRANCES H. GREEN (1805-1878)

Song of the North Wind

From the home of Thor,[1] and the land of Hun,
Where the valiant frost-king defies the sun,
Till he, like a coward, slinks away
With the spectral glare of his meager day—
And throned in beauty, peerless Night,
In her robe of snow and her crown of light,
Sits queen-like on her icy throne.
With frost-flowers in her pearly zone —
And the fair Aurora[2] floating free,
Round her form of matchless symmetry —
An irised mantle of roseate hue,
With the gold and hyacinth melting through;
And from her forehead, beaming far,
Looks forth her own true polar star.
From the land we love — our native home —
On a mission of wrath we come, we come!
Away, away, over earth and sea!
Unchained, and chainless, we are free!

As we fly, our strong wings gather force.
To rush on our overwhelming course:
We have swept the mountain and walked the main.
And now, in our strength, we are here again;
To beguile the stay of this wintry hour.
We are chanting our anthem of pride and power;
And the listening earth turns deadly pale —
Like a sheeted corse,[3] the silent vale
Looks forth in its robe of ghastly white,
As now we rehearse our deeds of might.
The strongest of God's sons are we —
Unchained, and chainless, ever free!

---

[1] *Thor.* Norse god of thunder.
[2] *Aurora.* Not Aurora, the goddess of dawn, but the Northern Lights, Aurora Borealis.
[3] *Corse.* Archaic variant of "corpse."

<170>

We have looked on Hecla's[4] burning brow,
And seen the pines of Norland bow
In cadence to our deafening roar,
On the craggy steep of the Arctic shore;
We have waltzed with the maelstrom's[5] whirling flood,
And curdled the current of human blood,
As nearer, nearer, nearer, drew
The struggling bark to the boiling blue —
Till, resistless, urged to the cold death-clasp,
It writhes in the hideous monster's grasp —
A moment — and then the fragments go
Down, down, to the fearful depths below!
But away, away, over land and sea —
Unchained, and chainless, we are free!

We have startled the poising avalanche.
And seen the cheek of the mountain blanch,
As down the giant Ruin came.
With a step of wrath and an eye of flame;
Hurling destruction, death, and wo.
On all around and all below,
Till the piling rocks and the prostrate wood
Conceal the spot where the village stood;
And the choking waters vainly try
From their strong prison-hold to fly!
We haste away, for our breath is rife
With the groans of expiring human life
Of that hour of horror we only may tell —
As we chant the dirge and we ring the knell,
Away, away, over land and sea —
Unchained and chainless — we are free!

---

[4] *Hecla*. Famous volcano in Iceland, long believed to include a gateway to Hell.
[5] *Maelstrom*. Any one of many famous oceanic whirlpools, strong enough to dash ships to destruction. The most famous are in Scandinavian waters. The date of composition of this poem is not known, but Frances Green would certainly have read Poe's tale, "Descent into the Maelstrom."

<171>

Full often we catch, as we hurry along,
The clear-ringing notes of the Laplander's song.
As, borne by his reindeer, he dashes away
Through the night of the North, more refulgent than day!
We have traversed the land where the dark Esquimaux
Looks out on the gloom from his cottage of snow;
Where in silence sits brooding the large milk-white owl,
And the sea-monsters roar, and the famished wolves howl;
And the white polar bear her grim paramour hails,
As she hies to her tryste through those crystalline vales.
Where the Ice-Mountain stands, with his feet in the deep.
That around him the petrified waters may sleep;
And light in a flood of refulgence comes down,
As the lunar beams glance from his shadowless crown.
We have looked in the hut the Kamschatkan[6] hath reared,
And taken old Behring[7] himself by the beard,
Where he sits like a giant in gloomy unrest,
Ever driving asunder the East and the West.
But we hasten away, over mountain and sea.
With a wing ever chainless, a thought ever free!

From the parent soil we have rent the oak —
His strong arms splintered, his sceptre broke:
For centuries he has defied our power.
But we plucked him forth like a fragile flower,
And to the wondering Earth brought down
The haughty strength of his hoary crown.
Away, away, over land and sea —
Unchained and chainless — we are free!

We have roused the Storm from his pillow of air,
And driven the Thunder-King forth from his lair;
We have torn the rock from the dizzening steep,
And awakened the wilds from their ancient sleep;
We have howled o'er Russia's desolate plains.
Where death-cold silence ever reigns,
Until we come, with our trumpet breath,

6 Kamchatka, a peninsula in Siberia.
7 *Behring.* Vitus Bering, the discoverer of the Bering Strait, which separates
Russia from Alaska.

<172>

To chant our anthem of fear and death!
The strongest of God's sons are we —
Unchained and chainless — ever free!

We have hurled the glacier from his rest
Upon Chamouni's[8] treacherous breast;
And we scatter the product of human pride,
As forth on the wing of the Storm we ride,
To visit with tokens of fearful power
The lofty arch and the beetling tower;
And we utter defiance, deep and loud.
To the taunting voice of the bursting cloud;
And we laugh with scorn at the ruin we see
Then away we hasten — for we are free!

Old Neptune we call from his ocean-caves
When for pastime we dance on the crested waves;
And we heap the struggling billows high
Against the deep gloom of the sky;
Then we plunge in the yawning depths beneath,
And there on the heaving surges breathe,
Till they toss the proud ship like a feather,
And Light and Hope expire together;
And the bravest cheek turns deadly pale
At the cracking mast and the rending sail,
As down, with headlong fury borne,
Of all her strength and honors shorn.
The good ship struggles to the last
With the raging waters and howling blast.
We hurry the waves to their final crash,
And the foaming floods to phrensy lash;
Then we pour our requiem on the billow,
As the dead go down to their ocean pillow —
Down — far down — to the depths below,
Where the pearls repose and the sea-gems glow;
Mid the coral groves, where the sea-fan waves
Its palmy wand o'er a thousand graves,

---

[8] Chamouni. The famous glacier in Switzerland, part of every Romantic's "grand tour."

<173>

And the insect weaves her stony shroud,
Alike o'er the humble and the proud,
What can be mightier than we,
The strong, the chainless, ever free!

Now away to our home in the sparkling North,
For the Spring from her South-land is looking forth.
Away, away, to our arctic zone,
Where the Frost-King sits on his flashing throne,
With his icebergs piled up mountain high,
A wall of gems against the sky —
Where the stars look forth like wells of light,
And the gleaming snow-crust sparkles bright!
We are fainting now for the breath of home;
Our journey is finished — we come, we come!
Away, away, over land and sea —
Unchained and chainless — ever free!

<174>

JOHN GREENLEAF WHITTIER (1807-1892)

The Double-Headed Snake of Newbury

Far away in the twilight time
Of every people, in every clime,
Dragons and griffins and monsters dire,
Born of water, and air, and fire,
Or nursed, like the Python, in the mud
And ooze of the old Deucalion flood,
Crawl and wriggle and foam with rage,
Through dusk tradition and ballad age.
So from the childhood of Newbury town
And its time of fable the tale comes down
Of a terror which haunted bush and brake,
The Amphisbaena, the Double Snake![1]

Thou who makest the tale thy mirth,
Consider that strip of Christian earth
On the desolate shore of a sailless sea,
Full of terror and mystery,

Half redeemed from the evil hold
of the wood so dreary, and dark, and old,
which drank with its lips of leaves the dew
When Time was young, and the world was new,
And wove its shadows with sun and moon,
Ere the stones of Cheops' were squared and hewn.
Think of the sea's dread monotone,
of the mournful wail from the pine-wood blown,
of the strange, vast splendors that lit the North,
Of the troubled throes of the quaking earth,
And the dismal tales the Indian told,
Till the settler's heart at his hearth grew cold,
And he shrank from the tawny wizard boasts,

---

[1] "Concerning ye Amphisbaena, as soon as I received your commands, I made diligent inquiry: .... he assures me yt it had really two heads, one at each end; two mouths, two stings or tongues." Rev. Christopher Toppan to Cotton Mather — JGW.

<175>

And the hovering shadows seemed full of ghosts,
And above, below, and on every side,
The fear of his creed seemed verified;—
And think, if his lot were now thine own,
To grope with terrors nor named nor known,
How laxer muscle and weaker nerve
And a feebler faith thy need might serve;
And own to thyself the wonder more
That the snake had two heads, and not a score!
Whether he lurked in the Oldtown fen
Or the gray earth-flax of the Devil's Den,
Or swam in the wooded Artichoke,
Or coiled by the Northman's Written Rock,
Nothing on record is left to show;
Only the fact that he lived, we know,
And left the cast of a double head
In the scaly mask which he yearly shed.
For he carried a head where his tail should be,
And the two, of course, could never agree,
But wriggled about with main and might,
Now to the left and now to the right;
Pulling and twisting this way and that,
Neither knew what the other was at.
A snake with two heads, lurking so near!-
Judge of the wonder, guess at the fear!
Think what ancient gossips might say,

The Common Pasture for sheep or kine,
The terrible double-ganger heard
In leafy rustle or whir of bird!
Think what a zest it gave to the sport,
In berry-time, of the younger sort,
As over pastures blackberry-twined,
Reuben and Dorothy lagged behind,
And closer and closer, for fear of harm,
The maiden clung to her lover's arm;
And how the spark, who was forced to stay,
By his sweetheart's fears, till the break of day,
Thanked the snake for the fond delay!

<176>

Far and wide the tale was told,
Like a snowball growing while it rolled.
The nurse hushed with it the baby's cry;
And it served, in the worthy minister's eye,
To paint the primitive serpent by.
Cotton Mather came galloping down
All the way to Newbury town,
With his eyes agog and his ears set wide,
And his marvelous inkhorn at his side;
Stirring the while in the shallow pool
Of his brains for the lore he learned at school,
To garnish the story, with here a streak
Of Latin, and then another of Greek:
And the tales he heard and the notes he took,
Behold! are they not in his Wonder-Book?
Stories, like dragons, are hard to kill.
If the snake does not, the tale runs still
In Byfield Meadows, on Pipestave Hill.
And still, whenever husband and wife
Publish the shame of their daily strife,
And, with mad cross-purpose, tug and strain
At either end of the marriage-chain,
The gossips say, with a knowing shake
Of their gray heads, "Look at the Double Snake!
One in body and two in will,
The Amphisbaena is living still!"

Shaking their heads in their dreary way,
Between the meetings on Sabbath-day!
How urchins, searching at day's decline
The Common Pasture for sheep or kine,
The terrible double-ganger heard
In leafy rustle or whir of bird!
Think what a zest it gave to the sport,
In berry-time, of the younger sort,
As over pastures blackberry-twined,
Reuben and Dorothy lagged behind,
And closer and closer, for fear of harm,
The maiden clung to her lover's arm;

<177>

And how the spark, who was forced to stay,
By his sweetheart's fears, till the break of day,
Thanked the snake for the fond delay!
Far and wide the tale was told,
Like a snowball growing while it rolled.
The nurse hushed with it the baby's cry;
And it served, in the worthy minister's eye,
To paint the primitive serpent by.
Cotton Mather came galloping down
All the way to Newbury town,
With his eyes agog and his ears set wide,
And his marvelous inkhorn at his side;
Stirring the while in the shallow pool
Of his brains for the lore he learned at school,
To garnish the story, with here a streak
Of Latin, and then another of Greek:
And the tales he heard and the notes he took,
Behold! are they not in his Wonder-Book?
Stories, like dragons, are hard to kill.
If the snake does not, the tale runs still
In Byfield Meadows, on Pipestave Hill.
And still, whenever husband and wife
Publish the shame of their daily strife,
And, with mad cross-purpose, tug and strain
At either end of the marriage-chain,
The gossips say, with a knowing shake
Of their gray heads, "Look at the Double Snake!
One in body and two in will,
The Amphisbaena is living still!"

<178>

ALFRED, LORD TENNYSON (1809-1892)

The Lady of Shalott

On either side the river lie
Long fields of barley and of rye,
That clothe the wold and meet the sky;
And thro' the field the road runs by
To many-tower'd Camelot;

And up and down the people go,
Gazing where the lilies blow
Round an island there below,
The island of Shalott.

Willows whiten, aspens quiver,
Little breezes dusk and shiver
Through the wave that runs for ever
By the island in the river
Flowing down to Camelot.

Four grey walls, and four grey towers,
Overlook a space of flowers,
And the silent isle imbowers
The Lady of Shalott.

By the margin, willow veil'd,
Slide the heavy barges trail'd
By slow horses; and unhail'd
The shallop flitteth silken-sail'd
Skimming down to Camelot:

But who hath seen her wave her hand?
Or at the casement seen her stand?
Or is she known in all the land,
The Lady of Shalott?

<179>

Digital art after J.W. Waterhouse, *The Lady of Shallot* (1888).
Original at Tate Gallery, London.

<180>

Only reapers, reaping early,
In among the bearded barley
Hear a song that echoes cheerly
From the river winding clearly;
Down to tower'd Camelot;

And by the moon the reaper weary,
Piling sheaves in uplands airy,
Listening, whispers, ""'Tis the fairy
Lady of Shalott."

There she weaves by night and day
A magic web with colours gay.
She has heard a whisper say,
A curse is on her if she stay
To look down to Camelot.

She knows not what the curse may be,
And so she weaveth steadily,
And little other care hath she,
The Lady of Shalott.

And moving through a mirror clear
That hangs before her all the year,
Shadows of the world appear.
There she sees the highway near
Winding down to Camelot;

There the river eddy whirls,
And there the surly village churls,
And the red cloaks of market girls
Pass onward from Shalott.

Sometimes a troop of damsels glad,
An abbot on an ambling pad,
Sometimes a curly shepherd lad,
Or long-hair'd page in crimson clad
Goes by to tower'd Camelot;

<181>

And sometimes through the mirror blue
The knights come riding two and two.
She hath no loyal Knight and true,
The Lady of Shalott.

But in her web she still delights
To weave the mirror's magic sights,
For often through the silent nights
A funeral, with plumes and lights
And music, went to Camelot;

Or when the Moon was overhead,
Came two young lovers lately wed.
"I am half sick of shadows," said
The Lady of Shalott.

A bow-shot from her bower-eaves,
He rode between the barley sheaves,
The sun came dazzling thro' the leaves,
And flamed upon the brazen greaves
Of bold Sir Lancelot.

A red-cross knight for ever kneel'd
To a lady in his shield,
That sparkled on the yellow field,
Beside remote Shalott.

The gemmy bridle glitter'd free,
Like to some branch of stars we see
Hung in the golden Galaxy.
The bridle bells rang merrily
As he rode down to Camelot:

And from his blazon'd baldric slung
A mighty silver bugle hung,
And as he rode his armor rung
Beside remote Shalott.

<182>

All in the blue unclouded weather
Thick-jewell'd shone the saddle-leather,
The helmet and the helmet-feather
Burn'd like one burning flame together,
As he rode down to Camelot.

As often thro' the purple night,
Below the starry clusters bright,
Some bearded meteor, burning bright,
Moves over still Shalott.

His broad clear brow in sunlight glow'd;
On burnish'd hooves his war-horse trode;
From underneath his helmet flow'd
His coal-black curls as on he rode,
As he rode down to Camelot.

From the bank and from the river
He flashed into the crystal mirror,
"Tirra lirra," by the river
Sang Sir Lancelot.

She left the web, she left the loom,
She made three paces through the room,
She saw the water-lily bloom,
She saw the helmet and the plume,
She look'd down to Camelot.

Out flew the web and floated wide;
The mirror crack'd from side to side;
"The curse is come upon me," cried
The Lady of Shalott.

In the stormy east-wind straining,
The pale yellow woods were waning,
The broad stream in his banks complaining.
Heavily the low sky raining
Over tower'd Camelot;

<183>

Down she came and found a boat
Beneath a willow left afloat,
And around about the prow she wrote
The Lady of Shalott.

And down the river's dim expanse
Like some bold seer in a trance,
Seeing all his own mischance —
With a glassy countenance
Did she look to Camelot.

And at the closing of the day
She loosed the chain, and down she lay;
The broad stream bore her far away,
The Lady of Shalott.

Lying, robed in snowy white
That loosely flew to left and right —
The leaves upon her falling light —
Thro' the noises of the night,
She floated down to Camelot:

And as the boat-head wound along
The willowy hills and fields among,
They heard her singing her last song,
The Lady of Shalott.

Heard a carol, mournful, holy,
Chanted loudly, chanted lowly,
Till her blood was frozen slowly,
And her eyes were darkened wholly,
Turn'd to tower'd Camelot.

For ere she reach'd upon the tide
The first house by the water-side,
Singing in her song she died,
The Lady of Shalott.

<184>

Under tower and balcony,
By garden-wall and gallery,
A gleaming shape she floated by,
Dead-pale between the houses high,
Silent into Camelot.

Out upon the wharfs they came,
Knight and Burgher, Lord and Dame,
And around the prow they read her name,
The Lady of Shalott.

Who is this? And what is here?
And in the lighted palace near
Died the sound of royal cheer;
And they crossed themselves for fear,
All the Knights at Camelot;

But Lancelot mused a little space
He said, "She has a lovely face;
God in his mercy lend her grace,
The Lady of Shalott."

—1842 version

<185>

The Kraken

Below the thunders of the upper deep;
Far, far beneath in the abysmal sea,
His ancient, dreamless, uninvaded sleep
The Kraken[1] sleepeth: faintest sunlights flee
About his shadowy sides: above him swell
Huge sponges of millennial growth and height;
And far away into the sickly light,
From many a wondrous grot and secret cell
Unnumbered and enormous polypi
Winnow with giant arms the slumbering green.
There hath he lain for ages and will lie
Battening upon huge sea-worms in his sleep,
Until the latter fire shall heat the deep;
Then once by man and angels to be seen,
In roaring he shall rise and on the surface die.

—1830

---

[1] The Kraken is a legendary Norse sea monster, probably based on sightings of
giant squid. Its power is said to be so great that it can pull ships to the bottom of
the sea; hence, its association with the dreaded maelstroms and whirlpools of the
North Sea. At the time Tennyson wrote his poem, the first dinosaur skeletons
had already been shown in England. In 1821, the oceanic plesiosaurs were
identified as a separate group, and drawings were published in 1824 outlining
the sea-serpent-like skeletons of these extinct monsters. These fossils were found
in Britain, in Dorset. Tennyson's slumbering giant is alarmingly like the
hibernating monsters in Godzilla films.

<186>

EDGAR ALLAN POE (1809-1849)

The Raven

Once upon a midnight dreary,
    while I pondered, weak and weary,
Over many a quaint and curious
    volume of forgotten lore —
While I nodded, nearly napping,
    suddenly there came a tapping,
As of someone gently rapping,
    rapping at my chamber door —
" 'Tis some visitor," I muttered,
    "tapping at my chamber door —
Only this and nothing more."

Ah, distinctly I remember
    it was in the bleak December;
And each separate dying ember
    wrought its ghost upon the floor.
Eagerly I wished the morrow; —
    vainly had I sought to borrow
From my books surcease of sorrow —
    sorrow for the lost Lenore —
For the rare and radiant maiden
    whom the angels name Lenore —
Nameless *here* for evermore.[1]

---

[1] *For evermore.* Poe offered different "explanations" of "The Raven." As a character portrait of the obsessive-compulsive, it is in line with Poe's self-confessed complex of "The Imp of the Perverse." Poe told others that the poem is an exercise in elocution, with a didactic intent (this can be safely discounted). One possible inspiration, in both language and theme, is this verse from Chapter 18 of Sir Walter Scott's novel, *The Bride of Lammermoor*:
    "When the last Laird of Ravenswood to Ravenswood shall ride,
    And woo a dead maiden to be his bride,
    He shall stable his steed in the Kelpie's flow,
    And his name shall be lost for evermoe!"

<187>

And the silken, sad, uncertain
    rustling of each purple curtain
Thrilled me — filled me with fantastic
    terrors never felt before;
So that now, to still the beating
    of my heart, I stood repeating
" 'Tis is some visitor entreating
    entrance at my chamber door —
Some late visitor entreating
    entrance at my chamber door; —
  This it is and nothing more."

Presently my soul grew stronger;
    hesitating then no longer,
"Sir," said I, "or Madam, truly,
    your forgiveness I implore;
But the fact is I was napping,
    and so gently you came rapping,
And so faintly you came tapping,
    tapping at my chamber door,
That I scarce was sure I heard you"—
    here I opened wide the door; —-
  Darkness there and nothing more.

Deep into that darkness peering,
    long I stood there wondering, fearing,
Doubting, dreaming dreams no mortal
    ever dared to dream before;
But the silence was unbroken,
    and the stillness gave no token,
And the only word there spoken
    was the whispered word, "Lenore?"
This I whispered, and an echo
    murmured back the word, "Lenore"
  Merely this and nothing more.

<188>

Back into the chamber turning,
    all my soul within me burning,
Soon again I heard a tapping
    somewhat louder than before.
"Surely," said I, "surely that is
    something at my window lattice;
Let me see, then, what thereat is,
    and this mystery explore —
Let my heart be still a moment
    and this mystery explore; —
  'Tis the wind and nothing more!"

Open here I flung the shutter,
    when, with many a flirt and flutter,
In there stepped a stately Raven[2]
    of the saintly days of yore;
Not the least obeisance made he;
    not a minute stopped or stayed he;
But, with mien of lord or lady,
    perched above my chamber door —
Perched upon a bust of Pallas[3]
    just above my chamber door —
  Perched, and sat, and nothing more.

Then this ebony bird beguiling
    my sad fancy into smiling,
By the grave and stern decorum
    of the countenance it wore,
"Though thy crest be shorn or shaven,
    thou," I said, "art sure no craven,
Ghastly grim and ancient Raven
    wandering from the Nightly shore —
Tell me what thy lordly name is
    on the Night's Plutonian shore!"
  Quoth the Raven "Nevermore."

---

[2] Ravens are associated with the father god Odin in Norse myth, and are
depicted as messengers, and as harbingers of death.
[3] *Pallas.* Pallas Athena, goddess of wisdom. Here Poe has a Norse death symbol
perch atop the Greek icon of wisdom — reason deranged by grief.

<189>

Much I marveled this ungainly
    fowl to hear discourse so plainly,
Though its answer little meaning —
    little relevancy bore;
For we cannot help agreeing
    that no living human being
Ever yet was blessed with seeing
    bird above his chamber door —
Bird or beast upon the sculptured
    bust above his chamber door,
    With such name as "Nevermore."

But the Raven, sitting lonely
    on the placid bust, spoke only
That one word, as if his soul in that
    one word he did outpour.
Nothing farther then he uttered —
    not a feather then he fluttered —
Till I scarcely more than muttered
    "Other friends have flown before —
On the morrow *he* will leave me,
    as my Hopes have flown before."
    Then the bird said "Nevermore."

Startled at the stillness broken
    by reply so aptly spoken,
"Doubtless," said I, "what it utters
    is its only stock and store
Caught from some unhappy master
    whom unmerciful Disaster
Followed fast and followed faster
    till his songs one burden bore —
Till the dirges of his Hope that
    melancholy burden bore
    Of 'Never — nevermore.'"

<190>

But the Raven still beguiling
    my sad fancy into smiling,
Straight I wheeled a cushioned seat
    in front of bird, and bust and door;
Then, upon the velvet sinking,
    I betook myself to linking
Fancy unto fancy, thinking
    what this ominous bird of yore —
What this grim, ungainly, ghastly,
    gaunt and ominous bird of yore
  Meant in croaking "Nevermore."

This I sat engaged in guessing,
    but no syllable expressing
To the fowl whose fiery eyes
    now burned into my bosom's core;
This and more I sat divining,
    with my head at ease reclining
On the cushion's velvet lining
    that the lamplight gloated o'er,
But whose velvet-violet lining
    with the lamp-light gloating o'er,
  She shall press, ah, nevermore!

Then, methought, the air grew denser,
    perfumed from an unseen censer
Swung by seraphim whose footfalls
    tinkled on the tufted floor.
"Wretch," I cried, "thy God hath lent thee —
    by these angels he hath sent thee
Respite — respite and nepenthe
    from thy memories of Lenore;
Quaff, oh quaff this kind nepenthe[4]
    and forget this lost Lenore!"
  Quoth the Raven "Nevermore."

---

[4] *Nepenthe.* From Homer's Odyssey, *nepenthes pharmakon*, a magic potion that cures grief and induces forgetfulness.

<191>

"Prophet" said I, "thing of evil! —
   prophet still, if bird or devil! —
Whether Tempter sent, or whether
   tempest tossed thee here ashore,
Desolate yet all undaunted,
   on this desert land enchanted —
On this home by Horror haunted —
   tell me truly, I implore —
Is there — *Is* there balm in Gilead?[5] —
   tell me — tell me, I implore!"
   Quoth the Raven "Nevermore."

"Prophet!" said I, "thing of evil! —
   prophet still, if bird or devil!
By that Heaven that bends above us —
   by that God we both adore —
Tell this soul with sorrow laden
   if, within the distant Aidenn,[6]
It shall clasp a sainted maiden
   whom the angels name Lenore —
Clasp a rare and radiant maiden
   whom the angels name Lenore."
   Quoth the Raven "Nevermore."

---

[5] *Balm in Gilead.* Balm is the resin of the balsam tree, used for perfume and medicine, and associated in the Bible with the town of Gilead. The line is literally adapted from the Bible, "Is there no balm in Gilead?" (*Jeremiah* 8:22). As Poe is a nonbeliever, his question is posed, from a "desert land" as if to ask, "Is there a Holy Land, and is there balm there?" The Raven's answer negates all.
[6] *Aidenn.* Alternate spelling of Eden, probably from the Arabic *Adn*. In both this reference and the preceding mention of Gilead, Poe is equating Holy Land sites with Heaven itself.

<192>

"Be that word our sign of parting,
  bird or fiend!" I shrieked, upstarting —
"Get thee back into the tempest
  and the Night's Plutonian shore!⁷
Leave no black plume as a token
  of that lie thy soul hath spoken!
Leave my loneliness unbroken! —
  quit the bust above my door!
Take thy beak from out my heart,
  and take thy form from off my door!"
Quoth the Raven "Nevermore."

And the Raven, never flitting,
  still is sitting, *still* is sitting
On the pallid bust of Pallas
  just above my chamber door;
And his eyes have all the seeming
  of a demon's that is dreaming,
And the lamp-light o'er him streaming
  throws his shadow on the floor;
And my soul from out that shadow
  that lies floating on the floor
Shall be lifted — nevermore!

1844-1849

---

⁷ *Plutonian shore.* The other bank of the River Styx in Hades, where the souls if
dead dwell in Greek and Roman mythology. Twice in the poem Poe veers into
the pagan view of the afterlife, and lets the Raven be a messenger from that
world, whether the Hades of the Greek of the even more gloomy Hel of the
Norse myth.

<193>

The Bells

I

Hear the sledges with the bells —
Silver bells!
What a world of merriment their melody foretells!
How they tinkle, tinkle, tinkle,
In the icy air of night!
While the stars that oversprinkle
All the Heavens, seem to twinkle
With a crystalline delight;
Keeping time, time, time,
In a sort of Runic rhyme,
To the tintinabulation that so musically wells
From the bells, bells, bells, bells,
Bells, bells, bells —
From the jingling and the tinkling of the bells.

II

Hear the mellow wedding bells,
Golden bells!
What,? a world of happiness their harmony foretells!
Through the balmy air of night
How they ring out their delight!
From the molten golden-notes
And all in tune
What a liquid ditty floats
To the turtle-dove that listens while she gloats
On the moon!
Oh, from out the sounding cells,
What a gush of euphony voluminously wells!
How it swells!
How it dwells
On the Future! how it tells

<194>

Of the rapture that impels
To the swinging and the ringing
Of the bells, bells, bells, bells,
Bells, bells, bells —
To the rhyming and the chiming of the bells!

III

Hear the loud alarum bells —
Brazen bells!
What a tale of terror, now, their turbulency tells!
In the startled ear of Night
How they scream out their affright!
Too much horrified to speak
They can only shriek, shriek,
Out of tune,
In a clamorous appealing to the mercy of the fire —
In a mad expostulation with the deaf and frantic fire,
Leaping higher, higher, higher,
With a desperate desire
And a resolute endeavor.
Now — now to sit, or never,
By the side of the pale-faced moon.
Oh, the bells, bells, bells!
What a tale their terror tells
Of despair!
How they clang, and clash, and roar!
What a horror they outpour
In the bosom of the palpitating air!
Yet the ear it fully knows,
By the twanging,
And the clanging,
How the danger ebbs and flows: —

Yet the ear distinctly tells,
In the jangling,
And the wrangling,
How the danger sinks and swells,

<195>

By the sinking or the swelling in the anger
of the bells —
Of the bells —
Of the bells, bells, bells, bells,
Bells, bells, bells—
In the clamor and the clangor of the bells!

IV

Hear the tolling of the bells —
Iron bells!
What a world of solemn thought their monody compels!
In the silence of the night,
How we shiver with affright
At the melancholy meaning of the tone!
For every sound that floats
From the rust within their throats
Is a groan.
And the people — ah, the people —
They that dwell up in the steeple
All alone,
And who, tolling, tolling, tolling
In that muffled monotone,
Feel a glory in so rolling
On the human heart a stone —
They are neither man nor woman —
They are neither brute nor human —
They are Ghouls: —
And their king it is who tolls;
And he rolls, rolls, rolls, rolls
A Paean from the bells!
And his merry bosom swells
With the Paean of the bells!
And he dances and he yells;
Keeping time, time, time,
In a sort of Runic rhyme,
To the Paean of the bells —
Of the bells: —
Keeping time, time, time,

<196>

In a sort of Runic rhyme
To the throbbing of the bells —
Of the bells, bells, bells —
To the sobbing of the bells;
Keeping time, time, time,
As he knells, knells, knells,
In a happy Runic rhyme,
To the rolling of the bells —
Of the bells, bells, bells: —
To the tolling of the bells,
Of the bells, bells, bells, bells,
Bells, bells, bells —
To the moaning and the groaning of the bells.

July 1849

<197>

The Conqueror Worm

Lo! 't is a gala night
   Within the lonesome latter years!
An angel throng, bewinged, bedight
   In veils, and drowned in tears,
Sit in a theatre, to see
   A play of hopes and fears,
While the orchestra breathes fitfully
   The music of the spheres.

Mimes, in the form of God on high,
   Mutter and mumble low,
And hither and thither fly —
   Mere puppets they, who come and go
At bidding of vast formless things
   That shift the scenery to and fro,
Flapping from out their Condor wings
   Invisible Woe!

That motley drama — oh, be sure
   It shall not be forgot!
With its Phantom chased for evermore,
   By a crowd that seize it not,
Through a circle that ever returneth in
   To the self-same spot,
And much of Madness, and more of Sin,
   And Horror the soul of the plot.

But see, amid the mimic rout
   A crawling shape intrude!
A blood-red thing that writhes from out
   The scenic solitude!
It writhes! — it writhes! — with mortal pangs
   The mimes become its food,
And seraphs sob at vermin fangs
   In human gore imbued.

Out — out are the lights — out all!
  And, over each quivering form,
The curtain, a funeral pall,
  Comes down with the rush of a storm
While the angels, all pallid and wan,
  Uprising, unveiling, affirm
That the play is the tragedy, "Man,"
  And its hero the Conqueror Worm.

1842-1849

<199>

The City in the Sea

Lo! Death has reared himself a throne
In a strange city lying alone
Far down within the dim West,
Where the good and the bad
    and the worst and the best
Have gone to their eternal rest.
There shrines and palaces and towers
(Time-eaten towers that tremble not!)
Resemble nothing that is ours.
Around, by lifting winds forgot,
Resignedly beneath the sky
The melancholy waters lie.

No rays from the holy heaven come down
On the long night-time of that town;
But light from out the lurid sea
Streams up the turrets silently —
Gleams up the pinnacles far and free —
Up domes — up spires — up kingly halls —
Up fanes — up Babylon-like walls —
Up shadowy long-forgotten bowers
Of sculptured ivy and stone flowers —
Up many and many a marvelous shrine
Whose wreathèd friezes intertwine
The viol, the violet, and the vine.

Resignedly beneath the sky
The melancholy waters lie.
So blend the turrets and shadows there
That all seem pendulous in air,
While from a proud tower in the town
Death looks gigantically down.
There open fanes and gaping graves
Yawn level with the luminous waves;
But not the riches there that lie
In each idol's diamond eye —
Not the gaily-jeweled dead

<200>

Tempt the waters from their bed;
For no ripples curl, alas!
Along that wilderness of glass —
No swellings tell that winds may be
Upon some far-off happier sea —
No heavings hint that winds have been
On seas less hideously serene.

But lo, a stir is in the air!
The wave — there is a movement there!
As if the towers had thrust aside,
In slightly sinking, the dull tide —
As if their tops had feebly given
A void within the filmy Heaven.
The waves have now a redder glow —
The hours are breathing faint and low —
And when, amid no earthly moans,
Down, down that town shall settle hence,
Hell, rising from a thousand thrones,
Shall do it reverence.

1831-1845

<201>

Alalume

The skies they were ashen and sober;
   The leaves, they were
      crispèd and sere —
The leaves, they were withering and sere:
It was night, in the lonesome October
   Of my most immemorial year;
It was hard by the dim lake of Auber,[8]
   In the misty mid region of Weir:[9] —
It was down by the dank tarn of Auber,
   In the ghoul-haunted woodland of Weir.

Here once, through an alley Titanic,
   Of cypress, I roamed with my Soul —
   Of cypress, with Psyche, my Soul.
These were days when my heart was volcanic
   As the scoriac rivers that roll —
   As the lavas that restlessly roll
Their sulphurous currents down Yaanek
   In the ultimate climes of the Pole —
That groan as they roll down Mount Yaanek
   In the realms of the Boreal Pole.[10]

[8] *Auber.* No convincing explanation has ever been given for the place-names in this poem. The French composer Daniel François Auber premiered an opera titled *Le Lac des Fées (The Lake of the Fairies)* in Paris in 1839, based on a German ballad set in the Harz Mountains, with a libretto by Eugène Scribe. Scribe's libretto sets the opening act in a lake in the mountains. Scribe's libretti were published in book form in Paris in 1841, but it is uncertain how Poe would have been familiar with this opera or its text.

[9] *Weir.* One possible source for this name is the artist and painter Robert Walker Weir, (1803-1889) who lived in New York City and taught at the West Point Military Academy.

[10] The volcano Mt. Erebus in Antarctica was discovered in 1841, but there is no volcano at the "Boreal" (North) Pole.

<202>

Entrance to a Wood (1836) by Robert Walker Wier.

Our talk had been serious and sober,
     But our thoughts they were palsied and sere —
     Our memories were treacherous and sere —
For we knew not the month was October,
     And we marked not the night of the year —
     (Ah, night of all nights in the year!)
We noted not the dim lake of Auber —
     (Though once we had journeyed down here)
We remembered not the dank tarn of Auber,
     Nor the ghoul-haunted woodland of Weir.

<203>

And now, as the night was senescent,
    And star-dials pointed to morn —
    As the star-dials hinted of morn —
At the end of our path a liquescent
    And nebulous lustre was born,
Out of which a miraculous crescent
    Arose with a duplicate horn —
Astarte's[11] bediamonded crescent
    Distinct with its duplicate horn.[12]

And I said — "She is warmer than Dian;[13]
    She rolls through an ether of sighs —
    She revels in a region of sighs.
She has seen that the tears are not dry on
    These cheeks where the worm never dies,
And has come past the stars of the Lion,[14]
    To point us the path to the skies —
    To the Lethean peace of the skies —
Come up, in despite of the Lion,
    To shine on us with her bright eyes —
Come up through the lair of the Lion,
    With love in her luminous eyes."

---

[11] *Astarte.* The Greek name for Ishtar, Semitic fertility goddess, associated with the planet Venus.
[12] Like the moon, Venus displays a crescent phase, which can be seen with a telescope.
[13] *Dian.* The moon.
[14] *Lion.* The constellation Leo.

<204>

But Psyche,[15] uplifting her finger,
  Said, "Sadly this star I mistrust —
  Her pallor I strangely mistrust —
Oh, hasten! — oh, let us not linger!
  Oh, fly! — let us fly! — for we must."
In terror she spoke, letting sink her
  Wings till they trailed in the dust —
In agony sobbed, letting sink her
  Plumes till they trailed in the dust —
  Till they sorrowfully trailed in the dust.
I replied — "This is nothing but dreaming.
  Let us on, by this tremulous light!
  Let us bathe in this crystalline light!

Its Sybillic[16] splendor is beaming
  With Hope and in Beauty tonight —
  See! — it flickers up the sky through the night!
Ah, we may safely trust to its gleaming
  And be sure it will lead us aright —
We surely may trust to a gleaming
  That cannot but guide us aright
  Since it flickers up to Heaven through the night."

Thus I pacified Psyche and kissed her,
  And tempted her out of her gloom —
  And conquered her scruples and gloom;
And we passed to the end of the vista,
  But were stopped by the door of a tomb —
  By the door of a legended tomb;
And I said — "What is written, sweet sister,
  On the door of this legended tomb?"
  She replied — "Ulalume — Ulalume —
  'T is the vault of thy lost Ulalume!"

---

15 *Psyche.* The Soul.
16 The Sibyls were ancient oracles.

<205>

Then my heart it grew ashen and sober
    As the leaves that were crispèd and sere —
    As the leaves that were withering and sere;
And I cried — "It was surely October
    On *this* very night of last year
    That I journeyed — I journeyed down here! —
    That I brought a dread burden down here —
    On this night, of all nights in the year,
    Ah, what demon has tempted me here?

Well I know, now, this dim lake of Auber —
    This misty mid region of Weir —
Well I know, now, this dank tarn of Auber,
    This ghoul-haunted woodland of Weir."

Said we, then — the two, then — "Ah, can it
    Have been that the woodlandish ghouls —
    The pitiful, the merciful ghouls,
To bar up our way and to ban it
    From the secret that lies in these wolds[17] —
    From the thing that lies hidden in these wolds —
Have drawn up the spectre of a planet
    From the limbo of lunary souls —
This sinfully scintillant planet
    From the Hell of the planetary souls?"

1847-1849

---

[17] *Wolds.* Old English. Wood or forest, especially woodland on rocky, higher ground.

<206>

OLIVER WENDELL HOLMES (1809-1894)

The Comet

The Comet![1] He is on his way,
And singing as he flies;
The whizzing planets shrink before
The spectre of the skies;
Ah! well may regal orbs burn blue,
And satellites turn pale,
Ten million cubic miles of head,
Ten billion leagues of tail!

On, on by whistling spheres of light
He flashes and he flames;
He turns not to the left nor right,
He asks them not their names;
One spurn from his demoniac heel, —
Away, away they fly,
Where darkness might be bottled up
And sold for "Tyrian dye."[2]

And what would happen to the land,
And how would look the sea,
If in the bearded devil's path
Our earth should chance to be?
Full hot and high the sea would boil,
Full red the forests gleam;
Methought I saw and heard it all
In a dyspeptic dream!

---

[1] This poem was published in 1832, in anticipation of the return of Halley's
Comet in 1835. Every re-appearance of Halley's Comet was accompanied by
superstitious panic worldwide, and since the earth sometimes passed through the
tail of the comet, rumors were rife that the comet's "burning" tail could
extinguish life on Earth. In 1910, scientists detected poisonous cyanogen gas in
the comet's tail, but the gas is so diffuse that it can have no effect on the planet's
atmosphere. The poem is skeptical, and its horrors are attributed to bad
digestion.
[2] *Tyrian dye.* A deep purple dye made since classical times, from boiled snails.

<207>

I saw a tutor take his tube
The Comet's course to spy;
I heard a scream, — the gathered rays
Had stewed the tutor's eye;
I saw a fort, — the soldiers all
Were armed with goggles green;
Pop cracked the guns! whiz flew the balls!
Bang went the magazine!

I saw a poet dip a scroll
Each moment in a tub,
I read upon the warping back,
"The Dream of Beelzebub;"
He could not see his verses burn,
Although his brain was fried,
And ever and anon he bent
To wet them as they dried.

I saw the scalding pitch roll down
The crackling, sweating pines,
And streams of smoke, like water-spouts,
Burst through the rumbling mines;
I asked the firemen why they made
Such noise about the town;
They answered not, — but all the while
The brakes went up and down.

I saw a roasting pullet sit
Upon a baking egg;
I saw a cripple scorch his hand
Extinguishing his leg;
I saw nine geese upon the wing
Towards the frozen pole,
And every mother's gosling fell
Crisped to a crackling coal.

<208>

I saw the ox that browsed the grass
Writhe in the blistering rays,
The herbage in his shrinking jaws
Was all a fiery blaze;
I saw huge fishes, boiled to rags,
Bob through the bubbling brine;
And thoughts of supper crossed my soul;
I had been rash at mine.

Strange sights! strange sounds! Oh fearful dream!
Its memory haunts me still,
The steaming sea, the crimson glare,
That wreathed each wooded hill;
Stranger! if through thy reeling brain
Such midnight visions sweep,
Spare, spare, oh, spare thine evening meal,
And sweet shall be thy sleep!

<209>

WILLIAM BELL SCOTT (1812-1890)

The Norns Watering Yggdrasil

For a picture

Within the unchanging twilight
   Of the high land of the gods,
Between the murmuring fountain,
   And the Ash-tree, tree of trees,
The Norns, terrible maidens,
   For evermore come and go.

Yggdrasill the populous Ash-tree,
   Whose leaves embroider heaven,
Fills all the grey air with music —
   To gods and to men sweet sounds,
But speech to the fine-eared maidens
   Who evermore come and go.

That way to their doomstead thrones[1]
   The Aesir[2] ride each day,
And every one bends to the saddle
   As they pass beneath the shade;
Even Odin, the strong All-father,
Bends to the beautiful maidens
   Who cease not to come and go.

The tempest crosses the high boughs,
   The great snakes heave below,
The wolf, the boar, and antlered harts
   Delve at the life-giving roots,
But all of them fear the wise maidens,
The wise-hearted water-bearers
   Who evermore come and go.

---

[1] *Doomestead thrones.* The Norse gods know that their world will be destroyed when Ragnarok comes to pass. They can only delay the time, but not prevent it.
[2] *Aesir.* Collective name for Odin and the Norse gods, as distinguished the rival Vanir, whom they had vanquished, similar to the relationship between Olympians and Titans.

<210>

And men far away in the night-hours
  To the north-wind listening, hear,
They hear the howl of the were-wolf,
  And know he hath felt the sting
Of the eyes of the potent maidens
  Who sleeplessly come and go.

They hear on the wings of the north wind
  A sound as of three that sing,
And the skald, in the blae mist wandering
  High on the midland fell,
Heard the very word of the o'ersong
  Of the Norns who come and go.

But alas for the ears of mortals
  Chance-hearing that fate-laden song!
The bones of the skald[3] lie there still, —
  For the speech of the leaves of the Tree
Is the song of the three Queen-maidens
  Who evermore come and go.

---

[3] *Skald.* Poet.

<211>

A Ghost

In the first watch of the night,
    One candle all my light,
I saw a Spirit near the door
Standing raised above the floor.
In the air he was, yet standing,
Feet placed flat as on some landing;
So I turned my elbowed chair.
    He stood still there, —
Like tarnished silver, dark yet bright,
    And edging his crisp hair,
His hands, — whatever parts were bare,
Except the soles of his firm feet,
Passed a line of phosphor light:
Then noiselessly I rose to greet
My visitor as it was meet;
    I had no fears;
His lips moved not, yet answered he,
Nor did I hear him through the ears;
    Ah, would I could
Repeat again his speech to Thee!
It satisfied and strengthened me,
It was Aeolian too, I heard,
But yet I think he spoke no word,

<212>

A Lowland Witch Ballad

The old witch-wife beside her door
    Sat spining with a watchful ear:
A horse's hoof upon the road
    Is what she longs for, longs to hear.

The mottled gloaming dusky grew,
    Or else we might a furrow trace,
Sowed with small bones and leaves of yew,
    Across the road from place to place.

Hark, he comes! The young bridegroom,
    Singing gaily down the hill,
Rides on, rides blindly to his doom:
    His heart that witch hath sworn to kill.

Up to the fosse he rode so free;
    There his steed stumbled and he fell.
He cannot pass, nor turn, nor flee;
    His song is done — he's in the spell.

She dances round him where he stands.
    Her distaff touches both his feet,
She blows upon his eyes and hands,
    He has no power his fate to cheat.

"Ye cannot visit her to-night,
    Nor ever again," the witch-wife cried;
"But thou shalt do as I think right,
    And do it swift without a guide.

"Upon the top of Tintock hill
    This night there rests the yearly mist,
In silence go, your tongue keep still,
    And find for me the dead man's kist.[4]

---

[4] *Kist.* Scottish for a storage chest.

<213>

"Within the kist there is a cup,
    Thou'lt find it by the dead man's shine,
Take it thus! Thus fold it up! —
    It holds for me the wisdom wine.

"Go to the top of Tintock hill,
    Grope within that eerie mist,
Whatever happens, keep quite still
    Until ye find the dead man's kist.

"The kist will open, take the cup,
    Heed ye not the dead man's shine,
Take it thus, thus fold it up,
    Bring it to me and I am thine."

He went, he could make answer none,
    He went, he found all as she said,
Before the dawn had well begun
    She had the cup from that strange bed.

Into the hut she fled at once,
    She drank the wine — forthwith, behold!
A radiant damozel advance
    From that black door in silken fold.

The little Circe flower[5] she held
    Towards the boy with such a smile
Made his heart leap, he was compelled
    To take it gently as a child.

She turned, he followed, passed the door,
    Which closed behind: at noon next day,
    Ambling on his mule that way,
The Abbot found the steed, no more.
    The rest was lost in glamoury.[6]

---

[5] *Circe flower.* Magician's Nightshade, as Scott explains "has the power attributed
to it of making any one accepting it in love with the giver."
[6] *Glamoury.* Magic power of witches and fairies to transform themselves into
other shapes. The Scottish word *glamour* derives from this.

<214>

Paracelsus[7]

Prayerless from the sacred well,
    From Castaly[8] and Hippocrene,[9]
He drank, and on the verge of Hell
Slept, and forgot where he had been,
When he returned to common day,
    Baptized by Hecate![10]

He was the aeronaut who flew
Through skies becoming black like night,
Above the rack and mountain range:
Saw his own shadow on the white
Cloud-world below that dazed his sight,
And with his lapsing sense scarce knew
That moving phantom, phantom strange,
Was his own shadow.[11] It was he
Who lay in fever frenziedly,
And chased the printed flowers that shed
A mad confusion around his bed,
Until at last they changed and past
Into vermin around the dead.

---

[7] *Paracelsus.* Philippus Aureolus Theophrastus Bombastus von Hohenheim (1493-1541), was a Renaissance physician as much revered as hated. He attempted to reform medieval medicine, defying its dicta and founding some of the principles of modern medicine. Even while practicing chemistry, he was a devoted astrologer who created his own alphabet for inscribing magical talismans. He also discovered laudanum, so the poem may be referring to the aftermath of an opium dream. He was so strident in his debunking of scholastic and medicinal nonsense that he was driven from post to post, and his works were prohibited.

[8] *Castaly.* Castalia, a legendary fountain on Mt. Parnassus, a home of the Muses.

[9] *Hippocrene.* A fountain on Mt. Helikon, sacred to the Muses. Since there were rival claims for these two fountains as home base for the Muses, the poet seems to indicate a quest by visitng both.

[10] *Hecate,* or Hekate, underworld goddess patroniszed by witches.

[11] *His own shadow.* These lines seem to be a description of the Brocken Spectre, an optical illusion caused by one's own shadow projected against fog.

<215>

ROBERT BROWNING (1812-1889)

Mesmerism

I.
All I believed is true!
I am able yet
All I want, to get
By a method as strange as new:
Dare I trust the same to you?

II.
If at night, when doors are shut,
And the wood-worm picks,
And the death-watch ticks,
And the bar has a flag of smut,
And a eat's in the water-butt —

III.
And the socket floats and flares,
And the house-beams groan,
And a foot unknown
Is surmised on the garret-stairs,
And the locks slip unawares —

IV.
And the spider, to serve his ends,
By a sudden thread,
Arms and legs outspread,
On the table's midst descends,
Comes to find, God knows what friends !

V.
If since eve drew in, I say,
I have sat and brought
(So to speak) my thought
To bear on the woman away,
Till I felt my hair turn grey —

<216>

VI.

Till I seemed to have and hold,
    In the vacancy
    'Twixt the wall and me,
From the hair-plait's chestnut gold
To the foot in its muslin fold —

VII.

Have and hold, then and there,
    Her, from head to foot,
    Breathing and mute,
Passive and yet aware,
In the grasp of my steady stare —

VIII.

Hold and have, there and then,
    All her body and soul
    That completes my whole,
All that women add to men,
In the clutch of my steady ken —

IX.

Having and holding, till
    I imprint her mst
    On the void at last
As the sun does whom he will
By the calotypist's skill —

X.

Then, if my heart's strength serve,
    And through all and each
    Of the veils I reach
To her soul and never swerve,
Knitting an iron nerve —

<217>

XI.

Command her soul to advance
And inform the shape
Which has made escape
And before my countenance
Answers me glance for glance —

XII.

I, still with a gesture fit
Of my hands that best
Do my soul's behest,
Pointing the power from it,
While myself do steadfast sit —

XIII.

Steadfast and still the same
On my object bent,
While the hands give vent
To my ardour and my aim
And break into very flame —

XIV.

Then I reach, I must believe,
Not her soul in vain,
For to me again
It reaches, and past retrieve
Is wound in the toils I weave;

XV.

And must follow as I require,
As befits a thrall,
Bringing flesh and all,
Essence and earth-attire,
To the source of the tractile fire:

<218>

XVI.
Till the house called hers, not mine,
With a growing weight
Seems to suffocate
If she break not its leaden line
And escape from its close confine.

XVII.
Out of doors into the night!
On to the maze
Of the wild wood-ways,
Not turning to left nor right
From the pathway, blind with sight —

XVIII.
Making thro' rain and wind
O'er the broken shrubs,
'Twixt the stems and stubs,
With a still, composed, strong mind,
Nor a care for the world behind —

XIX.
Swifter and still more swift,
As the crowding peace
Doth to joy increase
In the wide blind eyes uplift
Thro' the darkness and the drift:

XX.
While I — to the shape, I too
Feel my soul dilate
Nor a whit abate,
And relax not a gesture due,
As I see my belief come true.

<219>

XXI.
For, there! have I drawn or no
Life to that lip?
Do my fingers dip
In a flame which again they throw'
On the cheek that breaks a-glow?

XXII.
Ha! was the hair so first?
What, unfilleted,
Made alive, and spread
Through the void with a rich outburst,
Chestnut gold-interspersed?

XXIII.
Like the doors of a casket-shrine,
See, on either side,
Her two arms divide
Till the heart betwixt makes sign,
Take me, for I am thine!

XXIV.
"Now — now" — the door is heard!
Hark, the stairs! and near —
Nearer — and here —
"Now!" and at call the third
She enters without a word.

XXV.
On doth she march and on
To the fancied shape;
It is, past escape,
Herself, now: the dream is done
And the shadow and she are one.

<220>

XXVI.

First I will pray. Do Thou
That ownest the soul,
Yet wilt grant control
To another, nor disallow
For a time, restrain me now!

XXVII.

I admonish me while I may,
Not to squander guilt,
Since require Thou wilt
At my hand its price one day!
What the price is, who can say?

<221>

The Pied Piper of Hamelin:
A Child's Story

Written for, and inscribed to, W. M. the Younger.

I.

Hamelin Town's in Brunswick,
  By famous Hanover city;
The river Weser, deep and wide,[1]
Washes its wall on the southern side;
A pleasanter spot you never spied;
  But, when begins my ditty,
Almost five hundred years ago,
To see the townsfolk suffer so
  From vermin, was a pity.

II.

  Rats!
They fought the dogs and killed the cats,
  And bit the babies in the cradles,
And ate the cheeses out of the vats,
  And licked the soup from the cooks' own ladles,
Split open the kegs of salted sprats,
Made nests inside men's Sunday hats,
And even spoiled the women's chats
  By drowning their speaking
  With shrieking and squeaking
In fifty different sharps and flats.

---

[1] *Hamelin, Hanover, Brunswick, Weser.* The locales in this narrative poem are all real, and are accurately portrayed. The medieval legend of *Der Rattenfänger von Hamelin* had already been told by The Brothers Grimm, and in a poem by Goethe. The actual incident did not involve rats, but concerned the disappearance of 130 children. According to the Lueneberg manuscript (1440-50), "In the year 1284, on the day of Sts. John and Paul, on June 26. By a piper, clothed in many kinds of colors, 130 children born in Hamelin were led away, and lost at the place of execution (Calverie) near the *koppen [mountain]*." Speculation about the actual fate of the children ranges from their being removed because of plague, to their being taken away on one of the Crusades (this explanation was offered by Gottfried Leibniz).

<222>

III.
At last the people in a body
    To the Town Hall came flocking:
" 'Tis clear," cried they, "our Mayor's a noddy;
    And as for our Corporation — shocking
To think we buy gowns lined with ermine
For dolts that can't or won't determine
What's best to rid us of our vermin!
You hope, because you're old and obese,
To find in the furry civic robe ease?
Rouse up, sirs ! Give your brains a racking
To find the remedy we're lacking,
Or, sure as fate, we'll send you packing!"
At this the Mayor and Corporation
Quaked with a mighty consternation.

IV.
An hour they sate in council,
At length the Mayor broke silence:
"For a guilder I'd my ermine gown sell;
    I wish I were a mile hence!
It's easy to bid one rack one's brain —
I'm sure my poor head aches again,
I've scratched it so, and all in vain
Oh for a trap, a trap, a trap!"
Just as he said this, what should hap
At the chamber door but a gentle tap?
"Bless us," cried the Mayor, "what's that?"
(With the Corporation as he sat,
Looking little though wondrous fat;
Nor brighter was his eye, nor moister
Than a too-long-opened oyster,
Save when at noon his paunch grew mutinous
For a plate of turtle green and glutinous)
"Only a scraping of shoes on the mat?
Anything like the sound of a rat
Makes my heart go pit-a-pat!"

<223>

V.

"Come in!" — the Mayor cried, looking bigger:
And in did come the strangest figure!
His queer long coat from heel to head
Was half of yellow and half of red,
And he himself was tall and thin,
With sharp blue eyes, each like a pin,
And light loose hair, yet swarthy skin
No tuft on cheek nor beard on chin,
But lips where smile went out and in;
There was no guessing his kith and kin:
And nobody could enough admire
The tall man and his quaint attire.
Quoth one: "It's as my great-grandsire,
Starting up at the Trump of Doom's[2] tone,
Had walked this way from his painted tombstone!"

VI.

He advanced to the council-table:
And, "Please your honours," said he, "I'm able,
By means of a secret charm, to draw
All creatures living beneath the sun,
That creep or swim or fly or run,
After me so as you never saw!
And I chiefly use my charm
On creatures that do people harm,
The mole and toad and newt and viper;
And people call me the Pied Piper."
(And here they noticed round his neck
A scarf of red and yellow stripe,
To match with his coat of the self-same cheque;
And at the scarf's end hung a pipe;
And his fingers they noticed were ever straying
As if impatient to be playing
Upon his pipe, as low it dangled
Over his vesture so old-fangled.)
"Yet," said he, "poor Piper as I am,
In Tartary I freed the Cham,

---

[2] *Trump of Doom.* The trumpet call for The Last Judgement.

<224>

Last June, from his huge swarms of gnats,
I eased in Asia the Nizam
Of a monstrous brood of vampyre-bats:
And as for what your brain bewilders,
If I can rid your town of rats
Will you give me a thousand guilders?"
"One? fifty thousand!" — was the exclamation
Of the astonished Mayor and Corporation.

VII.
Into the street the Piper stept,
Smiling first a little smile,
As if he knew what magic slept
 In his quiet pipe the while;
Then, like a musical adept,
To blow the pipe his lips he wrinkled,
And green and blue his sharp eyes twinkled,
Like a candle-flame where salt is sprinkled;
And ere three shrill notes the pipe uttered,
You heard as if an army muttered;
And the muttering grew to a grumbling;
And the grumbling grew to a mighty rumbling;
And out of the houses the rats came tumbling.
Great rats, small rats, lean rats, brawny rats,
Brown rats, black rats, grey rats, tawny rats,
Grave old plodders, gay young friskers,
 Fathers, mothers, uncles, cousins,
Cocking tails and pricking whiskers,
 Families by tens and dozens,
Brothers, sisters, husbands, wives —
Followed the Piper for their lives.
From street to street he piped advancing,
And step for step they followed dancing,
Until they came to the river Weser
Wherein all plunged and perished!
— Save one who, stout as Julius Ceasar,
Swam across and lived to carry
(As he, the manuscript he cherished)

<225>

To Rat-land home his commentary:
Which was, "At the first shrill notes of the pipe,
I heard a sound as of scraping tripe,
And putting apples, wondrous ripe,
Into a cider-press's gripe:
And a moving away of pickle-tub-boards,
And a leaving ajar of conserve-cupboards,
And a drawing the corks of train-oil-flasks,
And a breaking the hoops of butter-casks:
And it seemed as if a voice
(Sweeter far than by harp or by psaltery
Is breathed) called out, 'Oh rats, rejoice!
The world is grown to one vast drysaltery!
So munch on, crunch on, take your nuncheon,
Breakfast, supper, dinner, luncheon!'
And just as a bulky sugar-puncheon,
All ready staved, like a great sun shone
Glorious scarce an inch before me,
Just as methought it said, 'Come, bore me!'
— I found the Weser rolling o'er me."

VIII.
  You should have heard the Hamelin people
Ringing the bells till they rocked the steeple
"Go," cried the Mayor, "and get long poles,
Poke out the nests and block up the holes!
Consult with carpenters and builders,
And leave in our town not even a trace
Of the rats!" — when suddenly up the face
Of the Piper perked in the market-place,
With a, "First, if you please, my thousand guilders!"

<226>

IX.

A thousand guilders! The Mayor looked blue;
So did the Corporation too.
For council dinners made rare havoc
With Claret, Moselle, Vin-de-Grave, Hock;
And half the money would replenish
Their cellar's biggest butt with Rhenish.
To pay this sum to a wandering fellow
With a gipsy coat of red and yellow!
"Beside," quoth the Mayor with a knowing wink,
"Our business was done at the river's brink;
We saw with our eyes the vermin sink,
And what's dead can't come to life, I think.
So, friend, we're not the folks to shrink
From the duty of giving you something to drink,
And a matter of money to put in your poke;
But as for the guilders, what we spoke
Of them, as you very well know, was in joke.
Beside, our losses have made us thrifty.
A thousand guilders! Come, take fifty!"

X.

The Piper's face fell, and he cried,
"No trifling! I can't wait, beside!
I've promised to visit by dinner-time
Baghdad, and accept the prime
Of the Head-Cook's pottage, all he's rich in,
For having left, in the Caliph's kitchen,
Of a nest of scorpions no survivor:
With him I proved no bargain-driver,
With you, don't think I'll bate a stiver!
And folks who put me in a passion
May find me pipe after another fashion."

<227>

XI.

"How?" cried the Mayor, "d' ye think I brook
Being worse treated than a Cook?
Insulted by a lazy ribald
With idle pipe and vesture piebald?
You threaten us, fellow? Do your worst,
Blow your pipe there till you burst!"

XII.

Once more he stept into the street,
And to his lips again
Laid his long pipe of smooth straight came;
And ere he blew three notes (such sweet
Soft notes as yet musician's cunning
 Never gave the enraptured air)
There was a rustling,
that seemed like a bustling
Of merry crowds jostling at pitching and hustling,
Small feet were pattering, wooden shoes clattering,
Little hands clapping and little tongues chattering,
And, like fowls in a farm-yard when barley is scattering,
Out came the children running.
All the little boys and girls,
With rosy cheeks and flaxen curls,
And sparkling eyes and teeth like pearls.
Tripping and skipping, ran merrily after
The wonderful music with shouting and laughter.

XIII.

The Mayor was dumb, and the Council stood
As if they were changed into blocks of wood,
Unable to move a step, or cry
To the children merrily skipping by.
— Could only follow with the eye
That joyous crowd at the Piper's back.
But how the Mayor was on the rack,
And the wretched Council's bosoms beat,
As the Piper turned from the High Street
To where the Weser rolled its waters

<228>

Right in the way of their sons and daughters!
However he turned from South to West,
And to Koppelberg Hill his steps addressed,
And after him the children pressed;
Great was the joy in every breast.
"He never can cross that mighty top!
He's forced to let the piping drop,
And we shall see our children stop!"
When, lo, as they reached the mountain-side,
A wondrous portal opened wide,
As if a cavern was suddenly hollowed;
And the Piper advanced and the children followed,
And when all were in to the very last,
The door in the mountain side shut fast.
Did I say, all? No; One was lame,
And could not dance the whole of the way;
And in after years, if you would blame
His sadness, he was used to say, —
"It's dull in our town since my playmates left!
I can't forget that I'm bereft
Of all the pleasant sights they see,
Which the Piper also promised me.
For he led us, he said, to a joyous land,
Joining the town and just at hand,
Where waters gushed and fruit-trees grew,
And flowers put forth a fairer hue,
And everything was strange and new;
The sparrows were brighter than peacocks here,
And their dogs outran our fallow deer,
And honey-bees had lost their stings,
And horses were born with eagles' wings;
And just as I became assured
My lame foot would be speedily cured,
The music stopped and I stood still,
And found myself outside the hill,
Left alone against my will,
To go now limping as before,
And never hear of that country more!"

<229>

Earliest known depiction of the Piper, from a painted church window in Hamelin. The mountain and its execution spot are shown at right; the walled town with the Weser River, and the Piper in a boat summoning the rats into the river, at center.

XIV.

Alas, alas for Hamelin!
There came into many a burgher's pate
A text which says that Heaven's gate
Opes to the rich at as easy rate
As the needle's eye takes a camel in!
The Mayor sent East, West, North, and South,
To offer the Piper, by word of mouth,
  Wherever it was men's lot to find him,
Silver and gold to his heart's content,
If he'd only return the way he went,
  And bring the children behind him.
But when they saw 'twas a lost endeavour,
And Piper and dancers were gone for ever,
They made a decree that lawyers never
  Should think their records dated duly
If, after the day of the month and year,
These words did not as well appear,

<230>

"And so long after what happened here
  On the Twenty-second of July,
Thirteen hundred and seventy-six:"
And the better in memory to fix
The place of the children's last retreat,
They called it, the Pied Piper's Street —
Where any one playing on pipe or tabor,
Was sure for the future to lose his labour.
Nor suffered they hostelry or tavern
  To shock with mirth a street so solemn;
But opposite the place of the cavern
  They wrote the story on a column,
And on the great church-window painted
The same, to make the world acquainted
How their children were stolen away,
And there it stands to this very day.
And I must not omit to say
That in Transylvania there's a tribe
Of alien people that ascribe
The outlandish ways and dress
On which their neighbours lay such stress,
To their fathers and mothers having risen
Out of some subterraneous prison
Into which they were trepanned
Long time ago in a mighty band
Out of Hamelin town in Brunswick land,
But how or why, they don't understand.

XV.
So, Willy, let me and you be wipers
Of scores out with all men — especially pipers!
And, whether they pipe us free from rats or from mice,
If we've promised them aught, let us keep our promise!

<231>

HEINRICH HEINE (1797-1856)

The Incantation

The young Franciscan sits alone
  In the dreary cloister cell;
He reads in a book of magic, called
  The Mastery of Hell.

So fierce at last his longing grew,
  When struck the midnight drear,
The powers of the Underworld
  Pale-lipped he bade appear.

"Ye spirits! fetch me from the grave
  The fairest woman dead.
If but this night she while away,
  The boon were great," he said.

He conjures with the awful word;
  His wish is straight allowed;
The poor dead beauty rises up
  In her white and ghostly shroud.

Her frozen bosom rent with sighs,
  In sorrow she has come.
She sits her down beside the monk;
  They gaze and they are dumb.

<232>

The Water Nymphs

There's a murmur of waves on the lonely strand,
    The moon o'er the deep has risen;
The warrior rests on the white sea sand,
    His dreams are a radiant prison.

The lovely nymphs in their filmy dress
    Mount up from the waters under;
They fancy the youth is asleep, and press
    Around him with stealthy wonder.

A marveling finger the first one laid
    On the plumes he wore in his bonnet;
With his woven armour another played,
    And the bandolier upon it.

With gleaming eyes then laughed the third,
    As she snatched from the sheath its treasure;
She leaned upon the naked sword,
    And smiled on the knight for pleasure.

The fourth drew near with a merry dance,
    And yearned till the words welled over:
"Fair mortal flower, sweet the chance
    If thou hadst been my lover!"

The hand of the knight the fifth held fast,
    And kissed it long and dumbly.
The sixth was coy, but she kissed at last
    His mouth and his cheeks so comely.

To the wily knight it seemed far from wise
    To wake, that the joy should miss him;
So motionless under the moon he lies,
    As long as they care to kiss him.

<233>

King Harold Harfager

The great King Harold Harfager[1]
    Sits in the sea below,
Beside his lovely water-fay;
    The years, they come and go.

He cannot live, he cannot die,
    Bewitched in his magic tomb;
Already for two hundred years
    He has dreed his blissful doom.

The head of the king on the lovely lap
    Of the woman lies, and still
He gazes upward on her eyes,
    He cannot gaze his fill.

His golden hair grows silver-grey,
    And, from his face so pale,
The bones of his cheek, like a ghost's, stick out,
    His body is withered and frail.

And many a time from his dream of love
    On a sudden he starts, and shakes,
For the billows on high are raging wild,
    And his crystal palace quakes.

And oft in the wind he seems to hear
    The Norseman's battle-call,
And lifts his arms in gleeful haste;
    Then sadly lets them fall.

---

[1] *Harold Harfager*. Haraldr Háfagri, or Harald Fairhair, c. 850-832 CE, the first king of Norway. King Harald's burial site was a mound near the town of Haugesund, near the strait of Karmsund. A national monument to Harald and later kings buried there, was erected in 1872. The lineal descent of other Norwegian kings from Harald is traced in Snorri Sturluson's *Heimskringla*.

<234>

And even the sailors he will hear,
   Who sing as they sail along,
And praise King Harold Harfager
   In a glorious hero-song.

And then the king from his inmost soul
   Will groan and sob and weep;
But the water-fay will quickly bend,
   And kiss his woe to sleep.

—From Heine. *New Poems (Works of Heinrich Heine, Vol. 10).*
Margaret Armour, trans. 1904. London: Heinemann

<235>

VICTOR HUGO (1802-1885)

The Djinns

Town, tower,
Shore, deep,
Where lower
Cliff's steep;
Waves gray,
Where play
Winds gay,
All sleep.

Hark! a sound,
Far and slight,
Breathes around
On the night
High and higher,
Nigh and nigher,
Like a fire,
Roaring bright.

Now, on 'tis sweeping
With rattling beat,
Like dwarf imp leaping
In gallop fleet
He flies, he prances,
In frolic fancies,
On wave-crest dances
With pattering feet.

Hark, the rising swell,
With each new burst!
Like the tolling bell
Of a convent curst;
Like the billowy roar
On a storm-lashed shore,—

<236>

Now hushed, but once more
Maddening to its worst.

O God! the deadly sound
Of the Djinn's fearful cry!
Quick, 'neath the spiral round
Of the deep staircase fly!
See, see our lamplight fade!
And of the balustrade
Mounts, mounts the circling shade
Up to the ceiling high!

'Tis the Djinns' wild streaming swarm
Whistling in their tempest flight;
Snap the tall yews 'neath the storm,
Like a pine flame crackling bright.
Swift though heavy, lo! their crowd
Through the heavens rushing loud
Like a livid thunder-cloud
With its bolt of fiery might!

Ho! they are on us, close without!
Shut tight the shelter where we lie!
With hideous din the monster rout,
Dragon and vampire, fill the sky!
The loosened rafter overhead
Trembles and bends like quivering reed;
Shakes the old door with shuddering dread,
As from its rusty hinge 'twould fly!
Wild cries of hell! voices that howl and shriek!
The horrid troop before the tempest tossed —
O Heaven! — descends my lowly roof to seek:

Bends the strong wall beneath the furious host.
Totters the house as though, like dry leaf shorn
From autumn bough and on the mad blast borne,
Up from its deep foundations it were torn
To join the stormy whirl. Ah! all is lost!

<237>

O Prophet! if thy hand but now
Save from these hellish things,
A pilgrim at thy shrine I'll bow,
Laden with pious offerings.
Bid their hot breath its fiery rain
Stream on the faithful's door in vain;
Vainly upon my blackened pane
Grate the fierce claws of their dark wings!

They have passed! — and their wild legion
Cease to thunder at my door;
Fleeting through night's rayless region,
Hither they return no more.
Clanking chains and sounds of woe
Fill the forests as they go;
And the tall oaks cower low,
Bent their flaming light before.

On! on! the storm of wings
Bears far the fiery fear,
Till scarce the breeze now brings
Dim murmurings to the ear;
Like locusts' humming hail,
Or thrash of tiny flail
Plied by the fitful gale
On some old roof-tree sere.

Fainter now are borne
Feeble mutterings still;
As when Arab horn
Swells its magic peal,
Shoreward o'er the deep
Fairy voices sweep,
And the infant's sleep
Golden visions fill.

Each deadly Djinn,
Dark child of fright,
Of death and sin,
Speeds in wild flight.

<238>

Hark, the dull moan,
Like the deep tone
Of Ocean's groan,
Afar, by night!

More and more
Fades it slow,
As on shore
Ripples flow,—
As the plaint
Far and faint
Of a saint
Murmured low.

Hark! hist!
Around,
I list!
The bounds
Of space
All trace
Efface
Of sound.

—1828

—Trans. John L. O'Sullivan.

<239>

Conversation with the Marble Faun

He seemed to shiver, for the wind was keen.
'Twas a poor statue underneath a mass
Of leafless branches, with a blackened back
And a green foot — an isolated Faun
In old deserted park, who, bending forward,
Half-merged himself in the entangled boughs,
Half in his marble settings. He was there,
Pensive, and bound to earth; and, as all things
Devoid of movement, he was there — forgotten.

Trees were around him, whipped by icy blasts —
Gigantic chestnuts, without leaf or bird,
And, like himself, grown old in that same place.
Through the dark network of their undergrowth,
Pallid his aspect; and the earth was brown.
Starless and moonless, a rough winter's night
Was letting down her lappets o'er the mist.
This — nothing more: old Faun, dull sky, dark wood.

Poor, helpless marble, how I've pitied it!
Less often man — the harder of the two.

So, then, without a word that might offend
His ear deformed — for well the marble hears
The voice of thought — I said to him: "You hail
From the gay amorous age. O Faun, what saw you
When you were happy? Were you of the Court?

"Speak to me, comely Faun, as you would speak
To tree, or zephyr, or untrodden grass.
Have you, O Greek, O mocker of old days,
Have you not sometimes with that oblique eye
Winked at the Farnese Hercules?[1] — Alone,
Have you, O Faun, considerately turned
From side to side when counsel-seekers came,
And now advised as shepherd, now as satyr? —

---

[1] *Farnese Hercules*. Hugo's Faun may be at the Chateau Vaux-le-Vicomte, since there is a Hercules statue there. See references to Vaux later in the poem.

<240>

Have you sometimes, upon this very bench,
Seen, at mid-day, Vincent de Paul instilling
Grace into Gondi?[2] — Have you ever thrown
That searching glance on Louis with Fontange,[3]
On Anne with Buckingham;[4] and did they not
Start, with flushed cheeks, to hear your laugh ring forth
From corner of the wood? — Was your advice
As to the thyrsus[5] or the ivy asked,
When, in grand ballet of fantastic form,
God Phoebus, or God Pan, and all his court,
Turned the fair head of the proud Montespan,[6]
Calling her Amaryllis? — La Fontaine,
Flying the courtiers' ears of stone, came he,
Tears on his eyelids, to reveal to you
The sorrows of his nymphs of Vaux?[7] — What said
Boileau[8] to you — to you — O lettered Faun,
Who once with Virgil, in the Eclogue, held
That charming dialogue? — Say, have you seen
Young beauties sporting on the sward? — Have you
Been honored with a sight of Molière[9]
In dreamy mood? — Has he perchance, at eve,
When here the thinker homeward went, has he,
Who — seeing souls all naked — could not fear
Your nudity, in his inquiring mind,
Confronted you with Man?"

---

[2] *Vincent de Paul ... Gondi.* St. Vincent de Paul (1581-1660), "the Great Apostle of Charity" was spiritual advisor to Madame di Gondi, who in turn helped finance many missionaries.

[3] *Louis with Fontagne.* Louis XIV and his mistress, the Marquise of Fontagne.

[4] *Anne with Buckingham.* George Viller, later Duke of Buckingham, and Anne of Brunswick (1574-1619), wife of James I.

[5] *Thyrsus.* A fennel-stalk wand symbolizing fertility and prosperity, probably phallic, topped with a pine cone and wrapped in ivy leaves. It is the staff of Dionysos.

[6] *Montespan.* Françoise Athénaïs de Rochechouart de Mortemart, Marquise of Montespan (1640-1707), the most famous of Louis XIV's mistresses. She and Fontagne were bitter rivals, and when Fontagne died suddenly, gossips said that Montespan had poisoned her.

[7] *La Fontaine ... Vaux.* Jean de la Fontaine, poet and fable-writer, penned an elegy to a disgraced and imprisoned patron (Fouquet) titled "Pleurez, Nymphes de Vaux," referring to the famed Chateau de Vaux-le-Vicomte and its gardens.

[8] *Boileau.* Nicolas Boileau-Despréaux (1636-1711), poet, satirist, critic.

[9] *Molière.* Molière's plays were performed at Vaux.

<241>

Under the thickly-tangled branches, thus
Did I speak to him; he no answer gave.

I shook my head, and moved myself away;
Then, from the copses, and from secret caves[10]
Hid in the wood, methought a ghostly voice
Came forth and woke an echo in my souls
As in the hollow of an amphora.

"Imprudent poet," thus it seemed to say,
"What dost thou here? Leave the forsaken Fauns
In peace beneath their trees! Dost thou not know,
Poet, that ever it is impious deemed,
In desert spots where drowsy shades repose —
Though love itself might prompt thee — to shake down
The moss that hangs from ruined centuries,
And, with the vain noise of thine ill-timed words,
To mar the recollections of the dead?"

Then to the gardens all enwrapped in mist
I hurried, dreaming of the vanished days,
And still behind me — hieroglyph obscure
Of antique alphabet — the lonely Faun
Held to his laughter, through the falling night.

I went my way; but yet — in saddened spirit
Pondering on all that had my vision crossed,
Leaves of old summers, fair ones of old time —
Through all, at distance, would my fancy see,
In the woods, statues; shadows in the past!

1837

— *"Il semblait grelotter." Trans. William Young*

---

[10] *Caves.* The gardens at Vaux included artificial grottoes. Later owners of the
Chateau, especially after the French Revolution, allowed the gardens to sink into
neglect, so Hugo may well have found the Vaux gardens a gloomy spot.

<242>

Cain

From *La Légende des Siècles*

Then, with his children, clothed in skins of brutes,
Disheveled, livid, rushing through the storm,
Cain fled before Jehovah. As night fell
The dark man reached a mount in a great plain,
And his tired wife and his sons, out of breath,
Said: "Let us lie down on the earth and sleep."
Cain, sleeping not, dreamed at the mountain foot.
Raising his head, in that funereal heaven
He saw an eye, a great eye, in the night
Open, and staring at him in the gloom.
"I am too near," he said, and tremblingly woke up
His sleeping sons again, and his tired wife,
And fled through space and darkness. Thirty days
He went, and thirty nights, nor looked behind;
Pale, silent, watchful, shaking at each sound;
No rest, no sleep, till he attained the strand
Where the sea washes that which since was Asshur.
"Here pause," he said, "for this place is secure;
Here may we rest, for this is the world's end."
And he sat down; when, lo! in the sad sky,
The selfsame Eye on the horizon's verge,
And the wretch shook as in an ague fit.
"Hide me!" he cried; and all his watchful sons,
Their finger on their lip, stared at their sire.
Cain said to Jabal (father of them that dwell
In tents): "Spread here the curtain of thy tent,"
And they spread wide the floating canvas roof,
And made it fast and fixed it down with lead.
"You see naught now," said Zillah then, fair child
The daughter of his eldest, sweet as day.
But Cain replied, "That Eye — I see it still."
And Jubal cried (the father of all those
That handle harp and organ): "I will build
A sanctuary;" and he made a wall of bronze,
And set his sire behind it. But Cain moaned,

<243>

"That Eye is glaring at me ever." Henoch cried:
"Then must we make a circle vast of towers,
So terrible that nothing dare draw near;
Build we a city with a citadel;
Build we a city high and close it fast."
Then Tubal Cain (instructor of all them
That work in brass and iron) built a tower —
Enormous, superhuman. While he wrought,
His fiery brothers from the plain around
Hunted the sons of Enoch and of Seth;
They plucked the eyes out of whoever passed,
And hurled at even arrows to the stars.
They set strong granite for the canvas wall,
And every block was clamped with iron chains.
It seemed a city made for hell. Its towers,
With their huge masses made night in the land.
The walls were thick as mountains. On the door
They graved: "Let not God enter here." This done,
And having finished to cement and build
In a stone tower, they set him in the midst.
To him, still dark and haggard, "Oh, my sire,
Is the Eye gone?" quoth Zillah tremblingly.
But Cain replied: "Nay, it is even there."
Then added: "I will live beneath the earth,
As a lone man within his sepulchre.
I will see nothing; will be seen of none."
They digged a trench, and Cain said: " 'Tis enow,"
As he went down alone into the vault;
But when he sat, so ghost-like, in his chair,
And they had closed the dungeon o'er his head,
The Eye was in the tomb and fixed on Cain.

—*Anon Trans, from Dublin University Magazine*

King Canute

From *La Légende des Siècles*

King Canute died.[11] Encoffined he was laid.
Of Aarhuus came the Bishop prayers to say,
And sang a hymn upon his tomb, and held
That Canute was a saint — Canute the Great,
That from his memory breathed celestial perfume,
And that they saw him, they the priests, in glory,
Seated at God's right hand, a prophet crowned.

I.

        Evening came,
And hushed the organ in the holy place,
And the priests, issuing from the temple doors,
Left the dead king in peace. Then he arose,
Opened his gloomy eyes, and grasped his sword,
And went forth loftily. The massy walls
Yielded before the phantom, like a mist.

There is a sea where Aarhuus, Altona,
And Elsinore's vast domes and shadowy towers
Glass in deep waters. Over this he went
Dark, and still Darkness listened for his foot
Inaudible, itself being but a dream.
Straight to Mount Savo went he, gnawed by time,
And thus, "O mountain buffeted of storms,
Give me of thy huge mantle of deep snow
To frame a winding-sheet." The mountain knew him,
Nor dared refuse, and with his sword Canute
Cut from his flank white snow, enough to make

---

[11] King Canute (c. 995 - 1035 CE) slew his old father, Sweno, to obtain the crown. His kingdom included England, Denmark, and Norway. He was King of England from 1016 until his death. His fight with the English lords who resisted the "Danelaw" included a siege of London. As in the preceding poem, "Cain," Hugo here employs supernatural themes to trace the concepts of guilt and conscience. Although this successful Viking king adopted Christianity and was even received at Rome, Hugo seems to doubt that any king from this bloodthirsty era could attain Heaven.

<245>

The garment he desired, and then he cried,
"Old mountain! death is dumb, but tell me thou
The way to God." More deep each dread ravine
And hideous hollow yawned, and sadly thus
Answered that hoar associate of the clouds:
"Spectre, I know not, I am always here."
Canute departed, and with head erect,
All white and ghastly in his robe of snow,
Went forth into great silence and great night
By Iceland and Norway. After him
Gloom swallowed up the universe. He stood
A sovran kingdomless, a lonely ghost
Confronted with Immensity. He saw
The awful Infinite, at whose portal pale
Lightning sinks dying; Darkness, skeleton
Whose joints are nights, and utter Formlessness
Moving confusedly in the horrible dark
Inscrutable and blind. No star was there,
Yet something like a haggard gleam; no sound
But the dull tide of Darkness, and her dumb
And fearful shudder. " 'Tis the tomb," he said,
"God is beyond!" Three steps he took, then cried:
'Twas deathly as the grave, and not a voice
Responded, nor came any breath to sway
The snowy mantle, with unsullied white
Emboldening the spectral wanderer.
Sudden he marked how, like a gloomy star,
A spot grew broad upon his livid robe;
Slowly it widened, raying darkness forth;
And Canute proved it with his spectral hands.
It was a drop of blood.

II.
But he saw nothing; space was black — no sound.
"Forward," said Canute, raising his proud head.
There fell a second stain beside the first,
Then it grew larger, and the Cimbrian chief
Stared at the thick vague darkness, and saw naught.
Still as a bloodhound follows on his track,

<246>

Sad he went on. There fell a third red stain
On the white winding-sheet. He had never fled;
Howbeit Canute forward went no more,
But turned on that side where the sword arm hangs.
A drop of blood, as if athwart a dream,
Fell on the shroud, and reddened his right hand.
Then, as in reading one turns back a page,
A second time he changed his course, and turned
To the dim left. There fell a drop of blood.
Canute drew back, trembling to be alone,
And wished he had not left his burial couch.
But, when a blood-drop fell again, he stopped,
Stooped his pale head, and tried to make a prayer.
Then fell a drop, and the prayer died away
In savage terror. Darkly he moved on,
A hideous spectre hesitating, white,
And ever as he went, a drop of blood
Implacably from the darkness broke away
And stained that awful whiteness. He beheld
Shaking, as doth a poplar in the wind,
Those stains grow darker and more numerous:
Another, and another, and another.
They seem to light up that funereal gloom,
And mingling in the folds of that white sheet,
Made it a cloud of blood. He went, and went,
And still from that unfathomable vault
The red blood dropped upon him drop by drop,
Always, for ever — without noise, as though
From the black feet of some night-gibbeted corpse.
Alas! Who wept those formidable tears?
The Infinite! — Toward Heaven, of the good
Attainable, through the wild sea of night,
That hath not ebb nor flow, Canute went on,
And ever walking, came to a closed door,
That from beneath showed a mysterious light.
Then he looked down upon his winding-sheet,
For that was the great place, the sacred place,
That was a portion of the light of God,
And from behind that door Hosannas rang.

<247>

The winding-sheet was red, and Canute stopped.
This is why Canute from the light of day
Draws ever back, and hath not dared appear
Before the Judge whose face is as the sun.
This is why still remaineth the dark king
Out in the night, and never having power
To bring his robe back to its first pure state,
But feeling at each step a blood-drop fall,
Wanders eternally 'neath the vast black heaven.

—Part I, Trans. R Garnett
Part II, Trans Anon., Dublin University Magazine

<248>

THÉOPHILE GAUTIER (1811-1872)

Coquetry in Death

I beg ye grant, when low I lie,
Before ye close my coffin-bed,
A little black beneath mine eye,
And on my cheek a touch of red!

Ah, make me beautiful as now!
For I would be upon my bier,
As on the night of his avow
Charming and bloomful, gay and dear.

For me no linen winding-sheet!
But gown me very grand and bright.
Bring forth my frock of muslin sweet,
With many ruffles soft and white.

My favourite frock! I wore it well,
Who wore it at love's flowering.
And since his look upon it fell,
I've kept it as a sacred thing.

For me no funeral coronet,
No tear-embroidered cushion place;
But o'er my fair lace pillow let
My hair droop free about my face.

Dear pillow! Often did it mark,
In mad, sweet nights our brows unlit,
And, all within the gondola dark,
Did count our kisses infinite.

<249>

About my waxen hands supine,
Folded in prayer at life's deep gloam,
My rosary of opals twine,
Blessed by His Holiness at Rome.

I'll finger it, when bedded cold
Where never one shall rise. How oft
His lips upon my lips have told
A *Pater* and an *Ave* soft!

<250>

Tombs and Funeral Pyres

No grim cadaver set its flaw
In happy days of pagan art,
And man, content with what he saw,
Stripped not the veil from beauty's heart.

No form once loved that buried lay,
A hideous spectre to appal,
Dropped bit by bit its flesh away,
As one by one our garments fall;

Or, when the days had drifted by
And sundered shrank the vaulted stones,
Showed naked to the daring eye
A motley heap of rattling bones.

But, rescued from the funeral pyre,
Life's ashen, light residuum
Lay soft, and, spent the cleansing fire,
The urn held sweet the body's sum,—

The sum of all that earth may claim
Of the soul's butterfly, soul passed,—
All that is left of spended flame
Upon the tripod at the last.

Between acanthus leaves and flowers
In the white marble gaily went
Loves and bacchantes all the hours,
Dancing about the monument.

At most, a little Genius wild
Trampled a flame out in the gloom,
And art's harmonious flowering smiled
Upon the sadness of the tomb.

<251>

The tomb was then a pleasant place.
As bed of child that slumbereth,
With many a fair and laughing grace
The joy of life surrounded death.

Then death concealed its visage gaunt,
Whose sockets deep, and sunken nose,
And railing mouth our spirits haunt,
Past any dream that horror shows.

The monster in flesh raiment clad
Hid deep its spectral form uncouth,
And virgin glances, beauty-glad,
Sped frankly to the naked youth.

Twas only at Trimalchio's board
A little skeleton made sign,
An ivory plaything unabhorred,
To bid the feasters to the wine.

Gods, whom Art ever must avow,
Ruled the marmoreal sky's demesne.
Olympus yields to Calvary, now;
Jupiter to the Nazarene!

Voices are calling, "Pan is dead!"
Dusk deepeneth within, without.
On the black sheet of sorrow spread,
The whitened skeleton gleams out.

It glideth to the headstone bare,
And signs it with a paraph wild,
And hangs a wreath of bones to glare
Upon the charnel death-defiled.

It lifts the coffin-lid and quaffs
The musty air, and peers within,
Displays a ring of ribs, and laughs
Forever with its awful grin.

<252>

It urges unto Death's fleet dance
The Emperor, the Pope, the King,
And makes the pallid steed to prance,
And low the doughty warrior fling;—

Behind the courtesan steals up,
And makes wry faces in her glass;
Drinks from the sick man's trembling cup;
Delves in the miser's golden mass.

Above the team it whirls the thong,
With bone for goad to hurry it,
Follows the plowman's way along,
And guides the furrows to a pit.

It comes, the uninvited guest,
And lurks beneath the banquet chair,
Unseen from the pale bride to wrest
Her little silken garter fair.

The number swells: the young give hand
Unto the old, and none may flee.
The irresistible sarabande
Compelleth all humanity.

Forth speeds the tall, ungainly fright,
Playing the rebeck, dancing mad,
Against the dark a frame of white,
As Holbein drew it — horror-sad; —

Or if the times be frivolous,
Trusses the shroud about its hips:
Then like a Cupid mischievous,
Across the ballet-room it skips,

And unto carven tombs it flies,
Where marchionesses rest demure,
Weary of love, in exquisite guise,
In chapels dim and pompadour.

<253>

But hide thy hideous form at last,
Worm-eaten actor! Long enough
In death's wan melodrama cast,
Thou'st played thy part without rebuff.

Come back, come back, O ancient Art!
And cover with thy marble's gleam
This Gothic skeleton! Each part
Consume, ye flames of fire supreme!

If man be then a creature made
In God's own image, to aspire,
When shattered must the image fade,
Let the lone fragments feed the fire!

Immortal form! Rise thou in flame
Again to beauty's fount of bloom
Let not thy clay endure the shame,
The degradation of the tomb!

<254>

CHARLES BAUDELAIRE (1821-1867)

The Revenant

Like the mild-eyed angels sweet
I will come to thy retreat,
Stealing in without a sound
When the shades of night close round.

I will give thee manifold
Kisses soft and moony-cold,
Gliding, sliding o'er thee like
A serpent crawling round a dike.

When the livid morn creeps on
You will wake and find me gone
Till the evening come again.

As by tenderness and ruth
Others rule thy life and youth,
I by terror choose to reign.

—Translated by John Squires, 1909

<255>

The Burial of An Accursed Poet

If haply one dark, dreary night
Some charitable soul appear
And 'neath old rubble stow from sight
The body that you held so dear —

What time the chaste stars veil their eyes,
Drowsy and fain for slumber, there
Spiders shall weave their traceries.
Vipers their spotted young shall bear.

Above your doomed head you will hear
Each night throughout the heavy year
The lean wolves' melancholy cries,
Famished hags' bowlings for a crust,
Lewd pastimes of old men who lust,
And scoundrels' dark conspiracies.

—Translated by John Squire, 1909

<256>

The Dance of Death

Carrying bouquet, and handkerchief, and gloves,
Proud of her height as when she lived, she moves
With all the careless and high-stepping grace,
And the extravagant courtesan's thin face.

Was slimmer waist e'er in a ball-room wooed?
Her floating robe, in royal amplitude,
Falls in deep folds around a dry foot, shod
With a bright flower-like shoe that gems the sod.

The swarms that hum about her collar-bones
As the lascivious streams caress the stones,
Conceal from every scornful jest that flies,
Her gloomy beauty; and her fathomless eyes

Are made of shade and void; with flowery sprays
Her skull is wreathed artistically, and sways,
Feeble and weak, on her frail vertebrae.
O charm of nothing decked in folly! they

Who laugh and name you a Caricature,
They see not, they whom flesh and blood allure,
The nameless grace of every bleached, bare bone,
That is most dear to me, tall skeleton!

Come you to trouble with your potent sneer
The feast of Life! or are you driven here,
To Pleasure's Sabbath, by dead lusts that stir
And goad your moving corpse on with a spur?

Or do you hope, when sing the violins,
And the pale candle-flame lights up our sins,
To drive some mocking nightmare far apart,
And cool the flame hell lighted in your heart?

<257>

Fathomless well of fault and foolishness!
Eternal alembic of antique distress!
Still o'er the curved, white trellis of your sides
The sateless, wandering serpent curls and glides.

And truth to tell, I fear lest you should find,
Among us here, no lover to your mind;
Which of these hearts beat for the smile you gave?
The charms of horror please none but the brave.

Your eyes' black gulf, where awful broodings stir,
Brings giddiness; the prudent reveler
Sees, while a horror grips him from beneath,
The eternal smile of thirty-two white teeth.

For he who has not folded in his arms
A skeleton, nor fed on graveyard charms,
Recks not of furbelow,[1] or paint, or scent,
When Horror comes the way that Beauty went.

O irresistible, with fleshless face,
Say to these dancers in their dazzled race:
"Proud lovers with the paint above your bones,
Ye shall taste death, musk scented skeletons!

"Withered Antinoüs, dandies with plump faces,
Ye varnished cadavers, and grey Lovelaces,
Ye go to lands unknown and void of breath,
Drawn by the rumour of the Dance of Death.

"From Seine's cold quays to Ganges' burning stream,
The mortal troupes dance onward in a dream;
They do not see, within the opened sky,
The Angel's sinister trumpet raised on high.

---

[1] *Furbelow.* A ruffle or frill on a cap or dress.

<258>

"In every clime and under every sun,
Death laughs at ye, mad mortals, as ye run;
And oft perfumes herself with myrrh, like ye
And mingles with your madness, irony!"

— From *The Poems and Prose Poems of Charles Baudelaire*.
James Huneker, ed. New York: Brentano's. 1919

The Ghost

Softly as brown-eyed Angels rove
I will return to thy alcove,
And glide upon the night to thee,
Treading the shadows silently.

And I will give to thee, my own,
Kisses as icy as the moon,
And the caresses of a snake
Cold gliding in the thorny brake.

And when returns the livid morn
Thou shalt find all my place forlorn
And chilly, till the falling night.

Others would rule by tenderness
Over thy life and youthfulness,
But I would conquer thee by fright!

— From *The Poems and Prose Poems of Charles Baudelaire*.
James Huneker, ed. New York: Brentano's. 1919

<259>

HERMAN MELVILLE (1819-1891)

The Maldive Shark

About the Shark, phlegmatical one,
Pale sot of the Maldive sea,
The sleek little pilot-fish, azure and slim,
How alert in attendance be.
From his saw-pit of mouth, from his charnel of maw
They have nothing of harm to dread,
But liquidly glide on his ghastly flank
Or before his Gorgonian head;
Or lurk in the port of serrated teeth
In white triple tiers of glittering gates,
And there find a haven when peril's abroad,
An asylum in jaws of the Fates!
They are friends; and friendly they guide him to prey,
Yet never partake of the treat —
Eyes and brains to the dotard lethargic and dull,
Pale ravener of horrible meat.

<260>

WILLIAM ALLINGHAM (1824-1889)

The fairies

Up the airy mountain,
    Down the rushy glen,
We daren't go a-hunting
    For fear of little men;
Wee folk, good folk,
    Trooping all together;
Green jacket, red cap,
    And white owl's feather!

Down along the rocky shore
    Some make their home,
They live on crispy pancakes
    Of yellow tide-foam;
Some in the reeds
    Of the black mountain lake,
With frogs for their watch-dogs,
    All night awake.

High on the hill-top
    The old King sits;
He is now so old and gray
    He's nigh lost his wits.
With a bridge of white mist
    Columbkill he crosses,
On his stately journeys
    From Slieveleague to Rosses;
Or going up with music
    On cold starry nights
To sup with the Queen
    Of the gay Northern Lights.

<261>

They stole little Bridget
    For seven years long;
When she came down again
    Her friends were all gone.
They took her lightly back,
    Between the night and morrow,
They thought that she was fast asleep,
    But she was dead with sorrow.
They have kept her ever since
    Deep within the lake,
On a bed of flag-leaves,
    Watching till she wake.

By the craggy hill-side,
    Through the mosses bare,
They have planted thorn-trees
    For pleasure here and there.
If any man so daring
    As dig them up in spite,
He shall find their sharpest thorns
    In his bed at night.

Up the airy mountain,
    Down the rushy glen,
We daren't go a-hunting
    For fear of little men;
Wee folk, good folk,
    Trooping all together;
Green jacket, red cap,
    And white owl's feather!

<262>

Goblin Market

Morning and evening
Maids heard the goblins cry:
"Come buy our orchard fruits,
Come buy, come buy:
Apples and quinces,
Lemons and oranges,
Plump unpecked cherries,
Melons and raspberries,
Bloom-down-cheeked peaches,
Swart-headed mulberries,
Wild free-born cranberries,
Crab-apples, dewberries,
Pine-apples, blackberries,
Apricots, strawberries; —
All ripe together
In summer weather, —
Morns that pass by,
Fair eves that fly;
Come buy, come buy:
Our grapes fresh from the vine,
Pomegranates full and fine,
Dates and sharp bullaces,
Rare pears and greengages,
Damsons and bilberries,
Taste them and try:
Currants and gooseberries,
Bright-fire-like barberries,
Figs to fill your mouth,
Citrons from the South,
Sweet to tongue and sound to eye;
Come buy, come buy."

<263>

Evening by evening
Among the brookside rushes,
Laura bowed her head to hear,
Lizzie veiled her blushes:
Crouching close together
In the cooling weather,
With clasping arms and cautioning lips,
With tingling cheeks and finger tips.
"Lie close," Laura said,
Pricking up her golden head:
"We must not look at goblin men,
We must not buy their fruits:
Who knows upon what soil they fed
Their hungry thirsty roots?"
"Come buy," call the goblins
Hobbling down the glen.
"Oh," cried Lizzie, "Laura, Laura,
You should not peep at goblin men."
Lizzie covered up her eyes,
Covered close lest they should look;
Laura reared her glossy head,
And whispered like the restless brook:
"Look, Lizzie, look, Lizzie,
Down the glen tramp little men.
One hauls a basket,
One bears a plate,
One lugs a golden dish
Of many pounds weight.
How fair the vine must grow
Whose grapes are so luscious;
How warm the wind must blow
Through those fruit bushes."
"No," said Lizzie, "No, no, no;
Their offers should not charm us,
Their evil gifts would harm us."
She thrust a dimpled finger
In each ear, shut eyes and ran:
Curious Laura chose to linger
Wondering at each merchant man.

<264>

One had a cat's face,
One whisked a tail,
One tramped at a rat's pace,
One crawled like a snail,
One like a wombat prowled obtuse and furry,
One like a ratel tumbled hurry skurry.
She heard a voice like voice of doves
Cooing all together:
They sounded kind and full of loves
In the pleasant weather.

Laura stretched her gleaming neck
Like a rush-imbedded swan,
Like a lily from the beck,
Like a moonlit poplar branch,
Like a vessel at the launch
When its last restraint is gone.

Backwards up the mossy glen
Turned and trooped the goblin men,
With their shrill repeated cry,
"Come buy, come buy."
When they reached where Laura was
They stood stock still upon the moss,
Leering at each other,
Brother with queer brother;
Signalling each other,
Brother with sly brother.
One set his basket down,
One reared his plate;
One began to weave a crown
Of tendrils, leaves, and rough nuts brown
(Men sell not such in any town);
One heaved the golden weight
Of dish and fruit to offer her:
"Come buy, come buy," was still their cry.
Laura stared but did not stir,
Longed but had no money:
The whisk-tailed merchant bade her taste
In tones as smooth as honey,

<265>

"_Buy from us with @ golden curl_"

The cat-faced purr'd,
The rat-faced spoke a word
Of welcome, and the snail-paced even was heard;
One parrot-voiced and jolly
Cried "Pretty Goblin" still for "Pretty Polly;" —
One whistled like a bird.

<266>

But sweet-tooth Laura spoke in haste:
"Good folk, I have no coin;
To take were to purloin:
I have no copper in my purse,
I have no silver either,
And all my gold is on the furze
That shakes in windy weather
Above the rusty heather."
"You have much gold upon your head,"
They answered all together:
"Buy from us with a golden curl."
She clipped a precious golden lock,
She dropped a tear more rare than pearl,
Then sucked their fruit globes fair or red:
Sweeter than honey from the rock,
Stronger than man-rejoicing wine,
Clearer than water flowed that juice;
She never tasted such before,
How should it cloy with length of use?
She sucked and sucked and sucked the more
Fruits which that unknown orchard bore;
She sucked until her lips were sore;
Then flung the emptied rinds away
But gathered up one kernel stone,
And knew not was it night or day
As she turned home alone.

Lizzie met her at the gate
Full of wise upbraidings:
"Dear, you should not stay so late,
Twilight is not good for maidens;
Should not loiter in the glen
In the haunts of goblin men.
Do you not remember Jeanie,
How she met them in the moonlight,
Took their gifts both choice and many,
Ate their fruits and wore their flowers
Plucked from bowers
Where summer ripens at all hours?

<267>

But ever in the noonlight
She pined and pined away;
Sought them by night and day,
Found them no more, but dwindled and grew grey;
Then fell with the first snow,
While to this day no grass will grow
Where she lies low:
I planted daisies there a year ago
That never blow.
You should not loiter so."
"Nay, hush," said Laura:
"Nay, hush, my sister:
I ate and ate my fill,
Yet my mouth waters still;
To-morrow night I will
Buy more:" and kissed her:
"Have done with sorrow;
I'll bring you plums to-morrow
Fresh on their mother twigs,
Cherries worth getting;
You cannot think what figs
My teeth have met in,
What melons icy-cold
Piled on a dish of gold
Too huge for me to hold,
What peaches with a velvet nap,
Pellucid grapes without one seed:
Odorous indeed must be the mead
Whereon they grow, and pure the wave they drink
With lilies at the brink,
And sugar-sweet their sap."

Golden head by golden head,
Like two pigeons in one nest
Folded in each other's wings,
They lay down in their curtained bed:
Like two blossoms on one stem,
Like two flakes of new-fall'n snow,
Like two wands of ivory

<268>

Tipped with gold for awful kings.
Moon and stars gazed in at them,
Wind sang to them lullaby,
Lumbering owls forbore to fly,
Not a bat flapped to and fro
Round their rest:
Cheek to cheek and breast to breast
Locked together in one nest.

Early in the morning
When the first cock crowed his warning,
Neat like bees, as sweet and busy,
Laura rose with Lizzie:
Fetched in honey, milked the cows,
Aired and set to rights the house,
Kneaded cakes of whitest wheat,
Cakes for dainty mouths to eat,
Next churned butter, whipped up cream,
Fed their poultry, sat and sewed;
Talked as modest maidens should:
Lizzie with an open heart,
Laura in an absent dream,
One content, one sick in part;
One warbling for the mere bright day's delight,
One longing for the night.

At length slow evening came:
They went with pitchers to the reedy brook;
Lizzie most placid in her look,
Laura most like a leaping flame.
They drew the gurgling water from its deep;
Lizzie plucked purple and rich golden flags,
Then turning homeward said: "The sunset flushes
Those furthest loftiest crags;
Come, Laura, not another maiden lags,
No wilful squirrel wags,
The beasts and birds are fast asleep."
But Laura loitered still among the rushes
And said the bank was steep.

<269>

And said the hour was early still
The dew not fall'n, the wind not chill:
Listening ever, but not catching
The customary cry,
'Come buy, come buy,'
With its iterated jingle
Of sugar-baited words:
Not for all her watching
Once discerning even one goblin
Racing, whisking, tumbling, hobbling;
Let alone the herds
That used to tramp along the glen,
In groups or single,
Of brisk fruit-merchant men.

Till Lizzie urged, "O Laura, come;
I hear the fruit-call but I dare not look:
You should not loiter longer at this brook:
Come with me home.
The stars rise, the moon bends her arc,
Each glowworm winks her spark,
Let us get home before the night grows dark:
For clouds may gather
Though this is summer weather,
Put out the lights and drench us through;
Then if we lost our way what should we do?"

Laura turned cold as stone
To find her sister heard that cry alone,
That goblin cry,
"Come buy our fruits, come buy."
Must she then buy no more such dainty fruit?
Must she no more such succous pasture find,
Gone deaf and blind?
Her tree of life drooped from the root:
She said not one word in her heart's sore ache;
But peering thro' the dimness, nought discerning,
Trudged home, her pitcher dripping all the way;
So crept to bed, and lay
Silent till Lizzie slept;

<270>

Then sat up in a passionate yearning,
And gnashed her teeth for baulked desire, and wept
As if her heart would break.

Day after day, night after night,
Laura kept watch in vain
In sullen silence of exceeding pain.
She never caught again the goblin cry:
"Come buy, come buy;" —
She never spied the goblin men
Hawking their fruits along the glen:
But when the noon waxed bright
Her hair grew thin and grey;
She dwindled, as the fair full moon doth turn
To swift decay and burn
Her fire away.

One day remembering her kernel-stone
She set it by a wall that faced the south;
Dewed it with tears, hoped for a root,
Watched for a waxing shoot,
But there came none;
It never saw the sun,
It never felt the trickling moisture run:
While with sunk eyes and faded mouth
She dreamed of melons, as a traveler sees
False waves in desert drouth
With shade of leaf-crowned trees,
And burns the thirstier in the sandful breeze.

She no more swept the house,
Tended the fowls or cows,
Fetched honey, kneaded cakes of wheat,
Brought water from the brook:
But sat down listless in the chimney-nook
And would not eat.

<271>

Tender Lizzie could not bear
To watch her sister's cankerous care
Yet not to share.
She night and morning
Caught the goblins' cry:
"Come buy our orchard fruits,
Come buy, come buy:" —
Beside the brook, along the glen,
She heard the tramp of goblin men,
The voice and stir
Poor Laura could not hear;
Longed to buy fruit to comfort her,
But feared to pay too dear.
She thought of Jeanie in her grave,
Who should have been a bride;
But who for joys brides hope to have
Fell sick and died
In her gay prime,
In earliest Winter time
With the first glazing rime,
With the first snow-fall of crisp Winter time.

Till Laura dwindling
Seemed knocking at Death's door:
Then Lizzie weighed no more
Better and worse;
But put a silver penny in her purse,
Kissed Laura, crossed the heath with clumps of furze
At twilight, halted by the brook:
And for the first time in her life
Began to listen and look.

Laughed every goblin
When they spied her peeping:
Came towards her hobbling,
Flying, running, leaping,
Puffing and blowing,
Chuckling, clapping, crowing,
Clucking and gobbling,
Mopping and mowing,

<272>

Full of airs and graces,
Pulling wry faces,
Demure grimaces,
Cat-like and rat-like,
Ratel- and wombat-like,
Snail-paced in a hurry,
Parrot-voiced and whistler,
Helter skelter, hurry skurry,
Chattering like magpies,
Fluttering like pigeons,
Gliding like fishes, —
Hugged her and kissed her:
Squeezed and caressed her:
Stretched up their dishes,
Panniers, and plates:
"Look at our apples
Russet and dun,
Bob at our cherries,
Bite at our peaches,
Citrons and dates,
Grapes for the asking,
Pears red with basking
Out in the sun,
Plums on their twigs;
Pluck them and suck them,
Pomegranates, figs." —

"Good folk," said Lizzie,
Mindful of Jeanie:
"Give me much and many:" —
Held out her apron,
Tossed them her penny.
"Nay, take a seat with us,
Honour and eat with us,"
They answered grinning:
"Our feast is but beginning.
Night yet is early,
Warm and dew-pearly,
Wakeful and starry:

<273>

Such fruits as these
No man can carry;
Half their bloom would fly,
Half their dew would dry,
Half their flavour would pass by.
Sit down and feast with us,
Be welcome guest with us,
Cheer you and rest with us." —
"Thank you," said Lizzie: "But one waits
At home alone for me:
So without further parleying,
If you will not sell me any
Of your fruits though much and many,
Give me back my silver penny
I tossed you for a fee." —
They began to scratch their pates,
No longer wagging, purring,
But visibly demurring,
Grunting and snarling.
One called her proud,
Cross-grained, uncivil;
Their tones waxed loud,
Their looks were evil.
Lashing their tails
They trod and hustled her,
Elbowed and jostled her,
Clawed with their nails,
Barking, mewing, hissing, mocking,
Tore her gown and soiled her stocking,
Twitched her hair out by the roots,
Stamped upon her tender feet,
Held her hands and squeezed their fruits
Against her mouth to make her eat.

White and golden Lizzie stood,
Like a lily in a flood, —
Like a rock of blue-veined stone
Lashed by tides obstreperously, —
Like a beacon left alone

<274>

In a hoary roaring sea,
Sending up a golden fire, —
Like a fruit-crowned orange-tree
White with blossoms honey-sweet
Sore beset by wasp and bee, —
Like a royal virgin town
Topped with gilded dome and spire
Close beleaguered by a fleet
Mad to tug her standard down.

One may lead a horse to water,
Twenty cannot make him drink.
Though the goblins cuffed and caught her,
Coaxed and fought her,
Bullied and besought her,
Scratched her, pinched her black as ink,
Kicked and knocked her,
Mauled and mocked her,
Lizzie uttered not a word;
Would not open lip from lip
Lest they should cram a mouthful in:
But laughed in heart to feel the drip
Of juice that syrupped all her face,
And lodged in dimples of her chin,
And streaked her neck which quaked like curd.
At last the evil people,
Worn out by her resistance,
Flung back her penny, kicked their fruit
Along whichever road they took,
Not leaving root or stone or shoot;
Some writhed into the ground,
Some dived into the brook
With ring and ripple,
Some scudded on the gale without a sound,
Some vanished in the distance.

<275>

In a smart, ache, tingle,
Lizzie went her way;
Knew not was it night or day;
Sprang up the bank, tore thro' the furze,
Threaded copse and dingle,
And heard her penny jingle
Bouncing in her purse, —
Its bounce was music to her ear.
She ran and ran
As if she feared some goblin man
Dogged her with gibe or curse
Or something worse:
But not one goblin skurried after,
Nor was she pricked by fear;
The kind heart made her windy-paced
That urged her home quite out of breath with haste
And inward laughter.

She cried "Laura," up the garden,
"Did you miss me?
Come and kiss me.
Never mind my bruises,
Hug me, kiss me, suck my juices
Squeezed from goblin fruits for you,
Goblin pulp and goblin dew.
Eat me, drink me, love me;
Laura, make much of me:
For your sake I have braved the glen
And had to do with goblin merchant men."

Laura started from her chair,
Flung her arms up in the air,
Clutched her hair:
"Lizzie, Lizzie, have you tasted
For my sake the fruit forbidden?
Must your light like mine be hidden,
Your young life like mine be wasted,
Undone in mine undoing,
And ruined in my ruin,
Thirsty, cankered, goblin-ridden?" —

<276>

She clung about her sister,
Kissed and kissed and kissed her:
Tears once again
Refreshed her shrunken eyes,
Dropping like rain
After long sultry drouth;
Shaking with aguish fear, and pain,
She kissed and kissed her with a hungry mouth.

Her lips began to scorch,
That juice was wormwood to her tongue,
She loathed the feast:
Writhing as one possessed she leaped and sung,
Rent all her robe, and wrung
Her hands in lamentable haste,
And beat her breast.
Her locks streamed like the torch
Borne by a racer at full speed,
Or like the mane of horses in their flight,
Or like an eagle when she stems the light
Straight toward the sun,
Or like a caged thing freed,
Or like a flying flag when armies run.

Swift fire spread through her veins, knocked at her heart,
Met the fire smouldering there
And overbore its lesser flame;
She gorged on bitterness without a name:
Ah! fool, to choose such part
Of soul-consuming care!
Sense failed in the mortal strife:
Like the watch-tower of a town
Which an earthquake shatters down,
Like a lightning-stricken mast,
Like a wind-uprooted tree
Spun about,

<277>

Like a foam-topped waterspout
Cast down headlong in the sea,
She fell at last;
Pleasure past and anguish past,
Is it death or is it life?

Life out of death.
That night long Lizzie watched by her,
Counted her pulse's flagging stir,
Felt for her breath,
Held water to her lips, and cooled her face
With tears and fanning leaves:
But when the first birds chirped about their eaves,
And early reapers plodded to the place
Of golden sheaves,
And dew-wet grass
Bowed in the morning winds so brisk to pass,
And new buds with new day
Opened of cup-like lilies on the stream,
Laura awoke as from a dream,
Laughed in the innocent old way,
Hugged Lizzie but not twice or thrice;
Her gleaming locks showed not one thread of grey,
Her breath was sweet as May
And light danced in her eyes.

Days, weeks, months, years
Afterwards, when both were wives
With children of their own;
Their mother-hearts beset with fears,
Their lives bound up in tender lives;
Laura would call the little ones
And tell them of her early prime,
Those pleasant days long gone
Of not-returning time:
Would talk about the haunted glen,
The wicked, quaint fruit-merchant men,
Their fruits like honey to the throat
But poison in the blood;
(Men sell not such in any town:)

<278>

Would tell them how her sister stood
In deadly peril to do her good,
And win the fiery antidote:
Then joining hands to little hands
Would bid them cling together,
"For there is no friend like a sister
In calm or stormy weather;
To cheer one on the tedious way,
To fetch one if one goes astray,
To lift one if one totters down,
To strengthen whilst one stands."

<279>

Repining

She sat alway thro' the long day
Spinning the weary thread away;
And ever said in undertone:
"Come, that I be no more alone."

From early dawn to set of sun
Working, her task was still undone;
And the long thread seemed to increase
Even while she spun and did not cease.
She heard the gentle turtle-dove
Tell to its mate a tale of love;
She saw the glancing swallows fly,
Ever a social company;
She knew each bird upon its nest
Had cheering songs to bring it rest;
None lived alone save only she; —
The wheel went round more wearily;
She wept and said in undertone:
"Come, that I be no more alone."

Day followed day, and still she sighed
For love, and was not satisfied;
Until one night, when the moonlight
Turned all the trees to silver white,
She heard, what ne'er she heard before,
A steady hand undo the door.
The nightingale since set of sun
Her throbbing music had not done,
And she had listened silently;
But now the wind had changed, and she
Heard the sweet song no more, but heard
Beside her bed a whispered word:
"Damsel, rise up; be not afraid;
For I am come at last," it said.

<280>

She trembled, tho' the voice was mild;
She trembled like a frightened child; —
Till she looked up, and then she saw
The unknown speaker without awe.
He seemed a fair young man, his eyes
Beaming with serious charities;
His cheek was white but hardly pale;
And a dim glory like a veil
Hovered about his head, and shone
Thro' the whole room till night was gone.

So her fear fled; and then she said,
Leaning upon her quiet bed:
"Now thou art come, I prithee stay,
That I may see thee in the day,
And learn to know thy voice, and hear
It evermore calling me near."

He answered: "Rise, and follow me."
But she looked upwards wonderingly:
"And whither would'st thou go, friend? stay
Until the dawning of the day."
But he said: "The wind ceaseth, Maid;
Of chill nor damp be thou afraid."

She bound her hair up from the floor,
And passed in silence from the door.

So they went forth together, he
Helping her forward tenderly.
The hedges bowed beneath his hand;
Forth from the streams came the dry land
As they passed over; evermore
The pallid moonbeams shone before;
And the wind hushed, and nothing stirred;
Not even a solitary bird,
Scared by their footsteps, fluttered by
Where aspen-trees stood steadily.

<281>

As they went on, at length a sound
Came trembling on the air around;
The undistinguishable hum
Of life, voices that go and come
Of busy men, and the child's sweet
High laugh, and noise of trampling feet.

Then he said: "Wilt thou go and see?"
And she made answer joyfully:
"The noise of life, of human life,
Of dear communion without strife,
Of converse held 'twixt friend and friend;
Is it not here our path shall end?"
He led her on a little way
Until they reached a hillock: "Stay."

It was a village in a plain.
High mountains screened it from the rain
And stormy wind; and nigh at hand
A bubbling streamlet flowed, o'er sand
Pebbly and fine, and sent life up
Green succous stalk and flower-cup.

Gradually, day's harbinger,
A chilly wind began to stir.
It seemed a gentle powerless breeze
That scarcely rustled thro' the trees;
And yet it touched the mountain's head
And the paths man might never tread.
But hearken: in the quiet weather
Do all the streams flow down together? —

No, 'tis a sound more terrible
Than tho' a thousand rivers fell.
The everlasting ice and snow
Were loosened then, but not to flow; —
With a loud crash like solid thunder
The avalanche came, burying under
The village; turning life and breath
And rest and joy and plans to death.

<282>

"Oh! let us fly, for pity fly;
Let us go hence, friend, thou and I.
There must be many regions yet
Where these things make not desolate."
He looked upon her seriously;
Then said: "Arise and follow me."
The path that lay before them was
Nigh covered over with long grass;
And many slimy things and slow
Trailed on between the roots below.
The moon looked dimmer than before;
And shadowy cloudlets floating o'er
Its face sometimes quite hid its light,
And filled the skies with deeper night.

At last, as they went on, the noise
Was heard of the sea's mighty voice;
And soon the ocean could be seen
In its long restlessness serene.
Upon its breast a vessel rode
That drowsily appeared to nod
As the great billows rose and fell,
And swelled to sink, and sank to swell.

Meanwhile the strong wind had come forth
From the chill regions of the North,
The mighty wind invisible.
And the low waves began to swell;
And the sky darkened overhead;
And the moon once looked forth, then fled
Behind dark clouds; while here and there
The lightning shone out in the air;
And the approaching thunder rolled
With angry pealings manifold.
How many vows were made, and prayers
That in safe times were cold and scarce.
Still all availed not; and at length
The waves arose in all their strength,
And fought against the ship, and filled
The ship. Then were the clouds unsealed,

<283>

And the rain hurried forth, and beat
On every side and over it.

Some clung together, and some kept
A long stern silence, and some wept.
Many half-crazed looked on in wonder
As the strong timbers rent asunder;
Friends forgot friends, foes fled to foes; —
And still the water rose and rose.

"Ah woe is me! Whom I have seen
Are now as tho' they had not been.
In the earth there is room for birth,
And there are graves enough in earth;
Why should the cold sea, tempest-torn,
Bury those whom it hath not borne?"

He answered not, and they went on.
The glory of the heavens was gone;
The moon gleamed not nor any star;
Cold winds were rustling near and far,
And from the trees the dry leaves fell
With a sad sound unspeakable.
The air was cold; till from the South
A gust blew hot, like sudden drouth,
Into their faces; and a light
Glowing and red, shone thro' the night.

A mighty city full of flame
And death and sounds without a name.
Amid the black and blinding smoke,
The people, as one man, awoke.
Oh! happy they who yesterday
On the long journey went away;
Whose pallid lips, smiling and chill,
While the flames scorch them smile on still;
Who murmur not; who tremble not
When the bier crackles fiery hot;
Who, dying, said in love's increase:
"Lord, let thy servant part in peace."

<284>

Those in the town could see and hear
A shaded river flowing near;
The broad deep bed could hardly hold
Its plenteous waters calm and cold.
Was flame-wrapped all the city wall,
The city gates were flame-wrapped all.

What was man's strength, what puissance then?
Women were mighty as strong men.
Some knelt in prayer, believing still,
Resigned unto a righteous will,
Bowing beneath the chastening rod,
Lost to the world, but found of God.
Some prayed for friend, for child, for wife;
Some prayed for faith; some prayed for life;
While some, proud even in death, hope gone,
Steadfast and still, stood looking on.

"Death — death — oh! let us fly from death;
Where'er we go it followeth;
All these are dead; and we alone
Remain to weep for what is gone.
What is this thing? thus hurriedly
To pass into eternity;
To leave the earth so full of mirth;
To lose the profit of our birth;
To die and be no more; to cease,
Having numbness that is not peace.
Let us go hence; and, even if thus
Death everywhere must go with us,
Let us not see the change, but see
Those who have been or still shall be."

He sighed and they went on together;
Beneath their feet did the grass wither;
Across the heaven high overhead
Dark misty clouds floated and fled;
And in their bosom was the thunder,
And angry lightnings flashed out under,
Forked and red and menacing;

<285>

Far off the wind was muttering;
It seemed to tell, not understood,
Strange secrets to the listening wood.

Upon its wings it bore the scent
Of blood of a great armament:
Then saw they how on either side
Fields were down-trodden far and wide.
That morning at the break of day
Two nations had gone forth to slay.

As a man soweth so he reaps.
The field was full of bleeding heaps;
Ghastly corpses of men and horses
That met death at a thousand sources;
Cold limbs and putrefying flesh;
Long love-locks clotted to a mesh
That stifled; stiffened mouths beneath
Staring eyes that had looked on death.

But these were dead: these felt no more
The anguish of the wounds they bore.
Behold, they shall not sigh again,
Nor justly fear, nor hope in vain.
What if none wept above them? — is
The sleeper less at rest for this?
Is not the young child's slumber sweet
When no man watcheth over it?
These had deep calm; but all around
There was a deadly smothered sound,
The choking cry of agony
From wounded men who could not die;
Who watched the black wing of the raven
Rise like a cloud 'twixt them and heaven,
And in the distance flying fast
Beheld the eagle come at last.

<286>

She knelt down in her agony:
"O Lord, it is enough," said she:
"My heart's prayer putteth me to shame;
Let me return to whence I came.
Thou for who love's sake didst reprove,
Forgive me for the sake of love."

—1850

<287>

ALGERNON SWINBURNE (1837-1909)

The Ballad of Dead Men's Bay

The sea swings owre the slants of sand,
All white with winds that drive;
The sea swirls up to the still dim strand,
Where nae man comes alive.

At the grey soft edge of the fruitless surf
A light flame sinks and springs;
At the grey soft rim of the flowerless turf
A low flame leaps and clings.

What light is this on a sunless shore,
What gleam on a starless sea?
Was it earth's or hell's waste womb that bore
Such births as should not be?

As lithe snakes turning, as bright stars burning,
They bicker and beckon and call;
As wild waves churning, as wild winds yearning,
They flicker and climb and fall.

A soft strange cry from the landward rings —
"What ails the sea to shine?"
A keen sweet note from the spray's rim springs —
"What fires are these of thine?"

"A soul am I that was born on earth
For ae day's waesome span:
Death bound me fast on the bourn of birth
Ere I were christened man.

"A light by night, I fleet and fare
Till the day of wrath and woe;
On the hems of earth and the skirts of air
Winds hurl me to and fro."

<288>

"O well is thee, though the weird be strange
That bids thee flit and flee;
For hope is child of the womb of change,
And hope keeps watch with thee.

"When the years are gone, and the time is come,
God's grace may give thee grace;
And thy soul may sing, though thy soul were dumb,
And shine before God's face.

"But I, that lighten and revel and roll
With the foam of the plunging sea,
No sign is mine of a breathing soul
That God should pity me.

"Nor death, nor heaven, nor hell, nor birth
Hath part in me nor mine:
Strong lords are these of the living earth
And loveless lords of thine.

"But I that know nor lord nor life
More sure than storm or spray,
Whose breath is made of sport and strife,
Whereon shall I find stay?"

"And wouldst thou change thy doom with me,
Full fain with thee would I:
For the life that lightens and lifts the sea
Is more than earth or sky.

"And what if the day of doubt and doom
Shall save nor smite not me?
I would not rise from the slain world's tomb
If there be no more sea.

"Take he my soul that gave my soul,
And give it thee to keep;
And me, while seas and stars shall roll
Thy life that falls on sleep."

<289>

That word went up through the mirk mid sky,
And even to God's own ear:
And the Lord was ware of the keen twin cry,
And wroth was he to hear.

He's tane the soul of the unsained child
That fled to death from birth;
He's tane the light of the wan sea wild,
And bid it burn on earth.

He's given the ghaist of the babe new-born
The gift of the water-sprite,
To ride on revel from morn to morn
And roll from night to night.
He's given the sprite of the wild wan sea

The gift of the new-born man,
A soul for ever to bide and be
When the years have filled their span.
When a year was gone and a year was come,
O loud and loud cried they —

"For the lee-lang year thou hast held us dumb
Take now thy gifts away!"
O loud and lang they cried on him,
And sair and sair they prayed:

"Is the face of thy grace as the night's face grim
For those thy wrath has made?"
A cry more bitter than tears of men
From the rim of the dim grey sea; —

"Give me my living soul again,
The soul thou gavest me,
The doom and the dole of kindly men,
To bide my weird and be!"

<290>

A cry more keen from the wild low land
Than the wail of waves that roll; —
"Take back the gift of a loveless hand,
Thy gift of doom and dole,

The weird of men that bide on land;
Take from me, take my soul!"
The hands that smite are the hands that spare;
They build and break the tomb;

They turn to darkness and dust and air
The fruits of the waste earth's womb;
But never the gift of a granted prayer,
The dole of a spoken doom.

Winds may change at a word unheard,
But none may change the tides:
The prayer once heard is as God's own word;
The doom once dealt abides.

And ever a cry goes up by day,
And ever a wail by night;
And nae ship comes by the weary bay
But her shipmen hear them wail and pray,
And see with earthly sight

The twofold flames of the twin lights play
Where the sea-banks green and the sea-floods grey
Are proud of peril and fain of prey,
And the sand quakes ever; and ill fare they
That look upon that light.

<291>

The Witch Mother

"O where will ye gang to and where will ye sleep,
Against the night begins?" —
"My bed is made wi' cauld sorrows,
My sheets are lined wi' sins.

"And a sair grief sitting at my foot,
And a sair grief at my head;
And dule to lay me my laigh pillows,
And teen till I be dead.

"And the rain is sair upon my face,
And sair upon my hair;
And the wind upon my weary mouth,
That never may man kiss mair.

"And the snow upon my heavy lips,
That never shall drink nor eat;
And shame to cledding, and woe to wedding,
And pain to drink and meat.

"But woe be to my bairns' father,
And ever ill fare he:
He has tane a braw bride hame to him,
Cast out my bairns and me." —

"And what shall they have to their marriage meat
This day they twain are wed?" —
"Meat of strong crying, salt of sad sighing,
And God restore the dead." —

"And what shall they have to their wedding wine
This day they twain are wed?" —
"Wine of weeping, and draughts of sleeping,
And God raise up the dead."

<292>

She's tane her to the wild woodside,
Between the flood and fell:
She's sought a rede against her need
Of the fiend that bides in hell.

She's tane her to the wan burnside,
She's wrought wi' sang and spell:
She's plighted her soul for doom and dole
To the fiend that bides in hell.

She's set her young son to her breast,
Her auld son to her knee:
Says, "Weel for you the night, bairnies,
And weel the morn for me."

She looked fu' lang in their een, sighing,
And sair and sair grat she:
She has slain her young son at her breast,
Her auld son at her knee.

She's sodden their flesh wi' saft water,
She's mixed their blood with wine:
She's tane her to the braw bride-house,
Where a' were boun' to dine.

She poured the red wine in his cup,
And his een grew fain to greet:
She set the baked meats at his hand,
And bade him drink and eat.

Says, "Eat your fill of your flesh, my lord,
And drink your fill of your wine;
For a' thing's yours and only yours
That has been yours and mine."

Says, "Drink your fill of your wine, my lord,
And eat your fill of your bread:
I would they were quick in my body again,
Or I that bare them dead."

<293>

He struck her head frae her fair body,
And dead for grief he fell:
And there were twae mair sangs in heaven,
And twae mair sauls in hell.

<294>

ALEXANDER PUSHKIN

The Demons

The clouds whirl, the clouds scurry.
The moon, unseen, lights up
from above the flying snow.
Gloom-ridden sky, gloom-ridden night:
on my life, I can't find the way.
I drive, I drive on the endless steppe.
The little bell's *ding-ding-ding*
flies back to me, fearsome,
fearsome in spite of one's self,
lost bells amid an unknown plain!

— "Driver, don't stop! Keep going on!" —
"It's impossible, sir. It's a heavy go
for the horses against all this snow.
And my eyes are swelling shut, sir.
Who can make out where snow ends
and where the land begins?
All the roads are covered, I swear.
Kill me if you like. I've stopped,
for not a track is to be seen.
We are lost! What would you have me do?" —

"What have you been following, driver,
if you can see no road?" —

"Some Demon of the steppe, my lord,
is leading the horse and me. I thought
I recognized a turn or two, but no,
now we've been turned aside. We're lost!

<295>

"Look, there ahead beyond that drift
he huffs, and spits at me. My God,
he's almost led the stumbling team
into a steep ravine! Back, back!

"Did you not see him, sir? He stood
as thin as a weird mile-post before us.
(Here, take this cloth and clean
your fogged-up spectacles!)
Look there — that little spark was him,
and now he's gone into the empty dark."

The clouds whirl, the clouds scurry.
The moon, unseen, lights up
from above the flying snow.
Gloom-ridden sky, gloom-ridden night:
on my life, I can't find the way.
We have no strength to go onward:
there, look, our tracks again:
we have gone in a full circle!
The little bell is suddenly silent,
in a fog so thick it cannot tremble.
The horses stop. "What is that in the field?"

"Who knows, sir. It's just a tree stump.
No, *Bozhe moi*, I see a wolf!"
The snowstorm becomes furious,
the snowstorm howls and wails.
The snorting horses make sounds
of terror and try to break the reins.

"There — farther on — the Demon.
I saw him jump, sir. See there:
just those two eyes float deep,
red lamps inside the gray-white
nothingness of sky and snow."

<296>

Then comes a sudden silence,
a narrow path made visible
lures on the horses; the bell
makes tentative tinkles. I see
a line of phantoms assembled
on either side of us,
in the midst of the whitening plains.

Onward we go, the driver's
whispered litany of *Bozhe moi*,[1]
Bozhe moi and the silver ding
of the blessed sledge-bell
our only prow and pilot.
Endless and formless,
the Demons watch us
in the dim play of the moonlight;
they are legion, as leaves
on the ground in November.

How many are there? Where do they go
en masse in this blizzard night?
And, oh, they are singing. Hush, driver!
Listen to that plaintive melody!
Are they off to some hobgoblins' burial?
Is Baba Yaga[2] at last to be married?

The clouds whirl, the clouds scurry.
The moon, unseen, lights up
from above the flying snow.
Gloom-ridden sky, gloom-ridden night:
on my life, I can't find the way.

---

[1] *Bozhe moi.* Russian exclamation: "My God!"
[2] *Baba Yaga.* The famous witch of Russian folklore who has iron teeth and eats children. Her famous hut sits on four fowls' legs.

<297>

In faith the driver and the horses
plod on in the narrow passage,
the right-of-way the Demons grant us
as they swarm and swarm around us,
some walking on snow and treetop,
some leaping into the storm itself.

Home, if I make it there, will not be warm
enough, nor will any bright song erase
the funereal chant of the Demons,
whose mourning rends my heart.

Bozhe moi, ding-ding-ding,
Bozhe moi, ding-ding-ding
Bozhe moi, ding-ding-ding

1830, Translation and adaptation by Brett Rutherford, 2012.

In the spirit of M.G. Lewis, I have taken liberties with Pushkin's original. The
sleigh bells and "Bozhe moi!" are my inventions, to enhance a public reading of
the poem. — BR.

<298>

FYODOR SOLOGUB (1863-1927)

The Devil's Swings

Below a pine's rough shadow,
Where loud the river sings,
The hairy-handed devil
Pushes his devilish swings.

He swings, and gives a crow
　　　　To and fro
　　　　To and fro
The boards creak, bending low,
The taut rope rubbing slow
Against the heavy bows.

The board sways back, and bracing,
With a long creak swings wide,
The devil, still gimacing,
Guffaws and holds his side.

I tremble to let go;
　　　　To and fro
　　　　To and fro
I sway and cling, but no,
My languid glances grow
Fast where the devil tows.

Above the looming pine
The blue fiend's sniggers sting:
"You found the swings so fine?
Well, devil take you, swing!"

Below the shaggy pine
They squeak and whirl and sling:
"You found the swings so fine?
Well, devil take you, swing!"

<299>

The fiend will not release
The board that hangs too steep
Till I am thrust toward peace
By the dark hand's dread sweep.

Until the hemp turns round
Too long, and is worn free,
Until the broad black ground
Comes flying up at me.

Above the pine I'll fling
And bore into the mire.
Then swing, devil, swing —
Higher, higher, higher!

When, Heaving On the Stormy Waters

When, heaving on the stormy waters,
I felt my ship begin to sink,
I prayed, "Oh, Father Satan, save me,
Forgive me at death's utter brink!

"If you will save my soul embittered
From perishing before its hour,
The days to come, the nights that follow
I vow to vice, I pledge to power."

The Devil forthwith snatched and flung me
Into a boat; the sides were frail,
But on the bench the oars were lying
And in the bow an old gray sail.

And landward once again I carried
My outcast soul, bereft of kin,
Upon its sickly vicious sojourn
My body and its gift of sin.

And I am faithful, Father Satan,
Unto my evil hour's vow,
When from my drowning ship you saved me
And when I prayed you guide the prow.

To you descend my praises, Father,
No day from bitter blame exempt.
O'er worlds my blasphemy shall tower;
And I shall tempt — and I shall tempt.

Transl. B.A. Rudzinsky

<301>

Bibliography

Anon. *An Analysis of Goethe's Tragedy of Faust, in Illustration of Retsch's* [sic] *Series of Outlines.* Engraved by Henry Moses from the originals by Friedrich August Moritz Retzsch. 1820. London: Boosey and Sons.

Barlow, Joel. *Columbiad: A Poem.* 1809. Philadelphia: C. & A. Conrad.

Baudelaire, Charles. *Baudelaire: His Prose and Poetry.* T.R. Smith, ed. 1919. New York: The Modern Library.

———. *The Poems and Prose of Charles Baudelaire.* James Huneker, ed. 1919. New York: Brentano's.

Browning, Robert. *Poems.* 1872. New York: A.L. Burt.

———. *The Poetic Works of Robert Browning.* 1897. London: Smith, Elder & Co.

Burnet, T[homas]. *Archaeologicae Philosophiae.* 1692. London.

Darley, George. *Selections from the Poems of George Darley.* 1904. London: Methuen & Co.

De Castro, Adolfo. *La Historia de los Protestantes Españoles y de su Persecucíon por Felipe II.* 1851. Cadiz.

———. *The Spanish Protestants, and Their Persecution by Philip II.* Thomas Parker, trans. 1851. London: Charles Gilpin.

Deutsch, Babette, and Avram Yarmolinsky, trans. *Modern Russian Poetry.* 1921. New York: Harcourt, Brace & Co.

Clairmont, Claire. *The Journals of Claire Clairmont.* Marion K. Stocking, ed. 1968. Cambridge: Harvard University Press.

Coleridge, Samuel Taylor. *The Complete Poetical Works of Samuel Taylor Coleridge.* Ernest Hartley Coleridge, ed. 1912. Oxford: Clarendon Press.

Gautier, Théophile. *Enamels and Cameos and Other Poems.* Agnes Lee, trans. 1906. Cambridge: The Jenson Society.

Goethe, Johann Wolfgang von. *Faust.* Walter Kaufmann, trans. 1961. New York: Anchor Doubleday.

———. *Faustus.* 1834. London: Hodgson, Boys, & Graves, "From the German of Goethe, Embellished with Retsch's [sic] Series of Twenty-Seven Outlines, Illustrative of the Tragedy." Engraved by Henry Moses. [Anonymous translation of excerpts from Faust, actually by Coleridge, plus "An Appendix, containing the May-Day Night Scene, translated by Percy Bysshe Shelley."

———. *Faustus. From the German of Goethe.* Samuel Taylor Coleridge, trans. Frederick Burwick, James c. McKusick, eds. 2007. Oxford: Clarendon Press.

Graves, Robert. *Fairies and Fusiliers.* 1918. London.

<302>

———. *The Greek Myths.* 1955. Baltimore: Penguin Books.

Green, Frances H. "Song of the East Wind" and biographical sketch, in *The Female Poets of America.* Rufus Griswold, ed. 1859. Philadelphia: Parry & Macmillan.

Greene, William. *Manuel Matamoros and His Fellow-Prisoners.* 1863. London: Morgan & Chase.

Gregor, Padric, ed. *Modern Anglo-Irish Verse.* 1914. London: David Nutt.

Helps, E.L., Ed. *Songs and Ballads of Greater Britain.* 1913. London: J.M. Dent & Sons.

Lieder, Paul Robert. "Scott and Scandinavian Literature." *Smith College Studies in Modern Languages.* Vol II No. 1, October 1920, pp. 8-57.

Longfellow, Henry Wadsworth. *Tales of a Wayside Inn.* 1863. Boston: Ticknor and Fields.

———. *Tales of a Wayside Inn.* 1867. London: Bell and Daldy. [With 15 wood engravings from designs by leading artists.]

Rogers, Robert Cameron. *The Wind in the Clearing and Other Poems.* 1894. New York: G.P. Putnam's Sons.

Rossetti, Christina. *Goblin Market and Other Poems.* 1862. London: Macmillan.

Scott, Sir Walter. *The Poetical Works of Sir Walter Scott.* J. Logie Robertson, ed. (1904) 1964. London: Oxford University Press.

Scott, William Bell. *Poems.* 1875. London: Longmans, Green & Co.

———. *A Poet's Harvest Home: Being 100 Short Poems.* 1882. London: Elliot Stock.

Sotheby, William. "Address to the Tragic Muse." *European Magazine and London Review.* Vol. 37. February 1800, pp. 141-42.

Squire, John ["Jack"] Collins. *Poems and Baudelaire Flowers.* 1909. London: The New Age Press.

Yeats, William Butler. *Early Poems and Stories.* 1925. New York: The Macmillan Co.

<303>

Irwin, Joseph James. *M.G. "Monk" Lewis*. 1976. Boston: Twayne Publishers.

Lewis, Matthew Gregory. "Giles Jollup the Grave, and Brown Sally Green." *The Spirit of the Public Journals for 1798*. 1:321. 1799 London: James Ridgway.

———. *The Isle of Devils: A Historical Tale, Funnded* [sic] *on an Anecdote in the Annals of Portugal*. 1827. Kingston, Jamaica.

———. *The Monk*. Louis F. Peck, ed. (1796) 1952. New York: Grove Press. [Original text restored, with variant readings.]

———. *Raymond and Agnes; or, The Bleeding Nun*. The Romancist and Novelist's Library. 1841. London: J. Clements.

———. *Tales of Terror and Wonder*. Henry Morley, ed. 1887. New York: G. Routledge & Sons. [includes the spurious *Tales of Terror*.]

———. *Tales of Wonder*. 1801. London: J. Bell

———. *Tales of Wonder*. 1805. Dublin: P. Wogan.

———. *Tales of Wonder*. 1805. Vienna: R. Sammer. [A three-volume edition with many additional poems, including more selections from Percy's *Reliques*. The edition is badly typeset and has a fragment of "Porsenna, King of Russia" in the middle of another poem in Volume III. It is doubtful that Lewis had anything to do with this production.]

———. *Tales of Wonder*. Douglass H. Thomson, ed. 2010. Ontario: Broadview Editions. [A must-read for Lewis scholars. Includes poems I-XXXII, and LVI to LX of *Tales of Wonder*, seven poems from *Tales of Terror*, and extensive notes and excerpts on the critical reception of Lewis's work. Provocative discussion of Lewis, his sources, the confusing print history of *Tales of Wonder*, and the critical issues surrounding parody in these texts.]

Lockhart, John Gibson. *The Life of Sir Walter Scott*. Vol II. (1837) Abbotsford Edition (Edinburgh Univ. Press). n.d. Boston: Dana Estes & Co. [Details on Scott's correspondence and meetings with Lewis in 1798-99.]

MacDonald, D.L. *Monk Lewis: A Critical Biography*. 2000. Toronto: Univ. of Toronto Press.

<304>

Peck, Louis F. *A Life of Matthew Gregory Lewis*. 1961. Cambridge: Harvard University Press.

————. "Southey and Tales of Wonder." *Modern Language Notes*. December 1935. [Asserts that Southey may not have consented to his poems' inclusion in *Tales of Wonder*. Southey's eight poems from the first edition were dropped in the second edition of 1801. Southey's poems do appear in the subsequent 1805 Dublin edition; they are omitted from the 1887 *Tales of Terror* by Morley. Peck appears to mistake Scott's Kelso printing of *An Apology for Tales of Terror* for Lewis's first edition.]

SOURCES FOR GOTHIC BALLADS AND NARRATIVES

The following annotated bibliography documents the sources used in compiling the new Yogh & Thorn edition of Matthew Gregory Lewis's *Tales of Wonder*, published 2010-2012 in two volumes.

Anon. *The Anglo-Saxon Chronicle*.

Anon. *A Collection of Old Ballads* [Corrected from the best and most Ancient Copies Extant. With Introductions, Historical, Critical or Humorous]. 1723. London: J. Roberts. [Authorship attrib. to Ambrose Philips (1674-1749).]

Anon. *A Collection of Old Ballads* [Corrected from the best and most Ancient Copies Extant. With Introductions, Historical, Critical or Humorous]. Vol II. 1723. London: J. Roberts. [Authorship attrib. to Ambrose Philips (1674-1749).]

Anon. *A Collection of Old Ballads* [Corrected from the best and most Ancient Copies Extant. With Introductions, Historical, Critical or Humorous]. Vol III. 1725. London: J. Roberts. [Authorship attrib. to Ambrose Philips (1674-1749).]

Anon. *Poems of the Elder Edda*. Patricia Terry, trans. (1969) 1990. Philadelphia: University of Pennsylvania Press. [Includes a fine modern translation of "The Waking of Angantyr."]

Baring-Gould, Sabine. *Curious Myths of the Middle Ages*. Vol 2. 1868. London: Rivingtons. [Discusses "Porsenna, King of Russia" and also has an entire chapter on the legends of Bishop Hatto.]

Bartholin, Thomas [the Younger]. *Antiqvitatum danicarum de causis contemptae a danis adhuc gentilibus mortis libri tres*. (Danish Antiquities on the Causes of the Contempt of Death Felt by The Danish Peoples, in Three Books). 1689. Copenhagen. [With texts in Icelandic and Latin, one source of "King Hakon's Death Song."

<305>

The original of "The Fatal Sisters," in Icelandic and Latin are on pp. 617-19.]

Brullaughan, Domonick. *Opusculum de Purgatorio Sancti Patritii, Hybernae Patroni. (A Little Work on the Purgatory of St. Patrick, Patron Saint of Ireland)* 1735. Louvain: F. Vande Velde. (British Museum, Grenville 4340).

Child, Francis James, ed. *The English and Scottish Popular Ballads*. Part I. 1882. Boston: Houghton, Mifflin & Co.

————. *The English and Scottish Popular Ballads*. Part IV. 1886. Boston: Houghton, Mifflin & Co.

————. *The English and Scottish Popular Ballads*. Part V. 1888. Boston: Houghton, Mifflin & Co.

————. *The English and Scottish Popular Ballads*. Part VIII. 1892. Boston: Houghton, Mifflin & Co.

————. *The English and Scottish Popular Ballads*. Part X. 1898. Boston: Houghton, Mifflin & Co.

Collison-Morley, Lacy. *Greek and Roman Ghost Stories*. 1912. Oxford: B.H. Blackwell.

Costello, Dudley. *A Tour Through the Valley of the Meuse: With the Legends of the Walloon Country and the Ardennes*. Second edition. 1846. London: Chapman and Hall.

Dasent, George Webbe. *The Story of Burnt Njal, or Life in Iceland at the End of the Tenth Century, From the Icelandic of the Njals Saga*. Volume 2. 1861. Edinburgh: Edmonston and Douglas. [Victorian translation including the poem and framing narrative of "The Fatal Sisters."]

DeLattre, Floris. *English Fairy Poetry: From the Origins to the Seventeenth Century*. 1912. London: Henry Frowde.

Dryden, John. *The Sixth Part of Miscellany Poems*. 1716. London: "Printed for Jacob Tonson at Shakespear's Head." [Includes a translation of "The Incantation of Hervor," untitled, with a Latin introductory paragraph, on pp. 387-91. The translator is unattributed, although the poem is in the midst of a group of poems by Richard Corbet, (1582-1635). It seems to have been a random editorial insertion among Corbet's poems. Andrew Wawn states that this is a reprint of Hickes' translation of 1703-05.]

Edwards, George Wharton. *The Forest of Arden With Some of Its Legends*. 1914 New York: Frederick A. Stokes Company.

Emerson, Oliver Farrar. "The Earliest English Translations of Bürger's Lenore: A Study in English and German Romanticism." *Western Reserve University Bulletins*. xviii:3 May 1915. [Traces the complicated history of the seven different translations of "Lenora" published in 1796.]

<306>

Evans, Thomas. *Old Ballads, Historical and Narrative, With Some of Modern Date*. Second edition. 1784. London: T. Evans.

Evans, Thomas, and R. H. Evans. *Old Ballads, Historical and Narrative, With Some of Modern Date*. [A New Edition, Revised and Considerably Enlarged from Public and Private Collections, By His Son]. 1810. London: R. H. Evans

Farley, Frank Edgar. *Scandinavian Influences in the English Romantic Movement*. Studies and Notes in Philology and Literature IX. 1903. Boston: Ginn & Company.

———. "Three 'Lapland Songs'" *PMLA*. 21:1 (1906) 1-39.

Fowler, David C. *A Literary History of the Popular Ballad*. 1968. Durham, NC: Duke University Press.

Garlington, Aubrey S. " 'Gothic' Literature and Dramatic Music in England 1781-1802." *Journal of the American Musicological Society*. 15:1 (Spring 1962) 48-64.

von Goethe, Johann Wolfgang. *The Poems of Goethe: Translated in the Original Metres*. Edgar Alfred Bowring, trans. 1853. London: J.W. Parker.

———. *The Poems of Goethe*. F.H. Hedge and Leopold Noa, eds. 1882. Boston: S.E. Cassino. [Translation of Goethe by 12 translators, including Bowring, Carlyle, and Longfellow].

Le Grand d'Aussy, Pierre Jean Baptiste. *Fabliaux or Tales, Abridged from French Manuscripts of the XIIth and XIIIth Centuries*. G.L. Way, trans. 3 vols. 1815. London: J. Rodwell.

Gray, Thomas. *The Poetical Works of Thomas Gray, With the Life of the Author*. 1782. Edinburgh: "At the Apollo Press." "The Fatal Sisters," pp. 64-8. "The Descent of Odin," pp. 68-72.

———. *The Poetical Works of Thomas Gray*. 1799. London: "Printed for J. Scratcherd." [Includes a literal translation of the original of "The Descent of Odin," showing Gray's omission of the first five stanzas.]

Grose, Francis. *The Antiquities of Scotland: The First Volume*. 1797. London: Hooper & Wigstead. [First printing of Burns' "Tam O'Shanter."]

Gruntvig, Svend. *Danmarks Gamle Folkviser*. (1853).

Guthke, Karl S. "Some Unidentified Early English Translations from Herder's *Volkslieder*." *Modern Language Notes*, 73:1 (Jan 1958) 52-56.

Harvey, Wallace. *Chronicles of Saint Mungo, or, Antiquities and Traditions of Glasgow*. 1843. Glasgow: John Smith & Son.

Herd, David. *The Ancient and Modern Scots Songs, Heroic Ballads, &c.* 1769. Edinburgh: Martin & Wotherspoon. [Expanded to two volumes in 1776. Source for "Clerk Colvill" and "Fair Margaret and

Sweet Willliam." Volume II of the 1776 edition includes "Mary's
Dream."]

von Herder, Johann Gottfried. *Volkslieder.* (1778-79) 1840. Leipzig:
Genhart & Reisland.

———. *Volkslieder.* Part II. (1779) 1911. Munich: Georg Müller.

Hickes, George. *Linguarum Veterum Septentrionalium Thesaurus
Grammatico-Criticus et Archaeologicus.* 1703-1705. Oxford. [6 parts, in
2 vols. I have not seen this volume, and happily cite Andrew
Wawn's summary of its contents: "details of saga manuscripts,
summaries of saga stories, a supplemented version of Runólfur
Jónsson's 1651 Grammar, runic transcriptions and interpretations,
and numismatic information." (*Vikings*, 19) "The Incantation of
Hervor" appears here in Icelandic and in an English translation,
"the first ever published in Britain of a complete Old Icelandic
poem" (Wawn, *ibid*, 21)] An excerpt from Hickes' work was printed
in 1711 as *Grammatica anglo-saxonica ex Hickesiano Linguarum
septentrionalium thesauro excerpta* (1711). This work can be found at
archive.org.

Hutchinson, William. *A View of Northumberland, with an Excursion to The
Abbey of Mailross in Scotland.* Vol. II. (1776) 1778. Newcastle: Vesey
& Whitfield. [First publication of Robert Lambe's "The Laidley
Worm of Spindelston Heughs."]

Johnson, James. *The Scottish Musical Museum; Consisting of Upwards of
Six Hundred Songs.* Volume V. (1793) 1839. Edinburgh: William
Blackwood & Sons. [Probable source for the version of "Tam Lin"
adapted by Lewis.]

Jones, Henry. *Saint Patricks Purgatory, Containing the Description,
Originall, Progresse and Demolition of That Superstitious Place.* 1647.
London. [Now attributed to Bishop James Spottiswoode.]

Kahlert, Karl Friedrich, and Peter Teuthold. *The Necromancer: Or, The
Tale of the Black Forest, Founded on Facts. Translated from the German
of Lawrence Flammenberg* (pseud.). 1794. London: Printed for
William Lane at the Minerva Press.

———. *Scotish* (sic) *Descriptive Poems; with some Illustrations of Scotish*
(sic) *Literary Antiquities.* 1803. Edinburgh: Mundell & Son.

Magnus, Olaus. *Historia de Gentibus Septentrionalibus.* 1555. Rome. [One
source for the story of the "Old Woman of Berkeley," including an
illustration of her carried off on horseback by the Devil.]

Mallet, David. *Ballads and Songs.* With notes and a Memoir of the
Author by Frederick Dinsdale. 1857. London: Bell and Daldy.

Mallet, Paul-Henri. *Introduction à l'Histoire de Dannemarc.* 1755.
Copenhagen. [Translated into English in 1770 by Thomas Percy,
with many added notes, as *Northern Antiquities.*]

<308>

Malory, Sir Thomas. *Le Morte d'Arthur, or The Hole Book of Kynge Arthur and of His Noble Knyghtes of The Rounde Table.* Stephen A. Shepherd, ed. 2004 New York: W.W. Norton.

Marie de France. *L'Espurgatoire Seint Patriz: An Old French Poem of the Twelfth Century.* Thomas Atkinson Jenkins, ed. 1894. Philadelphia: Press of Alfred J. Ferris. [Complete text of Marie de France's poetic setting of "St. Patrick's Purgatory."]

————. *Saint Patrick's Purgatory.* Michael J. Curley, trans. and ed. 1993. Binghamton: Medieval & Renaissance Texts and Studies Vol. 94. [Side-by-side edition of "Saint Patrick's Purgatory in French and English.]

Mickel, Emanuel J., Jr. *Marie de France.* Twayne's World Authors Series 306: France. 1974. New York: Twayne Publishers Inc.

Mickle, William Julius. *The British Poets.* Vol LXVI: Mickle and Smollett. 1822. Chiswick, C. Whittingham.

Percy, Thomas. *Reliques of Ancient English Poetry: Consisting of Old Heroic Ballads, Songs, and Other Pieces of Our Early Poets.* Vol I. Fourth Edition. 1794. London: F. & C. Rivington.

————. *Reliques of Ancient English Poetry: Consisting of Old Heroic Ballads, Songs, and Other Pieces of Our Early Poets.* Vol III. Third Edition. 1775. London: J. Dodsley.

————. *Five Pieces of Runic Poetry Translated from the Icelandic Language.* 1763. London: R. & J. Dodsley. [Based upon Verelius and Hickes.]

————. *Northern Antiquities: Or A Description of the Manners, Customs, Religion and Laws of the Ancient Danes.* [Translated from Paul-Henri Mallet's *l'Introduction a l'Histoire de Dannemarc, etc.*"] (1770). 1809. Edinburgh: C. Stewart. [This influential volume was reprinted and expanded in 1847 by I.A. Blackwell, and was reprinted numerous times up to the turn of the 20th century.]

Pinkerton, William. "Saint Patrick's Purgatory. Part IV. Modern History." *Ulster Journal of Archaeology.* First series, Vol. 5 (1857), pp. 61-81. [Includes descriptions of St. Patrick's Purgatory, and the Bishop of Clogher's detailed depiction of its destruction in 1632.]

Railo, Eino. *The Haunted Castle: A Study of the Elements of English Romanticism.* 1927. London: George Routledge & Sons Ltd.

Ramsay, Allan. *The Tea-Table Miscellany: A Collection of Choice Songs, Scots and English. (1732-37)* 13th Edition. 1762. Edinburgh: A. Donaldson.

Robertson, John G. *A History of German Literature.* 1902. New York: G. P. Putnam's Sons.

Roger of Wendover. *Flowers of History, Comprising the History of England From the Descent of the Saxons to A.D. 1235.* [Formerly attributed to

<309>

Matthew Paris, a.k.a, Matthew of Westminster.] J.A. Giles, trans. (1567) 1849. London: Henry G. Bohn.

Ross, Margaret Clunies. *The Cambridge Introduction to The Old Norse-Icelandic Saga.* 2010. Cambridge: Cambridge Univ. Press. [A definitive overview of Norse-Icelandic sagas, including a fine chapter on the reception of sagas in the 17th to 19th centuries.]

———. *The Old Norse Poetic Translations of Thomas Percy.* Series: Making the Middle Ages, Volume 4, Center for Medieval Studies, Univ. Of Sydney, Australia. 2001. Turnhout, Belgium: Brepols Publishers.

Scheffer, Johannes Gerhard. *The History of Lapland.* 1674 Oxford: "At the Theatre." [Also, a second, expanded English edition in 1704, with Addenda.]

———. *Lapponia, id est, Regionibus Lapponum et Gentis Nova et Verissima Descriptio.* 1673. Frankfurt. [Original Latin version of *The History of Lapland,* with wood engravings illustrating Lapland customs, pagan religious practices and witchcraft.]

Scott, Sir Walter. *An Apology for Tales of Terror.* 1799. Kelso: "Printed at the Mail Office." Online version by Douglass H. Thomson at www.walterscott.lib.ed.ac.uk/works/poetry/apology/home.html

———. "Copy of An Original Letter by the Late Sir Walter Scott, Bart." *The Lady's Magazine and Museum.* Jan 1837:490. [A letter from Scott to Lewis concerning "Willy's Lady" and several other Scottish Ballads.]

———. "Essay on Imitations of the Ancient Ballad," in *The Complete Works of Sir Walter Scott.* Vol 1. 1833: New York: Cooner & Cooke. [Account of Scott's collaboration with Lewis, and of the publisher of *Tales of Wonder,* pp. 188-89].

———. "Evans's Old Ballads," in *The Miscellaneous Works of Sir Walter Scott,* Vol XVII. 1861 Edinburgh: Adam and Charles Black. 119-136.

———. *Minstrelsy of the Scottish Border.* (1802, 3 vols). One-volume edition. 1869. London: Alex Murray & Son. [First publication of the original version of "Willy's Lady," along with a note about Lewis's version of that ballad for *Tales of Wonder,* pp. 369-72.]

———. *The Pirate.* (Waverly Novels, Volume 23). (1821) 1831. Boston: Samuel H. Parker. [Notes in Volume 1 concerning the oral transmission of the original of "The Fatal Sisters" from the *Saga of Burnt Njal.*]

Scribe, Eugene and Germaine Delavigne. *La Nonne Saglante.* Opera libretto, 1854. Anne Williams, trans. Available online at www.rc.umd.edu/praxis/opera/williams/williams_translation.pdf

<310>

Service, James. *Metrical Legends of Northumberland: Containing the Traditions of Dunstanborough Castle, and Other Poetical Romances.* 1834. Alnwick: W. Davison. [Includes notes attempting to connect Lambe's "Laidley Worm of Spindleston Heughs" to historical events and to the struggle between Christianity and paganism in Northumberland.]

Shane, Leslie. *Saint Patrick's Purgatory: A Record from History and Literature.* 1932. London: Burns Oates & Washbourne Ltd. [A compilation of documents about Logh Derg, discussion over the controversy of the "original" cave, and details on the reception and transmisson of the text, including its use by Dante.]

Southey, Robert. *Metrical Tales and Other Poems.* 1805. London: Longman, Hurst, Rees, and Orme. [Includes poems that had appeared in *Tales of Wonder.*]

————. *The Poetical Works of Robert Southey.* New Edition. 1845. London: Longman, Brown, Green, and Longmans. [Includes the "Ballads and Metrical Tales" and the preface describing the discovery of the Latin text for "The Old Woman of Berkeley."]

Stempel, Guido H. *A Book of Ballads Old and New.* 1917. New York: Henry Holt & Co.

Sturluson, Snorri. *Heimskringla, or The Lives of the Norse Kings.* Trans. by A.H. Smith, trans. Erling Monsen, ed. (1932) 1990. New York: Dover Books. [Includes the full text of "King Hakon's Death Song" The original edition of this book is *Snorre Sturlessøns Norske kongers chronica* (1633, Copenhagen)].

Torfaeus (Þormóður Torfason). *Ancient History of Orkney, Caithness, & The North.* Rev. Alexander Pope, trans. 1861. Wick: Peter Reid.

————. *Orcades, Seu Rerum Orcadensium Historiae.* 1697. Copenhagen. [One of Thomas Gray's sources for "The Fatal Sisters," in Icelandic and Latin, pp. 36-7.]

Turberville, George. *Epitaphes, Epigrams, Songs and Sonnets, with a Discourse of the Friendly Affections of Tymetes to Pyndara His Ladie.* (1567). c. 1908. London: Henry Denham.

Vedel, Anders Sörensen and Peder Syv. *Et Hundrede udvalde Danske Viser, forögede med det andet Hundrede.* 1695. Copenhagen. [This Danish collection of Icelandic poems contains ballads rather than epic sagas, and is based on Vedel's edition titled *It Hundrede vduaalde Danske Vise* (1591, Ribe).]

Verelius, Olaus. *Hervarer Saga ok Heiðreks Konungs.* (The Saga of Hervor and Heidrekr) 1672. Uppsala. [Swedish with Latin footnotes; the first printed text of this saga.]

Virgil. *Eclogues, Georgics,* [and] *Aeneid.* Vol 1. H. Rushton Fairclough, trans. 1965. Cambridge: Harvard University Press.

<311>

Wann, Andrew. "The Post-Medieval Reception of Old Norse and Old Icelandic Literature." in *A Companion to Old Norse-Icelandic Literature and Culture*. Rory McTurk, ed. 2005. Malden, MA: Blackwell Publishing. pp. 320-337. [Detailed chronology of early editions and translations of Norse poetry and sagas.]

———— *The Vikings and the Victorians: Inventing the Old North in Nineteenth-Century Britain*. 2000. Cambridge: D.S. Brewer. [A magisterial survey of the reception of Norse myth and literature, including the publishing history of major source books (Hickes, Percy et al), and the later adoption of Norse themes into poetry and fiction. An indispensible and exhaustive study.]

Warrack, Alexander, comp. *The Scots Dialect Dictionary*. 1911. London: W.R. Chambers.

William of Malmesbury. *Chronicle of the Kings of England*. (1127) John Allen Giles, ed. (1847) 1904. London: George Bell & Sons [A revision of the 1815 translation by John Sharpe. Alternate source for the narrative of "The Old Woman of Berkeley."]

Willson, Anthony Beckles. "Alexander Pope's Garden in Twickenham." *Garden History*. 26:1 (Summer 1998) 31-59.

Wimberly, Lowry C. *Folklore in the English and Scottish Ballads*. 1928. New York: Frederick Ungar Publishing Co.

<312>

About This Book

This book was typeset using Aldine type, a face inspired by the designs of the great Venetian humanist printer and publisher, Aldus Manutius. Titles are set in Morris Troy, a typeface designed by William Morris for the Kelmscott Press.

British and archaic spellings, as found in the original poems, have been retained for the most part. Double quotes have been used throughout to denote quotations, with single quotes marking quotes-within-quotes. Poets' use of long dashes, sometimes combined with punctuation, have mostly been left as found. In keeping with the style of *Tales of Wonder*, I have, here and there, added long dashes to clarify changes of voice among quotations. The irregularities of "The Ancient Mariner" defied even this clarification, and Coleridge himself seemed content to let the Mariner's monologue be the heart of the poem without quotation marks. As the narrative becomes more complex, Coleridge introduces other voices with headings as though the poem were a play-script.

All footnotes, unless followed by the initials of the poet, are by the editor.

This book is also available in a PDF ebook edition.

<313>

www.ingramcontent.com/pod-product-compliance
Lightning Source LLC
Chambersburg PA
CBHW020535020726
47494CB00006B/1776